I'M CLEAR, WHAT'S IT LIKE UP YOUR END?

by
Tom Cotcher

Copyright © Tom Cotcher 2014
This book is sold subject to the condition that it shall not, by way of trade or otherwise, be lent, resold, hired out, or otherwise circulated without the publisher's prior consent in any form of binding or cover other than that in which it is published and without a similar condition including this condition being imposed on the subsequent publisher.
The moral right of Tom Cotcher has been asserted.
ISBN: 1500232246
ISBN-13: 978-1500232245

This book is dedicated to my wonderful wife Cookie and our fantastic boys Andrew and Edward, without whom I'd be a lot richer in pennies, but so much poorer in love.

Also to all those actors who shared and survived with me, the experiences recounted in this book.

CONTENTS

FOREWORD . . . . *i*

CHAPTER ONE *1*
   CURTAIN UP

CHAPTER TWO *18*
   TO BEGIN AT THE BEGINNING

CHAPTER THREE *28*
   SEE ME, SEE THESE SHIPYARDS

CHAPTER FOUR *36*
   ME? A COLLEGE BOY? YOU MUST BE JOKING!

CHAPTER FIVE *50*
   MY FIRST STINT AS A PRO

CHAPTER SIX *62*
   SEASON OF GOODWILL AND EMPLOYMENT

CHAPTER SEVEN *68*
   ORKNEY BECONS

CHAPTER EIGHT *83*
   MORE THAN A WINDY CITY

CHAPTER NINE *87*
   DUNDEE: I'M A NACTA AT LAST

CHAPTER 10	102
WORKING OVERSEAS	
CHAPTER ELEVEN	111
HURRICANES AND BUM BITERS IN CA	
CHAPTER TWELVE	126
JOB HUNTING ROUTES TO AVOID	
CHAPTER THIRTEEN	136
VIVE LA FRENCH? I DON'T THINK SO	
CHAPTER FOURTEEN	151
DUTCH CLAPS	
CHAPTER FIFTEEN	165
PLAYING AWAY FROM HOME	
CHAPTER SIXTEEN	174
THEY'RE GONNA PUT ME IN THE MOVIES	
CHAPTER SEVENTEEN	181
WITH FRIENDS LIKE THESE	
CHAPTER EIGHTEEN	188
CELEBRITY STATUS	
CHAPTER NINETEEN	199
PLAYING ANOTHER COP	
ABOUT THE AUTHOR	211

FOREWORD

During the course of this book you will see on occasion, but not always for fear it becomes over used, the word 'nacta'. In order to avert confusion please read the following:

Nacta : Actor (male) noun

Nactress : Actress (female) another noun

It is in fact the answer a thespian replies to the question when asked what he or she does for a living, e.g. "Am a nacta" or "Am a nactress".

N. B. Usually pronounced in this fashion, though not always specific, to those raised north of Gretna Green.

By the way, the word nacta can also mean nactress, but the word nactress refers specifically to a female nacta, which if left unexplained could have created even more confusion.

N. B. The same rule applies to the word 'author' e.g. nautha, which can of course be both either male or female as well.

While the word 'prostitute' can mean only one thing, it can also be either male or female. But as you will not encounter it anywhere in this tome, it shouldn't concern you unduly.

Still confused? Wait till you read this book!

I'M CLEAR WHAT'S IT LIKE UP YOUR END is a compilation of the kind of misfortunes that more than a few members of the acting profession have most likely fallen victim to. The fact that I was party to all the experiences herein recounted - indeed sometimes the root cause of them - should in no way have a negative influence on any producer, director, casting director, or any other individual, or group of individuals, who are in a position to engage me in a contract of work as a professional nacta.

Furthermore I would like to take this opportunity to state quite categorically here and now that my career to date has been a reasonably joyful one throughout, with many successes to my credit. I therefore remain, as before this book went to print, a potential super star in the making, though a somewhat older one than when I began writing it. If only I had become a somewhat wiser one as well.

Tom Cotcher

Tom Cotcher as Hector in Flickers on the set at ATV Elstree

Granville Saxton, Floor Manager and Tom Cotcher on the set of Flickers

Tom Cotcher as Lennox in The Scots Play

Tom Cotcher as Trofimov, Ursula Smith as Madama Ranyevskaia

Tom Cotcher as Judge Gaffney in Harvey

Jeni Giffen, Benny Young and Tom Cotcher in Look Back in Anger

Thelma Rogers (Mum), Tom Cotcher (Billy) and Robert Robertson (Dad) in Billy Liar

The cast of Loom of Lights on the steps of St. Magnus Cathedral, Kirkwall, Orkney.
Ron Bain, Sue Barry, Tom Cotcher, Jeni Angus, Benny Young, David Birch.
Circa 1972

Tom Cotcher as DC Alan Woods in The Bill

CHAPTER ONE
CURTAIN UP

Whilst it would be quite impossible to list individually all of life's uncertainties which any one of us may encounter from time to time and to varying degrees, there is only one absolute certainty in a lifetime full of uncertainties and it is one which everyone will experience... I'm talking about death. There is only one of them for each of us. At least that is what we are led to believe. Let me put the record straight here and now by telling you that I have found to my dismay, that there are indeed exceptions to this rule, which directly affect a select few of us i.e. I'm talking about professional nactas and nactresses. These stalwarts of the performing arts will have experienced a sort of death umpteen times on an opening night alone, some even before the curtain goes up. During the run of a show, many more potentially heart-stopping, disastrous incidents will occur with terrifying frequency, adding copiously to the number of these demises.

I conclude therefore that throughout their working lives, those in our profession who have been lucky enough to be in reasonably regular employment will experience a death of sorts many hundreds of times. Ergo, in answer to that age old question, "Is there life after death?" the reply is a categorical: "Yes, if you are a nacta." But be warned, it may not always be a barrel o' laughs.

It could be argued that the odds of a three-legged Impala with galloping pneumonia surviving an attack by a pack of hungry lions could be likened to a professional jobbing actor surviving against the odds of a back-drop of bad luck, missed opportunities, and facing looming serial unemployment simultaneously. Many actors owe their very existence on their innate ability just to survive when all around appears grim. Of course they are not threatened by the same physical dangers that a sickly Impala would be accustomed to. For there are no teeth and claws of carnivorous big cats waiting to rip them to bits. Instead it is often waspish critics, unruly audiences, unexpected mishaps, hopeless directors, missed cues, dodgy agents, and sometimes it is even themselves who are to blame. As often as not though, it is the frightening antics of their fellow players that bring them to the brink of losing their very sanity.

Unlike other professions we do not have the luxury of structured career paths, pension plans, or any guarantee of employment at the end of our training, assuming that we all had any sort of training in the first place, for it is not a prerequisite for entering the profession. There are no rules to the game.

Whatever their background, the majority of the acting community can find themselves more out of than in employment throughout their working lives. Indeed an actor in his twilight years can only look forward to playing a part like Old Firs, the servant in Anton Pavlovich Chekov's play *The Cherry Orchard*, who appears in the play's final death throes, says absolutely nothing, blows out a candle and exits forever. Providing of course his agent is still alive and coherent enough to have put him up for the job in the first place. It is also an absolute must that the aged client can manage to get through the entire audition process without falling asleep.

Thus I conclude that any young thing with stars in their eyes, hoping to embark on a career in the acting profession these days, should be looked upon as needing a strong dose of psychiatric counselling, followed by an ego detoxification. Alternatively, stinking rich parents will suffice. But if it is in their hearts to tread the boards, then I say good luck to them, and I will be the first to help them succeed if I can.

An interesting observation is that that even with all the odds stacked heavily against us, it is remarkable that we actors remain so very protective of our profession. When called upon to defend it in any way e.g. as in a 'Save Our Theatre Campaign' we will do it quite admirably, usually in a rather emotionally heated fashion, with sheer passion to the fore. And while we will quite rightly rage noisily against social injustices, we can just as easily gush forth with the same intense enthusiasm if we merely take a liking to someone, or something - such as a melon soufflé sprinkled with cinnamon, if it takes our fancy.

As another example I offer this classic line delivered to me in a rather over-the-top, breathy fashion from an actress who had just finished doing a play. In answer to my query asking what the director was like to work with, which is always good to know in case you find yourself working with him in the future, she replied very intensely and with complete conviction, "I had an out of this world experience, darling. He is such a wonderful director. I bent over backwards for him… the whole cast did."

That misplaced implication stopped me in my tracks.

Directing ain't an exact science and consequently anyone can have a go. I once worked with one who started off as a window dresser and ended up directing big shows. I guess he must have had an eye for the job. So… nothing ventured!

But it is a sad fact that the females in the business have had it even more difficult than the blokes, if that is at all possible. For history tells us that the majority of major parts were written for the guys… and many guys played female parts, and some still do, which of course only serves to add to the problem. What it must be like for the naturally gifted highly trained actresses, who have slogged so hard during years of drama school training, graduating with a determination totally dedicated to their craft, when uninvited habitual unemployment interspersed with sporadic bouts of mostly underpaid acting work is their only reward, I can only imagine.

It must be so difficult for them to restrain from retching when they watch untrained talentless so-called celebrities making their bid for fame and fortune by jumping on the bandwagon of some down market television reality show and using it as a springboard to a career in our business. Their fifteen minutes of telly fame is usually followed by an offer of an extremely well paid stint in pantomime or suchlike.

It ain't cheap for two adults and a couple of kids to go and see a panto these days. So it is especially irksome when the management boast of the show's stars being made up of some wannabes who are famous on television for their ability to perform basic stuff like household chores, or just because they happen to be the 'partner' of someone who is legitimately well known, or they know what horse shit is best for your garden etc., etc., etc. These chancers even turn up in legit theatre gawd forbid, where they then find themselves totally out of their comfort zone, facing live audiences who cannot even hear them. The result is that some even have to take voice and acting lessons... Jeeeeez! My advice to them would be to bog off and leave the job to us professionals. Actors on the other hand, love their jobs so much that they only ever delve into other areas of employment when needs absolutely must.

Celebrity casting is only one irritating side effect we all have to endure, both actors and audiences alike. Another problem in our industry is the lack of places for actors to work i.e. theatres. There have been far too many closures and cuts in the arts due to a lack of workable financial policies in the past, coupled with a lack of understanding by successive governments of arts funding in general. Council grants have been squeezed into oblivion and this has had a drastic knock on effect for theatres especially.

Thankfully I believe there are now better tax incentives in place to make films here in the UK, thus the future of our film industry looks somewhat brighter. We are up there with the best of them, leading the way in some cases, and will continue so to do. You only need to watch the awards ceremonies to realise what our films and television, as well as theatre and radio have achieved worldwide. Why? Because Great Britain is a treasure trove of professional talent, that's why. From wardrobe to set design, from lighting and sound to special effects, in musicals, comedies, dramas and documentaries - then there are the writers, directors, producers, stunt men and women, stunt coordinators, as well as the CGI specialists etc. The list goes on and on. That's before we look at the fantastic successes of our nactas, without whom we would all be much the poorer. It is interesting to note that across the board so many careers in the industry in general began in the theatre.

So, some of the tax revenue generated from our film industry could be hived off to help at its grass roots i.e. the theatre. It certainly deserves it. Less cuts, more aid is what is needed.

It is a never ending job for our union Equity to keep pace dealing with the obstacles actors have to put up with, from unscrupulous employers to unsympathetic income tax officers etc. The wonderful craft is quite simply one of the best jobs in the world in my opinion, but the business side has its downside of unfairness, lost chances and damned cold dressing rooms.

"Without the arts there is no culture. Without culture there is no society. Without society we're well and truly f--d!"

Tom Cotcher circa 2014.

That's my wee rant over you'll be glad to hear. Now back to the serious stuff.

On the whole, actors (m & f) have an extraordinary ability to bounce back from whatever adverse situations they find themselves in. To put it simply, they have to, even when their future looks beyond hope, and their valiant efforts to succeed appear foolhardy, which sometimes can be the case e.g. if you weren't the one chosen for a part you were up for, you need to forget about it and get on prepping for the next opportunity that may present itself.

Forced to use their finely tuned communicative talents in other creative genres has been the answer for some e.g. when it comes to having their very own written work published, they are damned good at it. Of course it is not in the least surprising to learn that here is an area where a great many have triumphed writing their memoirs, autobiographies, novels, cook books etc. whether out of necessity or just as a hobby which turned out to be a lucrative side line, or even a brand new squeaky clean career. After all, actors are naturally gifted at getting the message across. And for those whose literary work did not scale the dizzy heights of success, the meagre beer money raised from their efforts, was no doubt put to good use as survival fodder.

It does make me proud that fellow nactas have had the courage to dip their quills into the world of publishing, even if some have avoided giving their readers an insight into the backstage grittier aspects of their lives in the business e.g. when a career is blighted by an actor's uncanny ability to be in the wrong place at the wrong time, instead of the exact opposite. *Mais, c'est la business.*

I have noticed generally speaking, that authors from the acting genre wisely steer politically correct paths, preferring diplomatic styles of approach to what they commit to putting down on paper, in order I presume not to upset their readers. I confess this has been duly noted by me. So I will endeavour not to upset my readers, and will practice the art of adhering like a limpet to a politically correct agenda also. However, I have to confess I have also noticed over the years that I am not perfect, surprising as that may seem. Thus I feel at this juncture I should warn you, that my valiant efforts for this work to be acceptable to all, without favours or prejudices on my part, and without falling foul of the P C brigade, may well indeed fall far short of what is acceptable to them, and what is expected of me… thus landing me in the *merde*, which I am absolutely adept at accomplishing on a semi-regular basis. At times I might even lapse into using scurrilous vernacular and respectively request that I may be forgiven for any such misdemeanours, which may occur between this book's covers. It is certainly not my intention in any way to ridicule, upset, make angry, irritate, annoy or enter as a protagonist into any of the copious amount of 'ists' that lie hidden like explosive anti-personnel mines for the unwary innocent, such as me, to tread on. But as you have already bought this book and you must be already reading it to have got this far, it may already be too late for me to apologise for any misdemeanours I may have already entered into in hindsight. But I'll say sorry anyway and hope I have covered myself enough to avert any future mistakes… BOOM… too late!

Quite often if one autobiographic novel has even had a modicum of success, then it usually follows that the writer goes on to publish new revelations in umpteen more tomes of his or her life. I used to wonder why they couldn't have said it all first time round. You will deduce by my ignorance that I have not been born with a gifted business brain. But eventually the understanding that selling many more books makes much more profit did kick in.

So I have set myself this goal; should this book be a rip roaring success, you can bet your bottom dollar I'll be hastily writing as many sequels as I can. Even if I have to fill 'em with made up stories and lies about myself, instead of recounting the truth as I have done in this book, in order to amuse my readers, as well as make a healthy dent into my overdraft.

So, to make this book highly sellable, I have taken great care to head it towards the hilarity end of the light hearted spectrum, consequently an easy fun read... hopefully. If I had approached it without this aforethought, telling the story of an actor with the glass half empty approach to life, it could end up as a turgid sequence of words, shuddering along mournfully like an Ardvark with gout, and that just ain't me folks.

And I have studiously endeavoured not to take myself too seriously, consistently reminding myself throughout the highly enjoyable creative writing process not to get above myself either, for I'm not bloody Shakespeare, though like me he wasn't perfect either, which is the only thing me and the Bard have in common. There's nowt wrong with him of course. A Shakespeare production when done well will always make for amazing theatre; delighting, educating, humouring and entertaining audiences as they have done for hundreds of years.

My only advice for anyone unused to his work is to swat up on the plot of the play you are about to see a bit beforehand, otherwise it will be one hell of a confusing evening trying to make any sort of sense out of a flowery, bygone age English, spoken in an iambic pentameter rhythm, by characters who in bygone days wore doublets and hose, garters, thigh-length boots, dodgy looking wigs, stick-on goatee beards, heaps of makeup and cod pieces large enough to hold their breakfast, lunch and dinner at one sitting. The bloke playing Ophelia had the easiest outfit to wear compared with them, although it was an absolute proviso in his contract that he didn't forget to shave before going on stage, and not just his beard either. Nowadays anything goes... and I do mean anything. I was in a Shakespeare production of the Scots play, when the costumes we wore were Judo outfits and the set was made of scaffold poles. We nactas weren't sure whether to put on hard hats as well and start throwing the scaffold around the stage in preparation to building a house.

I will also try to give a body swerve to the use of other people's fame in the 'star name dropping' routine. But I warn you that it will happen on occasion, so do please bear with me and allow me a little self-indulgence along the way, where I have deemed it absolutely necessary for the sake of enhancing a particular story.

Dear reader, should you ever come upon continuous dropping of names between any book's covers, I would suggest that you immediately put that book aside. You should then turn on the telly and tune in to watching those who are hell bent in shortening their time on earth, by going for the burn in some bloody awful body thrashing keep-fit programme. These are always good for a laugh.

Alternatively watching Morris Dancers strut their stuff, after having emptied pint after pint of local ale down their oesophagi with aplomb (some even whilst dancing) is the next best thing. Half-pissed, so-called grown up men wearing jingly bells tied around their legs and whacking one another with sticks during dubious looking dance routines has never ceased to have me in fits of laughter.

I wonder if there were Morris Dancers back in Shakespeare's time? If so, maybe it was them who inspired him to create the characters for his plays. They wore some daft outfits back then too as hitherto mentioned, sometimes even with bells on. Substitute swords for sticks and there we have it. Grown men, plenty of ale, lots of bashing one another, howls of pain and anguish, murderous blows to the pates (Shakespearean speak for 'heads'). Difficult to tell them apart. Ergo forsooth, I pose this enigma; were Sir Toby Belch and his mates just a bevy of half arsed Morris Dancers out on the piss? Incredulous if true. Marvellous even!

There is one aspect of the wonderful craft which ain't so marvellous. Consequently we actors try like hell to avoid it. It is… fear. Of course no-one in their right mind likes to be fearful, but for an actor plying his trade to a live audience it is ten times worse when it arrives unheralded, unwanted and is consequently unbearable. In fact, fear is the mother of all obstacles an actor will ever face. One can only surmise that this particular nasty piece of work has been created for the sole purpose of putting an early demise high on the agenda of an actor's life span, simply because the business is oversubscribed and our Maker has reckoned that a bit of self culling would do it good. This dreaded beast called fear makes its appearance in head-splitting, buttock-clenching moments, which would have lesser mortals immediately enrolling to retrain to artificially inseminate a fully consciuos grizzly mother bear suffering from a strong dose of PMT, rather than walk on stage and performing to a live audience ever again.

It can manifest itself anywhere, anytime, before pouncing mercilessly on unsuspecting victims without prior warning. 'Tis then that utter helplessness rules, giving rise to well-known harrowingly plaintive shrieks.

It can be found in dressing rooms:

"Oh for f-- 's sake… ah've ripped ma tights… right at the f--g crotch… I'm on in a minute too!"

Lurking in the wings:

"I haven't a bloody clue where or when I come on next!"

In an onstage thought:

"Is it me? Oh my gawd what is my line?"

A realisation when onstage:

'Oh my gawd no, I was sure it was a fart!'

The last one was tragic for the actor as it was a Christmas show he was performing in, and the character he was playing was dressed in an all in white jump suit. I know this to be true because I was there, and before you jump to any conclusions, no it wasn't me! I was told he retired early from the business. Not early enough for him, obviously.

Re: an actor forgetting what his next line is scenario; it happens extremely rarely, but when it does strike the panic is usually accompanied by a subtle if somewhat frantic mime acted out to fellow players, in order to get them to understand that their fellow actor is in dire trouble, and hasn't the foggiest idea what's he's supposed to say next. Consequently everyone on stage is enlisted into this spreading pandemic of fear, which has been ignited for no apparent reason by a bout of acting amnesia.

I give the following as an example:

Ada Rehan (1857-1916) was a famous Irish American actress who once played a heroine in a romantic comedy. During the play she said a line to a young nervous actor, then paused waiting for his reply. But the actor had forgotten what his reply should be, which apparently was, "You don't reply."

And so the prompter in the wings called out to him "You don't reply… you don't reply," repeating it so as to jog his memory. The young actor was by this time frantic with fear and shouted loudly back "How the hell can I reply when I don't know what to say!"

It is true that these types of scenarios are played out time and time again in nightmarish dreams every actor experiences countless times in his life.

These nightmares can occur anytime, usually during the rehearsal period, though in general it is in the final few nights leading to the play's opening which is when they strike most often, but they can even occur even after a show is up and running.

A very fearful moment I experienced myself was during a Shakespeare piece when a fellow thesp failed to appear for one of his entrances. These events also happen very occasionally thank goodness, but when they do you just have to get on with the play as best you can until the errant actor eventually makes his appearance. In this instance I was left alone for what seemed a hell of a long time on stage in front of many hundreds of pairs of eyes watching me, all trying to fathom out what was going on, or not going on in this case.

The silent gap on stage had to be filled somehow, during which the missing actor really needed to be found. I decided to kill time by using a bit of bravado. Wandering slowly downstage, as near to the audience as is possible without actually joining them in the front row of the stalls, I blew into my hands to signify that it was a cold night. Unfortunately the noise I made sounded suspiciously like I was blowing a raspberry at them. I decided to then change tack and proceeded to try and out-stare the faces staring up at me. This resulted in more than a few restless shuffles in the first few rows by those who felt intimidated by me. From the corner of my eye I saw a junior member of the stage management team in the wings shrug their shoulders signalling dismay, confusion and panic, which also signalled that I had more time to fill. The thing was I had a damn good idea where the missing actor was, and would have pocketed a fortune on a one hundred to one bet that he was indeed with an actress he had his eye on from day one of rehearsals. But how was I to let stage management know? I couldn't exactly mime him trying to get his leg over could I?

With nothing to lose I summoned up the courage and called out, "Sometimes he doth sleep a late."

Using the word 'sleep' I thought might give those in the wings a big hint of what he was trying to get up to and where he may possibly be, without me actually having to mime the act of copulation. At this point another cast member suddenly appeared on stage, but not the one I was hoping for, probably to give me moral support as he could see I was 'dying' on stage.

"Forsooth, I shall go awake him," he dutifully replied, then immediately sodded off again as quickly as he had appeared.

"Please!" I called back through gritted teeth and with mounting apprehension in my voice. The stage manager, who was now also watching from the wings, looked in a state of heightened astonishment when he heard our rewriting of the world's most renowned playwright's sacrosanct words. It was the best I could think of at the time, though in retrospect it probably threw the audience into a modicum of confusion and consternation as to why the missing character was prone to oversleeping.

Eventually the actor was found by the frantic searching of the posse backstage, which was made up of anyone who happened to be around, and made it onto the stage. Apparently the audience seemed oblivious to my torment and we carried on regardless of the delay, the show a great success once more. But for me, I'm sure another few years were knocked off my longevity.

Unbeknownst to me, there was an actor in the audience whom I knew. He told me afterwards that never in the 450-year history of any Shakespeare play, was the one word 'PLEASE' ever uttered from the mouths of any of Shakespeare's characters. Och well, fear can make you say some weird things I guess.

Then there was the time when I was cast in a play which was receiving critical acclaim - quite right too because it boasted what was a rather excellent cast made up of highly talented actors, a stellar cast allegedly, and I was one of 'em. I was certainly kept on my toes as I didn't want to let me, or the side down. All went well until one night the actress playing my wife, who up to that point had been absolutely terrific, went into a blind panic in the wings, literary two minutes before we were to make our first entrance together. Apparently she had had a sly look through a crack in the set at the audience and saw someone from her past she had hoped never to see again. Gawd knows why!

I knew something was wrong when she wasn't her usual free spirited self going through her odd warm up routine in the wings to calm her nerves. This included bending so low down from the waist that I perceived her to be looking up her skirt, presumably to check she hadn't forgotten to don her underwear. She would then rise slowly up again expelling an amazing amount of air for such a slender frame; luckily for me via her mouth. This was her way apparently of centring herself she told me, "for the job in hand". I was highly amused at her turn of phrase, but was gentlemanly enough at the time to refrain from saying that I didn't have the time for a hand job as we were about to go on stage.

Her routine had certainly worked for her up till then, as she always looked serene and in control when she completed it and gave a fabulous and flawless performance every time. I had thought I might try to copy her, but decided against the idea because I couldn't see whether or not my underwear was where it should be as I was wearing trousers and didn't fancy dropping them… enough said… what goes on in the wings stays in the wings!

On the night in question, just prior to her voyeuristic knicker observation routine as I said, she peeked at the audience… big mistake. When she turned back to look at me she resembled the ubiquitous frightened rabbit caught in a lorry's headlights. Visibly shaking she then announced in a stage whisper which could be heard in Dundee (another city many miles away from where we were) that she couldn't go on. Time was of the essence to get her back on planet earth as a normal working thespiana. The two actors already onstage and well into the first scene, fully expected me and the wife to enter at the appointed time, which was becoming sooner by the second. In retrospect I think I was exceedingly kind to her, considering I believed that by then even if she did somehow make it onstage, we would experience a catastrophic catastrophe in front of a live audience.

I cajoled in hushed tones, "C'mon babe, please don't do this now!" I heaped quiet praises. "You're fabulous… best actress I've worked with… ever… honest." I cuddled her, whispering close to her ear, "No tongues, I promise." I even begged her, mouthing the words, "Please I beg of you… pull yourself together."

Then with mere seconds to go, I reverted to miming a fast train and a jumbo jet crashing into one another with bits of bodies being thrown into the air. That did it. She turned away from me and waltzed straight onstage as if nothing was untoward. She was as magnificent as usual. I on the other hand, having been somewhat distracted by the experience to say the least, walked on behind her with an innate humourless grin on my face, sporting a spaced-out, distinct-lack-of-sanity look, as if I had recently joined a weird religious sect whose leader had just informed me that I was Jesus's barber, and asked if I would nip up the hill and give him a quick short back and sides, no names no pack drill.

Fear can also hit you with a mighty erratically aimed blow by a double handed sword made of real metal, atop of your shiny costume helmet made of real plastic made to look like real metal, during an opening night in the middle of a stage swordfight routine. Suddenly all attempts at kid-on fighting exit out of the window as you are left fighting for your very life. This awful situation you find yourself in without doubt will have been instigated by the irrational behaviour of a colleague on stage, when he realises for the very first time that there are many hundreds of pairs of eyes out there in that black dark void called the auditorium, watching his every move. Why it hadn't dawned on him previously that this would be the case with a live audience beggars belief. And so he carries on strutting his manly stuff, experiencing an overdose of highly charged testosterone coursing through his veins, the outcome of which causes him to have an oversized uncontrolled ego trip. Subsequently all the moves the pair of you have been rehearsing together for the past three arse-grindingly, body bruising weeks are lost in the ether of his red mist. For reasons at the time quite unfathomable to you, he decides to up the ante and invents unorthodox slashing sword actions, which a Samurai warrior would have trouble defending himself against. You are horrified as it dawns on you that his very sanity is now in question. Consequently he has every chance of scoring a direct hit at any given moment and with rising frequency absolutely anywhere upon your person without prior warning.

Actors such as those are known in the business as being paid up members of THE NO CONTROL BRIGADE. It has been my misfortune to have experienced at first hand, on two separate occasions, what it was really like to fight on stage against such madmen. The paying punters who witnessed these terrifying spectacles of raw violence unfold in front of them, reflected in their faces the awesome horrors they felt obliged to witness. They had just paid out a small fortune plus VAT for the privilege and so were reluctant to leave, for they knew a refund on their evening's entertainment investment wouldn't be an option. How could they leave their seats just because they felt squeamish watching an actor screaming in real fear and agony? They probably believed it was great acting, which was my only consolation. Though they'd no doubt already witnessed a plethora of violence in the cinema and on television, it was probably far more exciting though quite discomfiting watching it on a live stage. Unlike them, the thick line between reality and play acting just didn't exist in the now twisted minds of my adversaries. These episodes were simply terrifyingly all too bloody real… literally!

I tremble to think what the outcomes would have been if the sequences hadn't been rehearsed by a fight arranger. Probably so very much worse and tantamount to legalised attempted murder if actors were left to their own devices and had to conjure up their own stage fights. Then again they couldn't have been much worse.

It is worth noting here that those who practise the craft of fight arranging i.e. professional stunt coordinators are shit hot at it and can make the simplest of routines look spectacular, thrilling and extremely dangerous, when in fact the fight sequences have been choreographed to perfection, with safety always being at the forefront of every pre rehearsed action. I'd work with them anytime.

But I'd rather down a couple of pints of warm plankton infested real ale, during an energetic sex fantasy with an angry wasp, whilst sleeping on a hammock 50 feet up a snake infested tree in the Amazonian jungle during a monsoon downpour, than have a live stage fight ever again with a paid up merchant of the NO CONTROL BRIGADE.

So what does go through an actor's mind on stage during a live performance to a paying audience when a colleague, or dare I say opponent, starts to move in for the kill? The answer I can assure you is exactly what a sick, three-legged Impala is probably thinking when he sees a hungry pride of lions eyeing him up for supper.

As an example I will describe my experience in a show I hope never to do business with ever again… *Treasure Island*. I know what I'm talking about here because I've been in it twice; in fact it nearly did for me… twice. I have a strong suspicion that *Treasure Island* is jinxed for me and that if I ventured another crack at it I may not survive the outcome a third time.

Don't get me wrong for it is a fine piece of work. I believe the book to be a wonderful piece of writing, a master class in adventure, marvellous for young and old alike, but it is a difficult piece to transfer to the live stage. The opening scenes of the piece can be a bit wordy as the plot has to be set. If overwritten you lose the kids' attention. If underwritten no-one knows what's happening. It is simply an uphill battle to keep the youngsters listening and concentrating for any length of time until the real action starts. After all, what they have come to see is a bunch of supposedly grown up nasty looking egomaniacal pirates knocking seven colours out of one another, and the sooner it happens the better as far as they are concerned. So for those writers considering adapting the novel for the stage, do be aware of the pitfalls of using too much dialogue in the early stages.

On the two occasions early in my career when I was unfortunately cast in it, I played pirates both times and had the hazardous experience of working with fight arrangers who fell somewhat short in the fight arranging expertise stakes. They simply weren't up to scratch. The problem was that they weren't professional stunt coordinators, but actors who I can only presume attended some sort of stagefighting course and had turned up at the auditions offering their services as multi skilled fight arranging actors. I presume the theatre managements they approached thought it a real money saving coup to hire actors who could double as fight arrangers, rather than have to pay the proper price for the real ones as well. And so it came to pass that they were hired. Maybe if they had been female then they would have been better at the multitasking bit.

But as a fellow actor it was none of my bloody business to intervene. If they could make a few extra bob offering their fighting services as well as playing pirates then good luck to them I say. Jobbing actors get paid little enough as it is. I just got unlucky with the two I had to work with.

Of course neither of these two twats actually looked the part of swashbuckling, devil-may-care, psychotic killers of the seven seas we are so used to seeing in Hollywood blockbuster movies. But that didn't matter too much at the time, as these stage shows weren't anything remotely resembling high adventure, action packed Hollywood blockbuster movies. But the problem was that the kids who came to see the shows were expecting just that: high adventure, action packed Hollywood blockbusting movie type shows.

The first so-called fight arranger who also doubled as a pirate suffered an attack of R M S (Red Mist Syndrome) on our opening night and thus immediately joined the ranks of the aforesaid NO CONTROL BRIGADE when he introduced an unrehearsed boot up my arse half way through our fight routine. It is bad enough for an actor to lose control in front of an audience, but ten times worse when the fight arranger screws up in this way; especially so when any retaliation on my part would have been seen as a challenge and which no doubt would have been parried by a crudely directed swipe with his real metal sabre at gawd only knows what part of my anatomy. Ergo in his dressing room at half time, with the threat of his bollocks being mangled in a vice, I pointed out that it just wasn't cricket to behave in such a way in front of all these paying guests. I am happy to report that he never booted me up the arse again, nor did he invent any other dangerous unrehearsed fighting moves throughout the play's run. I guess it must have been something to do with his bollocks suffering a fate worse than death itself that got him back on track.

The next time I was stupid enough to sign a contract for yet another *Treasure Island* experience, the dodgy fight arranger didn't exactly fill the cast with confidence on our first day of rehearsals. When he tried to demonstrate the art of 'how to fall safely' by gently lowering himself onto a soft mat then attempting to accomplish a forward roll, he only succeeded in dislocating his shoulder.

Quite simply in my experience the best in the business for putting together the most spectacular and safest fight routines are professional stunt coordinators who specialise in their craft and whom I have the greatest trust, admiration and respect, a world away from the two daft buggers I had to work with.

There seems to be room to accommodate a variety of all sorts into our crazy business even if there aren't enough jobs to go round. As Shakespeare himself said, "All the world's a stage…" So in the words of the late and great Tony Hancock, courtesy of Ray Galton and Allan Simpson, "I'm going to dip in and have a basin full of anything I fancy."

I now seek to give you a wee look at these moments in my auspicious career to date, the majority of which I experienced in my early years in the business, when the best laid plans o' mice and myself went AWOL. In order to do this I would like to take you back in time to when I first got the acting bug. Or to be absolutely honest, to when I thought acting would be a better bet than having to work for a living - a misjudgement I realised all too quickly when I became a fully-fledged professional nacta, having gained a Diploma in Dramatic Art circa 1971, a product of the three year Acting Course at the Royal Scottish Academy of Music and Drama in Glasgow, my home town.

As my research for this book was based entirely on my personal memory, the most recent mishaps were naturally recalled first as they were freshest in my mind. My original plan was to work back through time, thus earlier mishaps would in turn, I hoped, be recalled to mind. But working in a sort of reverse chronological order proved to be beyond me, thus I abandoned this confusing exercise at an early stage.

I decided, in the words of Dylan Thomas, "To begin at the beginning." Thereafter it should be noted that there are no order of events, which in its idiosyncratic way reflects the ups and downs and sideways movement of a career in the acting business, or indeed the very lack of it. My fear of not being able to remember these occasional hiccups I experienced whilst plying my trade on a journey to international stardom, all too soon disappeared, for my past came at me in an uninterrupted flow like train delay apology announcements.

CHAPTER TWO

TO BEGIN AT THE BEGINNING

There were two pupils in my class at school who were actively encouraged to take time off without having to play the truant card. Whatever scam they were pulling I wanted a piece of the action. You may have gathered by now that education was a low priority on my agenda. The truth is that they were heading for the bright lights; boy actors doing stints in the Glasgow pantomime scene and on television. So when I found out what they were up to, I devised what I thought was a master plan which involved me joining the school's drama club. In fact joining the drama club was the only plan I had, so it had to work.

Our English teacher, a very decent chap called Mr Christie, also doubled as the school's drama club producer. So midway through a lesson when all other heads were bent low over desks studiously carrying out his scholarly demands, I chose to cautiously approach him in the vague hope that I too could get time off school... legally. I especially wanted never to have to sit through one more science class where a prematurely balding (which I am now experiencing) frustrated rocket scientist was failing in his attempts to teach me physics.

I'M CLEAR, WHAT'S IT LIKE UP YOUR END?

"Mr Christie, sir?" I whispered, peering up at him over his desk.

"Not now, Cotcher, I'm busy," he growled back menacingly, his head buried in what I believed to be some great work of literature. With an attitude of never give up, which has carried me as an actor for some forty-odd years (why did I ever listen to it?) I tried again.

"Can I join the drama club please, sir?"

He paused from doing his pools coupon and looked up at me. With a look of total incomprehension in his eyes he raised his voice at least an octave.

"You?" he shrilled.

"Yes sir me sir," I whispered even more quietly than I had before, hoping that he would take the hint and follow suit. But the hint wasn't taken.

"Why do you want to join the school's drama club, son?" he hollered suspiciously, the class behind me now fully aware of what was going on. They were probably hoping that I'd fail in my endeavours and end up getting thwacked with the leather belt Mr Christie kept in his desk drawer, which most teachers then used with unfair regularity, usually on me.

"Thought it might help me understand Shakespeare better, sir."

Though the class all giggled, to my astonishment he bought my ruse and one week later I started to rehearse the part of the one line footman in *A Man for All Seasons*. I'll never forget my line: "Master Rich is here Sir Thomas."

If only I had remembered it properly on the night; to be fair though, it wasn't entirely my fault.

"Honest Mr Christie, sir."

I had dutifully turned up on time to every rehearsal, said my line perfectly, on cue and loud enough to be heard by someone hard of hearing in the back row of The Coliseum in Rhodes. However, Mr Christie pointed out to me that the decibels were unnecessary as we were to perform in a studio theatre club in Glasgow, with an auditorium capable of seating a mere one hundred and twenty souls. It was called the Close Theatre and was attached quite literally to Glasgow's famous Citizens Theatre.

The first night, which was also the last night of the show, arrived. It went swimmingly well and without a hitch as I watched from the wings waiting to do my bit. About a page before I was about to step forth and give my all I felt a hand on my shoulder. The appointed stage manager and fellow pupil whispered in my ear that Mr bloody Christie had decided without my knowledge to change the timing of my entrance.

I whispered back, "Couldn't the old bugger have told me before the curtain went up? We've only been rehearsing it for five f--g weeks."

"Nothin' to do wi' me pal, ah'm just the messenger."

Through gritted teeth I reminded him that messengers in plays bearing bad tidings were usually slaughtered.

"So when do I go on now?" I demanded.

"No not now... I'll tell you when."

"I didn't mean now for Christ's sake... I meant...!"

"Look Lawrence Oh f--n' Livier... I'll gae ye a dunt in the back then you go on and do yur bit... got it...?" came the rather loudly whispered reply.

Up to then I had been totally relaxed though a tad excited and really looking forward to 'doing my bit', but with this rule change all sorts of feelings which I later learned to control when I was more experienced, came into play. The first thing I noticed was that my legs began to visibly shake. Then it was the turn of my mouth to misbehave as it began to lose saliva at an alarming rate. Following this my lips felt cold to the touch and I began to need to pee, very, very badly indeed.

Maybe if the stage manager hadn't tapped me again on the shoulder to warn me to get ready I wouldn't have thought that this was the new cue for me to go on stage. But he did and I did and subsequently I made what is called in the business 'a false entrance'. The audience's attention was immediately drawn to me, the gangly actor who appeared momentarily during someone else's bit, before being pulled unceremoniously off again by the stage manager. That was the first laugh I ever got as an actor, albeit an unrehearsed and unwanted one.

"What the...?"

"Not now!"

"Aw thanks. Why did you tap me on the..?"

"NOW! Go now for Christ's sake... you're on, you're on!" the stage manager hissed at me as he pushed me back onstage.

In later years I heard the story about that marvellous Scottish comedian Chic Murray. During a show he was sitting in his dressing room when at that moment he apparently should have been on stage. An irate stage manager came rushing in, saying, "Mr Murray... Mr Murray... you're on, you're on!"

Chic Murray replied in that dry way of his. "Am I? How am I doing?"

And so I lumbered in an ungainly manner back on to the stage. The audience who were within touching distance started to giggle. I don't blame them. After all, here was the actor who moments earlier had appeared quite suddenly, only to disappear again the next moment without uttering a sound, then suddenly reappear a second time shortly afterwards. The tittering died down slightly as the audience waited apprehensively for me to do something... anything. I spotted a mate of mine in the third row. He had a handkerchief stuffed in his mouth and tears were streaming down his face. I looked around at my fellow actors. The expression on each terror struck face told the same story... Fear!

I looked back at my mate. For some reason the handkerchief was gone. Privately I hoped the bugger had swallowed it. Then I took a loud deep breath... then... cocked it up... big time.

"Master Thomas it's Rich here... ummm... och he's here waitin' for you... the rich one," or words very similar, but certainly not the words I was supposed to say or in the order that I was supposed to say them.

Then I proceeded to exit off stage, backing all the way and bowing as low as I could without falling on my face. I wasn't supposed to bow at all but it was the only way I could get off without looking at the audience, who were by this time convulsed with laughter.

But I was determined to get as much time off school that the two budding starlets were getting so I turned up at the drama club again when they were casting for their next epic in the vague hope that my past performance as the footman had been forgotten. It came as a big surprise to me when Mr Christie did indeed give me another chance, even though he mentioned that he "hadn't forgotten my last bloody effort as the footman."

This time, however, it wasn't in a straight play but in the end of term revue in the school hall. I made damn sure that there would be no last minute changes, warning the stage manager that if he so much as coughed in the wings I wouldn't go on. This was my first and only bout of being a drama queen. Most of the school turned up to watch as word had got round.

"Cotch is in it, so it's bound to be a gas, if his f--g nacting debut is anything to go by," I overheard being said in the boys' bog.

The day of the performance arrived and so did I. On cue I strode purposefully onto the stage, the audience genuinely surprised that I didn't bugger off again immediately. In my hands I held a road traffic sign which depicted a motorbike above a car. I waited, listening to the hush of expectation, then shouted aloud, "THIS... IS A LOW FLYING MOTORBIKE."

The audience roared with laughter. It was a wonderful moment for me. I held up various other road signs, timed the punch lines and got the laughs. At half time I sat on the floor backstage with a mate called Bobby Jessamine, who was a fellow performer, our backs pressed against the hot pipes, sharing a can of warm lager. For him this was just another show. He had been in the drama club far longer than me. He was a veteran and a damned good actor as well as a brilliant artist. For me, this was uncharted territory and I was shell shocked. Not by stage fright, but because I had at last found something I thought I could do, and the experience was actually enjoyable.

"You're enjoying this experience, aren't you, Cotch?"

'Cotch' was my nickname, which was passed down to my eldest son and then dutifully given to his younger brother.

"Uh hu." I was at that age when a two syllable grunt would suffice for an answer.

"So why don't you try for drama school?"

"Wha's 'at then?"

"Where you learn to be a... nacta."

"Yeh?"

"Yeh."

"Nah, me parents wouldnae buy that idea."

But my fellow star wasn't to be beaten and had what I thought was the perfect answer. "Just tell them it's good character training."

"Yeh? Yeh! That's a brill idea. Thanks Bobby."

"Nae problem, Cotch."

When I met him a couple of years later, he was studying at the world renowned Glasgow Art School. Though our paths have never crossed since, I really hope that he has become a success. He was a good friend, a great bloke, and with all that natural creative talent, if anyone deserved to succeed in his chosen career then he did.

Me? I wasn't brilliant at anything. It wasn't that I was 'academically challenged' as would probably be said these days. Back then I won't dare tell you what the description of my academic abilities would be, so tough luck to the PC Brigade! Let me put it this way: I was just somewhat lazy and uninterested in being taught by psychopathic teachers, of which my school had a couple who were hell bent on not trying to teach me. However I do make an exception re my stunning looking history teacher, who was a vision which I can never, nor will I ever forget, in a short pink woolly skirt and black tights. I presume they were tights, as up to that point my efforts at sexual encounters with the opposite sex included tights every time. Scottish winters are absolutely mercenary with more than their fair share of the chill factor. And I was certainly chilled out quite a few times in my romantic endeavours.

Every morning at sparrows' fart, rain hail or shine, I would slog the five miles on my bike doing my paper run. But it was worth it, because my history teacher was one of my customers. Each time I climbed up the stairs of the dark tenement towards her third floor flat in Pollokshields, I would silently pray that she would suddenly appear at her door wearing a flimsy, short, low-cut nightie and bend over to pick up her bottle of milk before beckoning me inside (her flat). Sadly for me but happily for her I never did get my prayers answered. However what I did get was ninety-six percent for my history exam. Funny that.

This was offset, however, by getting a mere seven percent in physics. Me and the science teacher? We never did get on. Anyway he wouldn't have looked good in tights and a mini skirt. When I first entered his Physics class he somehow instinctively knew that I was not going to be cut out to be a future scientist. He was sadly proven right by my lack of interest I showed for the subject closest to his heart.

By contrast, both my elder sister and younger brother were academically more switched on than I was. But to be fair I had missed a bit of my early schooling due to being prone to accident and illness e.g. an early bout of pneumonia as an infant, then years later a broken leg when only seven and a half, namely the femur or thigh bone. The surgeon was baffled as to how I had come to break the strongest bone in the body by simply falling against a parked car. But on reading my medical history, he noted that I had a very rare and extremely painful recurring bone condition which I had from infancy. I am delighted to report that it went away along with the last zits of adolescence. Being X-rayed so many times all the way into my teens I am somewhat surprised to have survived. But I genuinely believe that the laying on of hands ritual by our local church Minister, which I was given when a I was a wee toddler, has a lot to do with me still being here to this day.

The year was 1957, I was seven and three quarters years old and in Glasgow's wonderful Yorkhill Hospital for Sick Children… again… this time recovering from the broken leg. My stay in the hospital lasted nearly five months. It should have been shorter but I took a long time to heal, so I am told. To a seven year old it felt a lot longer than just twenty weeks. My ward was of the Victorian variety, rectangular in shape and with very high ceilings. To this day high ceilinged rooms, which are admired by so many, leave me with a feeling of deep foreboding.

Mornings started early at around five thirty, with huge noisy hoover type machines heralding the start of a new empty day for me, bedbound as I was with my leg in a splint raised up at an angle of approximately thirty degrees. The mechanical cleaning giants were pushed along by hard working cleaning ladies who took great pride in their job. Not one speck of dust was left untouched. MRSA hadn't been invented then.

The beds were parked along the length of each wall facing each other. At the top of the ward there was a day room which looked out onto the well-manicured lawns. It was typical of my father when he broke all the rules by driving the family's new car, a Morris 1000 registration number VUS 411 into the hospital grounds and onto the neatly trimmed grass outside the day room, just so I could get a peek at it. He did this to cheer me up. It most certainly did... especially when I saw the look on Matron's face. The fact was that our previous car, an Austin A30 registration number OGA 990 was the one I fell against and broke my leg. Dad couldn't bear to even look at it after that. So he sold it and managed to cobble together enough for the Morris. Funny how I have remembered their reg numbers.

At night I used to lie in my hospital bed and through a gap in the window blinds opposite would watch the lights from the ships' masts and upper works as they sailed up and down the River Clyde. Little did I know at the time, that nine short years later I would be destined to work in the these very same yards. My imagination was given a free reign when my Dad suggested to me that I should try and work out where each ship had come from, where it was going to, what their cargoes would be, what countries the ships' crews were from etc. He had a gift for making things exciting, firing up my imagination.

He brought me a small wooden radio and set it up beside my bed. I had a fork attached to where the aerial had broken off which subsequently provided excellent reception. At night as I watched the ships pass by, I would listen to plays and stories with the volume turned down low so as not to disturb my fellow patients. Thus began my love for the radio medium, which I was lucky enough to work in as an actor many years later.

The fact that my grandfather was killed in 1918 a month before the Armistice when my Dad was only two and a half years old may well have gone some way towards making him such a dedicated family man. And he did manage to do some crazy things to keep his little family happy. Take Christmas Eve circa very early 1950s. Our first floor tenement flat overlooked St. George's Cross in the heart of Glasgow. As kids my elder sister and I we were so excited at the prospect of Santa Claus coming down our lum (chimney) we were still wide awake as midnight approached. We had been told that if we were still awake when Santa came he wouldn't leave us any presents... but so far that threat hadn't done the trick. So our Dad climbed out of the scullery (wee kitchen) window at the back of the tenement taking a small musical box with him. He worked his way along a narrow ledge. When he got to our bedroom window, he opened the top of the musical box. The moment we heard 'Jingle Bells' playing, my sister and I immediately fell fast asleep... apparently. A former Glasgow polis (policeman) he was as courageous as he was kind.

One time when we went to an Auld Firm game at Ibrox, the Rangers v Celtic derby, the crowd behind us started swaying forwards and backwards. We were in the terraces at the Rangers end of course, with only hand rails in front of us for support. As the nightmare unfolded these handrails became more of a dangerous obstacle than an aid as we were being pushed against them. Dad somehow managed to get me and my younger brother to safety on the other side of them. There must have been hundreds of supporters all thinking it a great wheeze to sway in unison, not giving a thought to the consequences of what might be happening to their fellow supporters further down the terraces towards the pitch, being crushed against the hand rails. When there was a lull in play and the crowd stopped swaying momentarily, Dad managed to turn around and face them.

He shouted at the top of his voice, "The next man that pushes will be a better man than me!"

That did it. No-one took up the challenge. They never swayed again. It was a magic moment that I will never forget. He wasn't a particularly tall man (around five foot eleven) nor was he of a powerful build, but his strength of character was enough to silence a mob. I am happy to report that years later the stadium was redesigned.

A few years later we moved to a housing estate in the south side of Glasgow. Dad was a country boy at heart, having been brought up in a wee town called Sauchie in Clackmananshire. He saw the move away from the city centre and out to the suburbs where the air was clearer, as a necessity for the good health of his young growing family. It is also where I started to spread my wings a bit.

Around that time I was beginning to start my apprenticeship as a young tearaway. There were two scout huts on the estate. To alleviate our boredom, me and a couple of mates used to hide in the bushes outside one of the huts, until we heard the scouts inside bouncing on their trampoline. We would then sneak in through the door and throw the main light switch. As we scarpered off we could hear the yelps of whoever the unfortunate scouts were who'd crash-landed in the pitch darkness. It never occurred to us the danger we were putting these lads in. We would then make our way to the other scout hut to see what chaos we could inflict there.

This all went swimmingly well until the scouts got smart to our calamitous and highly dangerous capers. When we heard them all shout, "Who's next for the trampoline?" we three daft bastards naturally assumed that they were happily trampolining away and so we threw the light switch as was our MO. But the only screams we heard came from the scout master and his troop of thirty or so who had been waiting for our visit. Consequently they roared out of the hall and chased us for our lives.

So off we trolled to the next scout hut to see what chaos we could cause there. What we didn't know was that the other lot had been forewarned that we bad boys were on the prowl. When we sneaked up to their scout hut we didn't see them sneaking up on us from behind the bushes and so we were caught red-handed. Instead of getting a good hiding, which we deserved and I believe we should have got, the scout master invited us into the scout hall to join in. It was probably the best thing that could have happened to me at the time. My two mates never went back. Some years later one of them became a highly respected art teacher! But I carried on in the scouts, so my early sojourn into juvenile delinquency was halted before it took hold. I thank you Drew Elliot, the Scout Master of Glasgow's 61st Scout Group wherever you are.

CHAPTER THREE

SEE ME, SEE THESE SHIPYARDS

As far as my future employment was concerned, I had had enough of hospitals, so medicine as a career was out. I once had a slight disagreement, which I won, with a particularly obnoxious nasty snob who turned out to be a barrister, so I don't think entering the Bar would have worked either. I just wouldn't have fitted in. But it was the sixties and unemployment was a thing of the future. There were numerous jobs to be had thank goodness. The trouble was I didn't fancy any of them. The only things I fancied wore skirts and makeup and were very pretty. I did happen to mention to my parents that I wanted to be a farmer, but they managed to dissuade me saying that it would be rather difficult as I lived in the city and so far they hadn't noticed any cows or sheep hanging around the place… so farming was out. So when it was time to let my school get along without me, I still hadn't a clue what sort of job I wanted to do for a living, let alone what sort of career may actually be available to me with my four O Levels, the total result of my twelve years of schooling. So any future career for me was in the hands of chance and opportunity.

I'M CLEAR, WHAT'S IT LIKE UP YOUR END?

T'was then that I remembered my school mate Bobby's suggestion. At last I felt I had a direction in life. One evening as I watched television with my family, I sat twiddling my scout woggle between sweaty fingers, trying to pick the right moment to tell my parents that one day they would watch me on the telly.

"I want to be... a nacta," I said.

"A what?"

"I want to go to drama school and learn to be a nacta."

"Drama what... to be a what?"

This wasn't going well. Then I suddenly remembered my school mate's immortal line and silently thanked my Maker for his good and wise advice. With new found confidence I stuttered on.

"It's good... drama school... for character training."

A few days later with my parents' encouragement, guidance and blessing I applied for the position of Apprentice Ships' Draughtsman at the Charles Connell & Co Shipyard in Scotstoun Glasgow. My audiences would have to wait a while for me yet.

It was in that very shipyard that I learned a few sobering lessons. One of which I would have to face up to... seven years later. T'other included a song and dance act, a lost journey and an awful lot of alcohol.

It was Christmas season in the shipyards and we two apprentice boys, me and Davie Beck - a good mate of mine who happened to have gone to the same school though he didn't study history - had to do an act for our Christmas box i.e. a collection of money from the draughtsmen in the drawing office to thank us for our work over the previous six months. This entailed making their teas and coffees, as well as buying their sandwiches and fags (cigarettes) from the local shops. Everyone knew I had a penchant for the doublet and hose bit, so they were in high expectation of a sonnet or two from the Bard at least - Rabbie Burns, that is, and not the English one called Will, who may turn out to be an imposter if some learned academic scholars of Shakespeare are to be believed. They are of the opinion that William didn't write all that has been attributed to him at all... allegedly!

At lunch times me and Davie would sit on the rocks down by the River Clyde waterfront eating our pieces (Scots for 'sandwiches') and chat about what 'act' we could do for our Christmas box as we watched the French fleets float by.

N.B. French fleets: armadas of used condoms escaping from the sewers into the River Clyde.

Our back drop was the shipyard where giant monoliths were beginning to take shape as the ships of the future.

If the draughtsmen had been disappointed when we opted for a wee song and dance routine atop an office table, to the tune of The Goons 'Ying Tong Tiddle I Po', they didn't show it, for they did us proud and stuffed our pockets with readies.

Later that afternoon in a local pub we two underage drinkers got sloshed on the proceeds. I cannot remember which pub it was that endangered their licence by selling alcohol to us, nor do I have any recall of leaving it, or as to how or when I arrived at Glasgow's Central Station from Scotstoun which was miles to the west, but somehow with the luck of a drunk I got there. My next memory - and it is the only vividly clear one - is pulling out of my pockets the remains of my share of the hard won cash from our routine and counting it in full view of everyone on the station concourse. I do not know to this day who he was, but if he reads this and remembers the swaying figure of a seventeen year old dropping pound notes like confetti, then I would like to thank that man for picking up the money, stuffing it back in my jacket pocket, and seeing me safely onto my train… truly a saint.

As you may have gathered we were not the perfect apprentice ships' draughtsmen. Out of sheer boredom we would draw risqué cartoons on the various ships' plans, much to the annoyance of the proper draughtsmen who had spent many hours painstakingly measuring, calculating sizes, tracing and finally drawing them. We used to watch from a hidden vantage point in the outer office as their completed plans were presented to the Chief Draughtsman and his deputy in his office. All would appear to go well until the Chief would do a double-take on spying a cartoon of a naked dervisher or something horribly similar, hanging from the masts and derrick fittings. We were roasted more than once by the ever patient fellow.

As a punishment, the budding Gileses would be sent down to the yard to measure some obscure bracket, or something hopelessly difficult to get at, high up on whatever of the three ships that were being built at the time.

I'M CLEAR, WHAT'S IT LIKE UP YOUR END?

In order to do this hair-raising deed, the apprentice in question would be kitted out for health and safety reasons... yes we had 'em in the sixties though they weren't nearly as adhered to or as strict as today. So all these encumbrances we had to wear were for insurance purposes. On one such occasion I was 'kitted out' in over-sized overalls with holes in the pockets, over-sized boots and an over-sized hard-hat, which if I turned my head too quickly, would stay facing front. When I turned around again it would then sit side-ways on top of my head like a rapper of today trying to be a cool dude. I believe all the clobber was oversized in order that it would fit an assortment of apprentices.

A policeman's hat of roughly the same size was given to me as part of my costume in the first ever movie I was cast in, and which you can read about later. But in the meantime, it's back to the shipyard.

Of course once I had struggled down to the yard I would find that I was the only one wearing anything like protective clothing, apart from the welders, who had to wear a hard hat device with a specially shaded eye safety visor for obvious reasons. But we were never given these which were in my opinion, the singular most important piece of safety equipment that we should have had. Instead we were told to avoid looking at what the welders were welding. This was no easy feat as the decks were strewn with debris of all sorts, from loose hanging wires to razor sharp discarded lumps of metal etc. It was difficult enough trying to circumvent these potentially hazardous obstacles without having to also avoid catching a glimpse of the welders' oxyacetylene flame.

In the shipyard itself the smell of white hot steel and the cacophony of deafening noise was and remains to this day, quite unforgettable. And so were the comments from the yard workers. Somehow I always managed to hear them above the din.

To add to my discomfort I had to carry with me one rule (one must never call it a ruler!) one pen, one retractable measuring tape, one rolled up complete plan of the ship, one rolled up plan of the specific area of the ship and a third rolled up plan depicting the bracket to be measured, which all added to the manoeuvrability problem caused by wearing oversized gear with holes for pockets. Thus the rule was placed between my teeth, the pen behind my ear, the retractable measuring tape in my left hand and all three maps wedged under my right arm.

On arriving at what little there was of the ship, at this stage only the basic skeletal shape of port and starboard sides with protruding half decks, I would unravel the first map and become immediately confused as to whether I was indeed actually looking up at the right ship. The shipyard workers thought it a great ruse to take the piss and often sent me to the wrong ship to start with. But once over this hurdle, I would roll up that plan and unravel the second. This too was of little help to me because I would be further confused as to which section of the ship I would have to find. I got lucky though when I saw part of the ship's bulwark which I recognised from the plan that I had earlier been caught cartooning a masturbating gargoyle on, which was the reason I had been sent down the yard on this occasion.

It was not long before I perceived my next problem. The bracket to be measured was approximately forty foot up and some five feet below the top of the ladder, which was precariously tied by a piece of rusty looking wire to a half-finished deck. There is an unwritten law in the shipyards i.e. when someone prepares to climb down a ladder they have precedence over the person preparing to climb up, providing the latter hadn't yet started. Thus many attempts can be made before the ladder is finally climbed. On this particular occasion I remember I had to make only two false starts so it wasn't too bad.

But by far the biggest problem I had was that I didn't have a wonderful head for heights, which meant that instead of leaning my body-weight away from the ladder as I climbed in order to give me more upwards leverage, I tended to cling close to the rungs and sort of slither upwards, with my knees protruding from each side looking no doubt like a cartoon character Roger Rabbit. Along with all the paraphernalia I was carrying, I can assure you this was a difficult, painful and terrifying exercise. But I finally made it, forty-six foot up on a ladder to be precise, which was not only vibrating from the riveters machines going at full throttle all around me, but on a swaying ladder being buffeted from irregular gusts of wind. With my left hand clutching the retractable tape, my right tentatively unrolling the final plan, I eventually spotted the elusive bracket and stuffed all three plans at an angle in between the rungs.

"How long you gonna be, pal?"

I glanced up and immediately felt dizzy. "Nearly finished mate… sorry to keep you."

It is not wise to offend anyone when you are perched high up a ladder and they have the advantage of being even higher than you, so it is always best to try to answer any query from above with the utmost politeness. What you really wanted to reply instead must always remain your very own secret.

With great care I passed the tape to my right hand then extended it until it passed the bracket. But as it was on a level with my eye line I couldn't see the tape's inch markings. The only way to see them was to lean away from the safety of the ladder, a death defying feat which I considered not worth the hassle and risk at my meagre wages of four pounds and ten shillings a week.

"Hurry up ya wee shite," the voice laughingly encouraged from above.

'Och sod it,' I thought, and shouted up, "All finished, pal."

Gripping the ladder as if my very life depended on it - as indeed it did - I made my way slowly back down to terra firma, Roger Rabbit style in reverse mode. I waddled back to the drawing office, my feet sliding around inside the boots. Later I wrote on the plan what I thought was a fair approximation of the bracket size and forgot about it until it returned to haunt me at Dundee Repertory Theatre seven years later.

Sitting backstage during rehearsals minding my own business I was deeply concentrating not on my line learning, which I should have been doing, but on reading a newspaper. Then I saw it, 'SHIP RUNS AGROUND'. It was my ship! Could it have been because of the measurement of that bracket? I had many a sleepless night over that. But there had been no casualties and I recall that my mate had previously drawn a cartoon on the same plan of two fornicating seagulls or something similar where my bracket should have been, so I didn't feel as guilty after that.

During my time at Dundee Rep I was what was called the Equity Deputy. That is to say I was the Actors' Union representative, or in another occupation a kind of shop steward. Surprising this, as my earlier experience of unions back in the shipyards nearly put me off them for life.

We apprentices had been told to join the union. Had I been asked to join there would have been no problem. Of course I was going to join, but I doggedly decided to do it in my own time. I realise with hindsight that I was being somewhat of an awkward pain in the arse just for the hell of it.

Unfortunately my seeming reluctance came to the attention of a greasy, long-haired, creepy bloke who was an ardent fan of a certain Russian called Trotksy or Lenin or whoever it was that wanted free beer for the workers. I didn't have a problem with that.

One afternoon as the office chores droned endlessly on, I nipped down to the gents for a pee and a puff. I had the occasional Kensitas cigarette in those days in order to relieve the lack of tension in my life. Unbeknownst to me the creepy one was waiting. Next thing I knew he had me in a strangle hold.

"Look here ya wee shite," he began. That was twice I had been called that, if it happened again I would begin to get worried. But this time it sounded like it was meant.

"What's wrong wi' you?" I managed to squeak. Reflected in the mirror opposite, I could see my eyes bulging as if I had advanced thyroiditis.

"I'll tell you whit's wrong wi' me… you is whit's wrong wi' me."

I shouldn't have told him to eff off at this point but I did.

"Why don't you join the union yah wee sod?"

Ah, that was it. Now I knew. "Because I don't want to… ok?"

"Well you don't have a choice pal. Wan oot, aw oot. That's the way it has tae be."

In truth I was not anti-union at all, but I wasn't going to let this creep know that. Two of my great uncles had been miners and if ever any trade needed a union (as well as the acting one) it was coal mining. However I tried to sound as if I had reasoned it out.

"In my opinion, pal, secondary picketing, block voting and violent intimidation aren't in anybody's interest, especially mine at this moment in time. So if you'd stop trying to f--g strangle me!"

Gawd was I bolshie back then. Just as I thought I had irreversibly overstepped the mark, my guardian angel arrived in the form of Big John, a tall good looking swarthy character, respected by everyone in the office. No-one messed with Big John. He wore thin ties and slightly creased grey suits which would not have looked out of place in the film *Casablanca*. In today's parlance he would be described as really cool. Ostensibly a quiet man, he was the strong silent type I guess women fall for. Though I wasn't strong I did try the silent bit with the women I met but it didn't work for me. I guess I must have been too noisy. When Big John spoke in that Glaswegian drawl of his people listened.

"Leave ra boy alone."

And that was all it took to save me from a pummelling.

"But Big John, he willnae join the union."

"It's his choice. It's a free country, remember."

As they walked away Big John looked back at me and shrugged. Left alone in the gents I quickly began to re-appraise postponing joining up. But before I could announce my new found allegiance to the great and mighty union, my path on the road to cinematic greatness, in the guise of makeup, wigs, doublets and hoes, was to take a new turn.

Both my fellow apprentice and I had come to the obvious conclusion that neither of us was cut out to be a ship's draughtsman. So we made a secret pact to save a few bob, leave the shipyards and hitch-hike round the world. But we had two problems to contend with before we could begin our adventure. The first was that our wages were pitiful, so we would probably have had to finish our apprenticeships by the time we had saved up anything like enough money to get us as far as Paisley (a town on the outskirts of Glasgow). Secondly, I wanted to give the acting thing one last go, otherwise I felt that it would be unfinished business… something I may regret. So I told Davie that I was going to apply for Drama School but that he needn't worry, because I stood as much chance of being accepted for the three year acting course as a vegan would relish eating a half-chewed bull's arse pie.

CHAPTER FOUR

ME? A COLLEGE BOY? YOU MUST BE JOKING!

And so it came to pass that I applied to be a student at The Royal Scottish Academy of Music and Drama. They duly sent me umpteen titles of plays from which I had to choose one speech and perform it at an audition. I was expected also to present one other speech of my own choosing which was not on their list. Unfortunately I had never read a whole play in my life. In *A Man for All Seasons* at school, I had only read up to the bit where my character entered by mistake, exited then came on again late! Subsequently I hadn't a clue what speech to choose from the play list or where to look for one that would suit my ability, or lack of it. The choice was soon made for me. As I stood in the bookshop leafing through the various options, the play *Andorra* by Max Frisch which was on the College's list turned out to be the cheapest. So I plumped for that. For my own contribution I chose a chunk out of Robert Burns' 'Tam O' Shanter' believing that no-one else would pick it for their second choice. I was right. On the day all the other candidates turned up with set pieces chosen from the list as requested then in addition, pieces from plays I didn't even know existed by playwrights I'd never heard of. I began to feel more than a little out of my depth. I also began to believe that this forthcoming audition had all the makings of a disaster for me.

Before I knew it, the appointed audition day arrived and I strolled into the auspicious Royal Scottish Academy of Music and Drama building in St. George's Place, Glasgow.

Interesting wee fact: one of our drama teachers, an exquisitely groomed and distinguished chap with the most refined of manners by the name of Cecil Williams, had tried to help Nelson Mandela in the early 1960s attend a meeting of the then banned ANC in South Africa. It was a highly dangerous escapade indeed which took some guts from both of them to try to accomplish. Nelson Mandela drove the car dressed as a chauffeur with Cecil acting the part of his 'boss'. Unfortunately they were stopped en route by the police and questioned. Cecil tried to blag their way out of the perilous situation they found themselves in, but to no avail. Subsequently they were both arrested and placed under house arrest. They were indeed men of much courage. I'm sure Cecil would have been absolutely delighted that the name St. George's Place, where the RSAMD was at the time, was renamed Nelson Mandela Place.

Back to the audition: I was led to various rooms by one of the third-year drama students where I was put through my paces. In the first room I entered I was met by the Movement teacher. She instructed me to walk up and down then roundabout a bit etc., etc., etc., so on and so forth, presumably to see if I could do so without tripping up, something I did quite often many years later as D C Woods in *The Bill*, much to the chagrin of my fellow players. Eventually I was released after I presume she was content that I had no noticeable postural problems and that all my limbs appeared to do what was expected of them when ordered.

The next stage was the music room where I had to tap out various rhythms to a piece of piano music. That bit was easy. When I was younger I used to play around with a snare drum and high-hat cymbals in a carpet warehouse in Hamilton with two other wannabe rock stars. That was until we inadvertently set of the burglar alarms alerting the local constabulary, heralding the end of any future career as a drummer in the music business. Rhythm I was definitely good at and I could bash out a few chords on the guitar.

I was then made to go through umpteen musical scales, sing from a music score which was hazardous for me as I couldn't read a note of music, some more music stuff that I cannot quite remember, then I was accompanied to the voice class for poetry recitation (to test my diction I presume) followed by an exercise to see if I could take direction.

So far so good I thought to myself. I hadn't felt that I had let myself down up to that point. But I was more than aware that there was still plenty of opportunity for me to cock up, especially as I was about to be called onstage for my audition pieces.

The realisation dawned that I was about to present myself as a potential student worth training in the craft of professional acting. But I wasn't overawed by the occasion for two reasons: firstly because ignorance is bliss, and secondly I had already convinced myself that it wasn't going to be me on stage because I would be hiding behind the character I was portraying. In the play *Andorra* I was playing a young Jewish chap happily embracing his religion, and in the other I was a narrator of Scottish poetry. Had I been asked to give a speech as myself, that would have been a totally different story altogether.

Interesting thing I've noticed: people who are not in the business fully expect actors to be outgoing, gregarious and chock-full of confidence. Let me tell you that for the majority of actors I have known for over forty years that it is definitely not the case. Whilst actors will with measured confidence spout forth copious amount of lines playing a character to a packed house, they don't usually warm to standing out from the crowd and giving speeches as themselves. That is a completely different kettle of fish and requires quite a different expertise. In these situations e.g. after dinner speaking, corporate presenting etc., we actors have nothing to hide behind, no costume, no lines written by a playwright. I will regale you with my experience of after dinner speaking later but I thought it worth mentioning at this juncture.

When I walked onto the stage of the College's Athenaeum Theatre, to my surprise there was no-one in the auditorium. Presuming that those running the auditions had nipped off for a cuppa, I began clowning around a bit, doing star jumps and the like, uttering weird noises to get my vocal chords warmed up. I thought that these were the sort of things real actors did and indeed I found out later that I wasn't far wrong.

Then a gruff voice upstage and behind me said, "When you're ready, we haven't got all day son." It was the imposing figure of the Deputy Head of the Royal Scottish Academy of Music and Drama, John (Johnny) Groves seated behind a desk. Beside him sat the equally imposing figure of the Head of College, Colin Chandler or as he became known to us budding thespians, The Boss.

During the three years I spent at the RSAMD I quickly grew to respect highly both these exceptional characters. They didn't try to shove some daft psychobabble approach to acting down our throats, or push us in directions we didn't want to go. Instead they gave us our rein, guiding us over the hurdles, the fences and the deep water jumps… until we passed the finishing post as fully fledged brand new squeaky-cleanish professional actors. They gained their rightful status by being honest with us, listening to us as individuals and wisely clearing a pathway allowing us to wonder at and learn as well as make mistakes. We eager young things soaked up the knowledge they shared unconditionally with us… well, I tried to anyway. The alternative for me was working in the shipyards and that wasn't going to be an option even if I had wanted to go back.

I got through the speeches without a hitch, that is to say I remembered all of the lines in the correct order and with I hope some style. How good my delivery actually was I of course had no idea, except that I was aware of a deafening silence from the two of them when I finished. After what seemed a millennium Johnny Groves asked me why I chose the extract from the play Andorra. I had the good sense not to reply that it was because it was the least expensive of the options, though in hindsight maybe I should have done, honesty always being the best policy. Instead I heard myself blurt out roughly the following:

"Well sir, I believe that the essence of the speech in *Andorra* is about the character realising the fact that he is Jewish and accepting it as a positive direction in his life. The route… no… the proper journey as I see it… chosen by him. Indeed in him… I suppose I see something of myself… though I'm not Jewish… not that it should mean anything anyway… it is acting after all… but the desire to be a nacta and the acceptance of that vocation is an enlightenment that I have fully accepted, and in doing so have at last found the path in life… that my journey should take…" I trailed off at that point.

Of course it was all a load of bollocks and the twinkle in all four of their eyes showed that they both saw right through my hastily presented ridiculous answer. At that moment I believed I had put the tin hat on any chance I had to gain entry into such an auspicious college as the RSAMD. Then it was The Boss's turn.

"Tom?"

"Yes sir?"

"What will you do if you are unsuccessful in your audition today?"

I was tempted to say that I would therefore bugger off with my mate from the shipyards and hitch-hike around the globe, but a little voice inside said, 'All may not be lost, give it another go Tommy.'

"Well sir, if I am not accepted this time round I will try again next year and the next until I am successful. So if I were you I would get me over and done with now."

Two weeks later and now a member of the union, I was apologising to my section leader back in the ship yard's drawing office for clocking on ten minutes late that morning when I was called to the phone. An unexpected phone call to your place of work is always disconcerting and a bit worrying. I was bracing myself for some sort of bad news. But it wasn't bad at all, though it was maybe bad for the acting profession, which I was told I had just been accepted into as a student.

In the Meantime

There were a few long weeks to kill between leaving the shipyards and officially becoming a student, so I decided that I would need a holiday as I probably wouldn't get another chance to have one for some years. How true that turned out to be. But to go on holiday I needed money and so I got a job as washer-checker-driver for a car hire firm based at Glasgow airport. It was a reasonably cushy number and apart from getting soaked umpteen times a day from washing the cars, I got to indulge myself in my second favourite past time... driving.

The year was 1968. The season was summertime and the sun was blisteringly hot. I was a few weeks away from my eighteenth birthday and driving a sparklingly clean big white automatic Ford Zodiac into the car hire drop-off zone at the front of the airport, where buses full of nubile young ladies off on their school trips abroad would unburden themselves of their highly sought after loads. With the car windscreen steaming up from the heat of my post pubescent ego, the radio blasted out the Beatles single 'Hey Jude'. All the mascara painted eyes inside the bus were on me as I screeched the car to an overdramatic emergency type stop, my arm dangling out of the open window like Jimmy Dean. I coolly threw open the door and swung my legs out, stood up and stretched blinking up at the bright sky. I felt like the guy in the Coca Cola adverts of the nineties, except for the fact that this was thirty years earlier. I thought all was going well and that I could have had my pick of any one of the giggling lovelies on the bus, until I realised that the sound they were making was not an excited sort of giggling noise made by girls of a certain age when they begin to realise what boys are for. Instead it was the giggling from girls of a certain age who were aware of what a prat I looked as I preened myself for what I thought was their benefit, forgetting that I was wearing big welly boots and with the car hire firm emblem emblazoned on my jersey. But the worst bit for me was the addition of the less than cool picture I was actually displaying as I hadn't realised that my trousers around the crotch area were splashing wet from having washed the sparkling clean white Zodiac car I had just parked.

For everyone else in the world who, like me, are fans of The Beatles and love the track 'Hey Jude', they must have so many wonderful memories which are triggered off every time they hear it played. For me it will always be etched in my memory as the time when it looked as if I'd pissed myself and proudly showed the result to a bus load of gorgeous birds.

I had a similar experience thirty years later at the five hundredth anniversary party in London's West End for a television series in which I happened to be a regular character for four years, but more of that later.

Occasionally, we washer-checker-drivers had to deliver cars to other destinations. One of the favourites was Prestwick airport. Apart from the fact that it would be at least a couple of hours away from the grafting side of the job, the road over the Fenwick Moor lent itself to opening up the cars' engines and having a bit of light hearted fun. It was easier to do daft stuff behind the wheel back then because there was so much less traffic around. We didn't wear seat belts as they hadn't even been invented, so it was a stupid and foolhardy practise to say the least. When I left that job to start Drama School, I had convinced myself that as I had miraculously survived my time as a washer checker driver, there just had to be something special waiting for me around the corner, something that was my destiny… surely it just had to be as a nacta? I think I was still trying to convince myself that I had made the right choice.

My Formal Training Looms

Prior to starting Drama School I was given a list of student requirements to buy. This included a black tee shirt, ballet shoes and a pair of black heavy denier footless tights all to be worn in the dance and movement classes which were part of the curriculum. When my wife went to her drama school the blokes not only had to wear the tee shirt, ballet shoes and black tights, but hairnets as well if they had longish hair.

Having just turned eighteen with a mind driven by a barely controllable urge to get laid on a regular basis, buying tights was not going to do my street cred any good.

Makeup wasn't as much of a problem for me because it was of the theatrical variety and therefore obviously not for personal use. But tights?! And so it came to pass that I found my way to the ladies lingerie department in a well-known Glasgow department store.

"Tights is it? For you, son? Black footless heavy denier wans an' aw, eh?"

I was acutely aware that every female within earshot had fine-tuned their ears into select hearing mode in order to confirm what I had just asked for. The female assistant had such a loud piercing voice that I swear customers arrived from other floors when they heard her just to witness my embarrassment. S'truth!

"What size of footless tights do you require?" she asked, upping the decibels.

I didn't even know that tights came in different sizes, so in my haste to get out of there pronto I whispered, "Large I suppose. I'm a man you see."

"Oh you're a man are you? Really? Och I'd never have guessed," came the droll reply, as she showed me the largest pair of black heavy denier footless tights she could find.

"Just give us the f--n' tights," is what I wanted to say. Instead I replied, "They'll do just fine, thank you."

I paid her and ran out into Sauchiehall Street, went straight to a pub and downed a couple of large whiskies. I began to have serious doubts about this nacting lark and was tempted to phone my mate in the shipyard to say, "pack a spare rucksack I'm coming with you."

There was a very pretty girl in my class at College called Jenny Twigge who was a gifted actress and went on to be a television star. She recalled the first Movement Class we had. It went something like this:

"We girls were told that we would be spending the next three years with the same guys in our class, so it wouldn't do to send them up when we saw them in their tights for the first time. Our Movement teacher explained it would probably be the first time that any of them had ever worn tights. We girls who were dressed in black leotards decided to be professional and carry on as normal when you boys came into the room. We wouldn't make any comments. That was until you came into the room Tommy. I'm sorry darling, but the look of utter fear and dejection on your face convulsed us all at once. Where did you get these tights? They were huge. The crotch was half-way down your thighs, and the leggings were so long there were folds upon folds."

Thanks, honey pie. We became good mates from then on. She reminded recently me of a play we did at College called the *Imperial Nightingale*, in which I played the White Wizard and had to perform magic. Our audiences full of kids loved all that stuff. For one of the tricks I did I had to juggle with hard-boiled eggs. Unbeknownst to me, some wag had swapped them for fresh eggs for a joke, so I was left literally with egg on my face.

When Jenny witnessed this she nearly wet herself in full view of the audience, which she eventually did do when the following occurred. During a later scene she was in, she happened to look into the wings and witnessed a bit of a commotion. The stage management team were frantically trying to make a mechanical bird fly across the stage on a wire, land on a wooden cherry tree branch, then burst into song. This sequence had always worked really well in rehearsals. But for some reason the damned bird would not play ball. As a last ditch attempt one of the team tried to get it launched by swinging it around above his head. Although it did take off, it had been swung so hard it flew headlong and at great speed missing Jenny by inches, and ended up impaled beak first in the tree's trunk instead, which happened to be in its flight path. The sound it emitted from its beak was not so much delightful singing, but more like the death throes of a frog landing on an electrified fence. That was the moment when Jenny lost control. Say no more.

She also recalled the time at college when she was asked in a movement class to appear as the smell of baking bread! Acting eh? You just can't beat it!

Another of my contemporaries at College was Benny Young, one of the most talented students of our three year Acting Course, and I am more than happy to say that he too has remained a lifelong friend. We became good mates early on in the course and would go out on the raz together often, always in the hope that we might get lucky with a 'couple of birds'. Failing that there was always a plethora of good pubs in Glasgow's West End as back up. During one of our more arty-farty sojourns we visited a theatre, where I managed with consummate ease to make a foopa. I was rather adept at those and still am.

As drama students we were naturally encouraged to see as many professional shows as possible. So one evening after classes finished and a pint or two was had, off me and Benny dutifully went. During the interval we were approached by the theatre manager who immediately recognised us as drama students. Gawd knows how; it wasn't as if we dressed flamboyantly in tights with sequined jock straps and spats or anything. But somehow she knew what we were, and that was her passport to zoom in on us. She was quite a formidable character with an incongruous deep voice, and dressed in a long flowing dark maroon coloured chiffon dress which made squiffing sounds when she walked.

"Are you enjoying the play darlings?" she breathed politely at us.

"Oh yes, immensely," I replied, sounding like I meant it.

She smiled, turned away and squiffed off to welcome other punters and I should have left it at that… but oh no not me. I had to try and impress. I called out to her in my best R P (Queen's English) accent which I had been struggling to master in voice class, but succeeded only in sounding more than a touch camp.

"I think it's one of his best pieces actually."

She stopped in her tracks, turned her head around so quickly that it damned nearly snapped off, then she squiffily lumbered her way back over to us.

"Really, well that is interesting. You know it well do you?"

"Yes of course," I replied, gaining in confidence by the second.

"What do you think of the way in which the first act was concluded?"

It is already probably obvious to you dear reader that I was lying through my teeth though I did so with great gusto. Of course I had never read the play, didn't even know it existed before that evening, and consequently knew sod all about it. But as I had just witnessed the end of the first act I thought I stood a good chance of sounding knowledgeable, so I bluffed on.

"The end of the first act… mmmh!" I mused with my version of an intellectual air. "Extremely Osbornesque," I offered.

"Yes, you are so very right."

So far so good, I thought to myself. But I noticed that Benny was ominously silent throughout this duologue.

"And the ending, do please tell me your thoughts on the finale."

I had by now run out of bluffing material, especially so as it was only half time. So I simply replied that it had been some years since I had read the piece and had forgotten how it had ended (I was nineteen years old at the time). By now my Glasgow accent was making a strong challenge to oust my camp version of Queen's English. Benny's top lip curled inwards. As time went on I learned that it was his way of registering impending doom, as well as restricting a guffawing laugh from exploding onto the scene.

"Oh?" she said, then squiffed off huffily.

"What did I say wrong?"

"Well for a start, it was one of his more recent plays."

"How recent?"

"Actually it's only six months old. Do you want me to go on?"

"Oh shit!"

The play was *Hotel in Amsterdam* by John Osborne. By saying it was 'Extremely Osbornesque' was sort of right, but more than a touch on the dramatic side of crap. Since that day, no matter how simple or obvious the answer to a question might be, if I'm at all unsure I admit it from the outset. And even though my intellectual capabilities may take a beating from so doing, I hope this approach will also show the more honest me.

My Debut

My first stint in professional theatre was as a student actor while still at Drama College. The famous Glasgow Citizen's Theatre situated in the heart of the Gorbals was doing a production of *Henry IV Part One* and they needed a few more bods to make up the numbers.

Many have heard of the infamous Gorbals and to some extent its infamy was well deserved, though I experienced only kindness and humour whenever I went there and never once any threat of violence during the play's run or at any time before or since. There was a pub next door to the theatre called the Seaforth, a typical spit and sawdust bar full of allsorts including we thesps, who would usually gather in the snug before curtain up. There was also a street gang in the area who were very protective of us theatre bods.

"Och youse poofy actors ur no a threat tae enywan. Weel look efter youse. Nae problem pal," which was what I was told by one of them. In their eyes we were incapable of defending ourselves and woe betide anyone who attempted to have a go at any of us. Ergo we were safe as houses in the Gorbals.

Being in a Shakespeare production was a good experience for a drama student and prudent accountancy from the theatre's point of view as we were unpaid labour. I was therefore employed as a one line courtier with added stage management duties. My line was "Jesus bless us", a request I secretly prayed for many times throughout my subsequent career in live theatre.

Working with professionals was a great insight into what life as a real actor would be like. The show was terrific and I was fascinated to watch these pros work at their craft during the rehearsal period then during performance. There was one hitch however. Isn't there always?

Along with my one-line courtier role, plus many other duties, I was also involved in the battle scene. Three weeks of rehearsals with a highly competent fight director of the stunt man variety, served to produce a spectacular fight sequence. It was thrilling to be part of. There were umpteen thespians on stage at the same time giving their all. They truly appeared to be belting and hacking seven colours of crap out of each other with formidable looking and potentially lethal broadswords, maces, battle axes etc. whilst being absolutely safe at the same time. The result was simply spectacular to watch apparently, until the dress rehearsal came along.

I had been directed to enter upstage right, behind an upturned truck, the type used in medieval Britain, I imagined, to transport unfortunates from dungeons to gallows. Simultaneously another fellow student was to appear down right and thus nearer the audience. We were then meant to advance on each other. He headed upstage towards me, whilst I headed downstage towards him. Then we were supposed to meet around the middle point of the upturned truck.

The other battlers were to join us onstage from various positions in the wings where upon battle would thus commence amidst a rowdy cacophony of highly choreographed, blood-curdling shrieking, snarling, accompanied by the clashing of weapons. It sounded real enough in rehearsals. But here's where things went awry.

The bloke in stage management, whose chore at that time was to direct a modicum of dry ice onto the stage thus adding a misty mystical ambience to the scene of battle, mistakenly put too much of the mix into the ice making machine. The result was as thick a pea-souper of a fog which any heavy industrial city in the land had ever seen, enveloping the entire stage with the stuff. There was indeed plenty of shrieking and growling as had been rehearsed. In fact there was much, much more of it than expected, coupled with genuine howls of pain and a few choice modern, un-Shakespearean oaths, as actors gave and received severe blows from each other, blinded as we all were by the thick mist.

When it eventually evaporated, the sight on stage looked every bit as real as an après battle battlefield could get. Not one of us escaped some bruising or bashing of one sort or another.

I made a very necessary mental note. From then on, I would be very respectful and extremely wary of any sort of special effects that I may ever have to encounter.

The Animal Lover

I learned about the hazards of working with animals on stage during a production of *A Midsummer Night's Dream* when I was cast as one of the mechanicals. I was playing the one with the dog. Now I have to say that I had a choice of a real dog or a stuffed one. Being an animal lover and not wanting to show that I couldn't control one on stage I decided on the real variety.

The dog I was given to work with had no pedigree, which I thought and hoped would work in my favour because pedigrees can be somewhat highly strung. And true to my thinking and hopes he performed brilliantly both in rehearsals as well as all through the first half of the opening night.

But unbeknownst to me during the interval the poor mutt had become quite ill backstage and was taken home by its owner. The Front of House Secretary's dog happened to be in the building and so it was swiftly pressganged in to replace it though no-one had told me. In the dimly lit wings I was handed the dog's lead and naturally presumed it to be the same dog attached to the other end. Innocently I walked onstage and was immediately greeted by uproarious laughter. At first I thought that I had forgotten to put on me tights or something until I glanced down to check that they were indeed where they should be. It was then that I realised what the audience found to be so amusing. From their point of view my dog had turned from being predominantly white with a few black patches to one which was jet black with a white nose. This unrehearsed animal, startled by the bright lights and the hoots of laughter, took off like an Exocet into the auditorium. Pandemonium ensued. And so my line, "And this dog is my dog," by Will Shakespeare (or whoever really wrote it) got another round of laughter as I had to speak it to a dogless lead.

By the way, to those of you who are dog lovers like me, I want to let you know that the first dog was very soon well again. Apparently he had been spoilt with too many biscuits given by the well-meaning cast and crew, who had grown extremely fond of him.

I wasn't to work with animals again for many years until I did a play about a mental asylum in which my character carried his pet snake, a python constrictor, around in a shoe box. Unfortunately the poor reptile died before the opening night. Stage management doused it in TCP to stop its cold, decaying body from smelling. I had my doubt about TCP being the answer but I was overruled. By the time I took it out of its box during the dress rehearsal, the combined stench of the TCP and dead snake, which by then had been warmed up from the heat of the stage lights, nearly made me pass out. And so I overruled the management and insisted on using a rubber snake as a substitute instead. As the audience had read in the local press that there would be a real live snake on stage they turned up on the opening night in their droves truly believing that the wriggling rubbery thing in my hands was the real McCoy. So I got away with it, much to the consternation of the snake bloke who had earlier claimed to be an expert on snakes. I was tempted to ask him, if he knew so much about the things, how come it died in his care? But for once I decided to keep schtuum.

CHAPTER FIVE

MY FIRST STINT AS A PRO

The three years at College soon went by and I was catapulted into the real world of the jobbing actor. My professional debut was in the famous Bradford Alhambra in a season of dreaded weekly rep. I say dreaded because it was such an absolutely exhausting experience that I dreaded ever having to do it again.

Weekly Rep meant exactly what it said; we only had one week to rehearse the following week's play during the days, whilst playing a totally different show in the evenings which had been rehearsed the previous week. It was damned hard graft both physically and mentally. The only saving grace was that an old chum of mine Jeni Giffen, who had been in the year above me at College, was also in the company. She and I had the auspicious titles of Acting ASMs. i.e. actors with assistant stage management duties. This meant that not only had we to act in the plays, thus having to learn lines, but also do all the stage management duties as well, six days a week. On the seventh day, the Sabbath, whilst everyone else in the UK was going to Church, or resting, or simply benefiting from a day off work, Jeni and I would do catch up on our chores e.g. our washing, shopping, writing home etc., and catching up with much needed rest.

A typical working day for us would start at nine o'clock when we would arrive to clear the furniture etc., from the previous night's show, sweep the stage, mark out the rehearsal set with gaffa tape and boil up the kettle for teas and coffees before the company of thespians arrived at ten. It would then be up to us to somehow get the cast to donate some pennies towards the ever diminishing tea and coffee fund, which is arguably one of the most difficult jobs in the history of the theatre.

Jeni or I would then be on the book. That is to say, one of us would sit through all the rehearsals marking in the actors moves in the prompt copy book and feed them their lines when they dried (forgot their lines) which was quite often in weekly rep as they had had only a week to try and learn them... in the right order... without tripping over the furniture.

Meanwhile the other Acting ASM would be sent around the town to beg or borrow whatever props were needed for the next week's play, rushing back to the theatre six or seven times a day in time to rehearse their own bit. Rehearsals would finish at around five o'clock when the actors would bugger off to prepare for their performances that evening, leaving the Acting ASMs to reverse the whole process on stage, and note how many had managed to avoid paying for their teas and coffees yet again.

Up would come the rehearsal markings from the stage, the set for that evening's show would have to be reset, tea and coffee cups washed, wigs dressed, costumes checked and if necessary mended before a quick meal break on the trot. Then it was back in to run the show that night, as well as acting in it. Finally when the play was put to bed around ten thirty at night, we would go back to our separate digs and learn our lines for the following day's rehearsal before hitting the sack around midnight.

My landlady was a Mrs Sobjec, a Checkoslovakian lady who let out her spare room. She was a wonderful, motherly type, an absolute angel who took pity on me, with breasts that you wanted to envelop you when things were going wrong. Every night when I crawled exhausted over the threshold of her welcoming house, she would have a mug of hot tea and sandwiches ready waiting for me.

Our season opened with a highly unfunny comedy which to the best of my knowledge has never been staged again. I was cast as a waiter. The director insisted that as I was fair-haired and as most waiters were of the dark-haired Latino variety - in his opinion - I should dye my locks black. This idea didn't please me too much but not wanting to create a rumpus so early on, Jeni and I dutifully dyed my hair boot-polish black. At the same time we did our week's washing, most of which subsequently ended up sporting a strange darkish hew from the residue of the hair dye that somehow got into the water system for the rest of the season. A few days later after the play had opened, one of the thesps sidled up to me in the wings and whispered conspiratorially in me ear just as I was about to go on stage, telling me that he had met the director's boyfriend in London.

"So what's the big deal?" I enquired.

He went on. "Thing is dear boy, not only are you remarkably like him in size, stature and general appearance, in fact you're a dead ringer… but the chap has jet black hair too… just like yours is now!"

Good grief!

Tiredness took its toll. I once lost the prompt copy minutes before curtain up on a first night. As I crept around in the wings hunting for it, the highly nervous company of actors wondered what the hell I was doing. I couldn't admit the loss, for it would have given them apoplexy on top of the varying degrees of nervous breakdowns they were already experiencing. No actor wants to hear that if they have the hellish experience of drying and ask for a prompt, the voice of the prompter calling back saying, "Sorry pal but I've gone and lost the bloody prompt copy so you'll just have to make it up. Good luck!"

Consequently I took the curtain up with an old unmarked copy and had to guess where the rehearsed cuts came, as well as all the sound and light cues. The prompt book eventually turned up two minutes before the end of the play. Some stupid sod had picked it up in the darkened wing space, mistakenly thinking it was his then waddled off to his dressing room to get ready for the show, oblivious to the terror he had just unleashed for me. My young head sprouted a few grey hairs on that occasion. By this time my hair was an assortment of black, grey, blue and orangey blonde colours, as Jeni and I had tried in vain to dye it back to its original colour after the play finished its run. And you should have seen the colour of my washing afterwards.

On another night I actually fell asleep as I sat in the prompt corner watching the script and listening to the actors drone on... and on... and on... zzz! When I awoke the play was nearing its natural end. Luckily, all the cast had got through the show without requiring the need of a prompt.

Much as I love my job, I am hopeless at watching it being done by others. My wife dreads going to the theatre with me as I tend to fall asleep more often than not. I blame this on my weekly rep days when I was too tired to stay awake in the wings as an overworked Acting ASM. As soon as the curtain goes up in the theatre my mind triggers off sleep mode and I blissfully drift off until rudely awakened usually by a sharp dig in the ribs, or by an actor belting out a line directed at me personally if he or she has caught me napping.

But I think my pal Jeni surpassed me for cock-ups when she was on the book and had to run a show. The play we were doing at the time was a typical whodunnit. During the interval she pre-set a luggage trunk on stage which should have had a blood-soaked lower torso hanging out of it, which was in reality half of a tailor's dummy. The idea was that as the curtain went up on the second half the two actors who were playing the murderers would be seen stuffing a corpse into the wooden trunk. But with all her other copious duties she had to cope with, she inadvertently forgotten to set the said dummy properly, leaving it sprawled over the trunk's closed lid instead. Minutes before the curtain went up on the second act, the two actors sauntered on stage, fags dangling from their heavily Leichner lipsticked lips and stood by the trunk gassing away to each other. Smoking on stage in these days wasn't in the Health and Safety 'not to do' list. If only they had had the sense to glance down and see that the dummy had not been set properly, it would have turned out so differently.

The next mistake Jeni made was when she pressed what she thought was the bar warning bell button in the prompt corner, telling the audience to return to their seats, for she had in fact pressed the curtain up button by mistake. The Flyman, who was an avid horse racing fan, was sitting in his chair high up in the gantry overlooking the stage, studying the form in the sporting section, when he should of course have been on stand-by, alert to what was going on some thirty odd feet below him. Ergo when he saw the green light flash on the wall beside him, he thought it was his cue to go into action. So he folded up his paper and hauled at the rope. And so the curtain went up.

It was a Saturday, the house was packed. For some reason most of the punters were already seated. The auditorium lights were still on, as were the working lights on stage i.e. the lights usually used when putting a set up or taking it down. When the curtain began to rise the whole theatre was lit up like a Christmas tree, revealing onstage firstly two pairs of actors legs, the wooden trunk, then the torso atop it, followed by the top halves of the two chatting, smoking thesps. At this point I was watching from the wings when I saw what was happening. So I tried in a loud whisper to warn the actors that the curtain was on its way up, but they were too busy chatting away and didn't hear me. It wasn't until the rising sound of laughter from the auditorium reached them that they realised what was going on. Their cigarettes were then unceremoniously thrown into the trunk, as was the dummy and the play kicked off again. Luckily no fire ensued. In the local pub after the show I bought Jeni a large drink to calm her down. It was worth it. It was the best laugh I'd had since the season started. I only wish it had been recorded but video was in its infancy then.

An actor called Wilf was the oldest member of our little band of nactas and was cast as a policeman in one of the plays. Nothing wrong with that, until he was found wandering out of the stage-door in full costume during the show, then started to march up and down the street as if on patrol and be a general pain in the arse. All this would have been a highly amusing exercise for the rest of the cast to watch, if they hadn't been on stage at the time fully expecting him to be there with them on cue doing his bit. Instead he chose to carry on with his absurd ritual until the stage manager would eventually find him and drag him back to the stage. Needless to say he missed his entrances on more than one occasion, leaving the others to fluff and bluff their way through the play without him. That was probably the nearest I got to watching a method actor practise their craft, albeit outside of a theatre. I suppose he could be called a street theatre performer in today's parlance.

On one memorable first night another member of the company who was playing a detective, dried stone dead on his first line, when he could not for the life of him remember the name 'Robin'. The sad bugger got as far as "Right then… the question is… who killed Cock… ?"

I heard he gave up the business not long after our season ended and went off to the Far East to study a little known religion. Hopefully for him, one in which he didn't have to memorise many prayers. Some years later he was spotted in Hackney driving a taxi. By the way, he was also the same daft idiot as previously mentioned, who had picked up the prompt copy I was desperately looking for in the wings before the first night curtain went up. In fairness though when a line goes out of your head there is absolutely nothing in the world you can do about it except to rely heavily on your fellow thesps to dig you out of the hole you find yourself in. Having said that, the name 'Robin', sort of flows after the word 'Cock'... doesn't it?

When our season ended I was more than pleased to be leaving weekly rep behind. It had taught me one sobering lesson which was... never to do it again. If it wasn't for the joy of the cock-ups, I don't know how I would have survived such a harrowing and exhausting experience. Certainly without my dear great friend Jeni Giffen to be there with me, I don't think I would have done.

As one door closes the wait for the next door to open can seem like light years in happening. Luckily for me the early seventies was a very productive time in the business. No sooner had I said bye-bye to the north of England on the Saturday, two days later I was heading to Scotland to join a band of players who were in rehearsals with three plays for a Highlands and Islands Schools' Tour on the Monday.

There is something deeply disturbing about having to perform at nine a.m. in a school hall with the morning's sunlight streaming in through the windows. But it was an acting job and someone had to do it. I was aware that I was still serving my time as an apprentice at the game, so a school tour would have to fit the bill in the meantime, even though I would have much preferred to have been cast in a big Hollywood blockbuster of a film, which may or may not surprise you.

There were six of us budding young thesps, five males and two females. I duly noted that the odds of getting lucky were more than slightly stacked against us males. And so our little troupe of travelling players set off to entertain our young audiences in a Ford Transit van.

On my immediate arrival in the delightful Scottish Highland town, I was whisked off to rehearsals the moment I got off the train. Around half past five when rehearsals finished and my fellow players adjourned to the pub, I was given a digs list and left to my own devices to find lodgings. Marvellous! Usually the company management would already have sent on the digs list to me long before my arrival, but as I had taken on the job at such short notice there had been a cock-up in that department. To be absolutely frank, I hadn't a clue where to start looking for good digs as I had never been in the town before in my life. After frantically searching for a room within the restraints of my tight budget I simply couldn't find any that I could afford. But one kindly cast member took me under his wing telling me that he had heard of rooms in a hotel on the outskirts of town which were very reasonably priced indeed. He also happened to mention that none of the rest of the cast had opted to stay there which surprised me. I was left wondering why. Thanking him anyway I set off with his directions scribbled on the back page of my script, dragging my seemingly reluctant large suitcase which was getting heavier by the minute. Trolley wheels on suitcases hadn't been invented then unfortunately.

I began to wonder why this hotel was so cheap but wasn't used by the other cast members and concluded as I tramped wearily on and on, that as it appeared to be situated some miles away from the theatre that this had to be the reason. I found out later that its far away location was only part of the problem.

To get to it I had to walk down the length of the High Street then turn right cutting through a camp site which bordered each side of the road. At a junction I turned left into a country road which seemed to go on forever before I finally turned right into a steep inclined tree lined track which was surrounded by what appeared to be dense forest of the type seen in a Sir Richard Attenborough South American jungle documentary. Eventually the trees and thick foliage thinned making way for an otherwise empty large clearing where the creepy looking hotel stood eerily before me, with a few empty farm buildings hiding amongst an overgrown garden in the background. From their general direction I whiffed a rather odious stench of rotten cow shit.

I love country smells and had enjoyed mucking out the byre in my youth, when we scouts camped in the fields of Dalnair Farm, Croftamie near Drymen. It was a blissful place and a blissful time for me. In fact it was this experience of farm work when I was eleven years old that gave me my first ambition, which was to be a farmer, as mentioned earlier.

But this cow stuff that was invading my nostrils didn't smell at all healthy. All in all, the place did not have anything like a welcoming ambience associated with a country establishment and was not the welcoming sight I had expected to see. Apart from the reek, incredibly spooky is how best to describe the place. Venturing into the silent empty reception area I tentatively called out. Minutes seemed to pass but still no one appeared. A few flies were buzzing about the place, probably down to the close proximity of the smelly farm buildings. I wandered back outside wondering whether to head back and try the campsite for a vacant tent instead, when a middle-aged, rather large and somewhat strong-looking woman appeared from around the side of the hotel carrying long ladders over her shoulder as if they were no heavier than a bag of peas. When I enquired if she knew if there was a room to rent, she slowly looked me up and down, sighed wearily then said in a reluctant sort of way, "There is a room indeed, but you should try very hard no tae lock yourself oot as an old bugger and her daft wee companion have just done. I had to climb through their upstairs windie wi' these ladders I'm carrying tae let them back in. Second time this week an aw!"

She placed them against the wall then motioned me to follow her, which I dutifully did, back into the hotel hauling my suitcase which now felt twice the weight it had been when I started out on the journey from the theatre, up a flight of stairs and along a short corridor at the end of which was my room. On the way she pointed at a closed door and whispered, "That's the silly auld coos, in there."

Once safely inside my room she explained that she was the joint owner of the hotel, her business associate having 'gone and got herself bloody engaged', which was not to her liking at all as she 'was now already too wrapped up with her new hubby to be, to share the work in the hotel'. Then she left me, shutting the door firmly behind her.

It was like a set from a horror movie. There was nothing I could put my finger on that made the room particularly scary, but everything about it had an air of cold fear. But there was no immediate alternative, for it was by now too late to retrace my steps to the camp site. I resigned myself to my new digs, unpacked the suitcase, had a quick bath, thankfully the water was hot and there was plenty of it, then ventured downstairs for dinner.

In the dining room I perused the other guests, fully expecting a bunch of weird looking individuals who wouldn't look out of place in a Hammer horror film. But to my relief they all appeared quite normal. There were some workers from a hydroelectric dam at one table, a gaggle of business people at another, some hikers at the next and a quiet young couple sitting in the table close to mine, who smiled shyly when I said hello. I sincerely hoped that this wasn't their honeymoon hotel otherwise it would have been the shortest marriage ever.

My acting observational instincts kicked in as I waited apprehensively for my order to arrive, not knowing what to expect culinary wise. I began to surreptitiously closely study those around me, wondering what their characters were like, where they came from, what their life stories were etc., when into the dining room came a rather stoutly built elderly lady with a much smaller middle aged female companion in attendance. I came to the conclusion that they must be the ladies afore mentioned by our hostess.

The companion nodded sagely, smiling at all us guests, whilst the old girl studiously ignored everyone. She hobbled along with her left hand grasping a walking stick, her right tucked under her friend's arm for balance as she leant against her. Why she relied so heavily on her smaller pal I simply couldn't fathom, for she definitely looked the stronger of the two by far.

Then something untoward and indeed unfortunate happened. No sooner had the pair sat down than the old bugger broke wind... loudly. She followed up with another two in quick succession. It was quite a feat to let rip a hat trick before she had even begun to eat I thought. Immediately her companion got up, smiled apologetically in my direction, presumably because I was the closest to them, then aided her windy pal to her feet, the trauma of farting obviously having taking its toll on her ability to stand without some sort of assistance. But once upright the windy emissions started up again and intermittently carried on as they made their way out of the dining room and up the stairs. I sincerely hoped that they had not forgotten their key again for I don't think I could have survived an encore.

Though it is shameful to admit, errant farting makes me laugh... every time. I find it extremely amusing especially when done in places where it would be prudent not to e.g. a hotel dining room. Looking around me I tried very, very hard to control myself, hoping that someone would burst out laughing first so that I could then feel free to join in. Put bluntly, I would have unashamedly guffawed loudly along with them, but as no-one did, I felt obliged to stifle my bad manners and instead chose to smile to my fellow guests in what I hoped looked in an empathic way instead. I so wanted to share the comedy moment but my better mannered diners were not going to play that game. They studiously avoided eye contact with me and carried on talking to each other as if nothing had happened. I thought to myself that she must have done this noisy exit of hers before and so it wasn't at all news to everyone else.

Surprisingly I stayed on at the hotel throughout the two week rehearsal period. Not because I was hoping for a repeat of the comedic episode, but because it was the cheapest digs around, and I really didn't fancy staying in a tent which was the only possible real alternative. There are certain things one draws the line at, even at the risk of forsaking their art. As it happens, my stay in the hotel, apart from that unfortunate windy episode, was quite uneventful.

The food was adequate and didn't give me food poisoning.

There was always plenty of hot water for a deep bath.

The bar was always open each night when I got back.

The problem was the journey from the theatre to the hotel in the woods.

We tended to rehearse to around nine every night which meant by the time we had finished and had a drink or two with the others, it was dark in the extreme. There was no problem walking down the dimly lit High Street, nor was it difficult to walk by the camp site as light from camp fires etc., spilled onto the road helping me to see along the way. Things only got bad when I hit the country road. It was damn near pitch black by then and very, very spooky. Needless to say I often tended to have a few more alcoholic beverages than I would usually have had, in order to give me the Dutch courage to venture back to the hotel each night.

On one memorable occasion having downed more than a few pints as well as a couple of drams, I waved merrily to my companions in the pub and waddled off into the night. Things went well until the country road. The night was as black as early hell's waistcoat. I felt like Tam O' Shanter, but without the support of Tam's grey mare Meg. Only once did a car pass by and I could make good headway venturing gingerly forward using light spill from its headlights to help me navigate. But that only lasted a short time before I was plunged into pitch darkness again.

The alcohol kept me feeling relatively carefree until I tripped and fell into a ditch. I hauled myself up with the aid of a wooden stake which had been cemented into the ground. Once upright I leant my whole bodyweight on the stake, which had a transverse piece of wood nailed onto it. I remember looking up at the sky and giggling drunkenly at my silly plight. But as I did so I started to become acutely aware of the eerie noise of the trees as their leaves rustled in the strengthening wind. High above me clouds were scudding hurriedly across the sky. The vision of a bright half-moon suddenly appeared for a few moments, allowing it a brief glimpse of mother earth, and allowing me a brief glimpse at the piece of wood I was leaning on. I saw that some words had been branded onto it in the way that a cowboy brands a steer in a Western movie. Intrigued I looked closer at what was written using the dying light from the moon to aid me. I read the following: TO THE CEMETERY. That was enough for me! To this day I have never sobered up as quickly as I did when I read that sign. In fact it has remained the most sobering moment of my life.

Throwing myself backwards off the sign, I turned and ran blindly down the country road stumbling, falling, getting up, running again, stumbling, falling etc., until half way up the path to the hotel I saw the glow from its lights. Normally that glow had been enough to send shivers of fear up my spine. Never would I have believed that it would ever be a welcoming sight, but that night nothing in the world was more welcome I can tell you. I raced the last fifty yards and arrived at full pelt into the reception area, which was perchance relatively full of party goers more than surprised to see this young man white with fear moaning incoherently about warlocks and witches as he made a bee line for the bar. After some more alcohol was consumed I took myself off to bed, vowing no matter how much it cost, I would get a taxi back each night from then on.

We seven eager young entertainers travelled around the Highlands and Islands of Scotland to our various venues, crushed together in a Ford Transit. Not only was the interior packed to the gunnels with our suitcases, costumes, props, plus all the other paraphernalia necessary for a troupe of travelling players, but the collapsible set had to come along too. It was tied precariously onto the roof rack, thus making the van top heavy. At least this was the excuse given by the actor who was the appointed driver, for the van toppling over onto its side. So we found ourselves marooned in a remote, boggy and bleak moorland that looked as if no other human being had ever

I'M CLEAR, WHAT'S IT LIKE UP YOUR END?

set foot before. The blinding horizontal rain didn't help either.

We had to empty the van of absolutely every sodding thing, before we could even begin to coax it back upright onto the rough muddy track. Luckily we had finished our shows for the day and were heading to our next town, so we didn't let any of our young audiences down by having to cancel. However, by that time, I couldn't have cared less.

We arrived at our next digs wet through, tired, hungry and just a little tetchy to say the least, only to find that the landlord, believing us to have reneged on our booking, had already gone to bed and locked up. This was a reasonable assumption as it was two o'clock in the morning. But he was a kindly soul and without malice opened up his B&B for us in the wee small hours. After what seemed like only five minutes kip we tucked into breakfast and set off once again, arriving at our next venue barely awake, let alone ready to perform.

It was around this time I realised that not all show business was tinsel and glitter. In fact I hadn't seen any tinsel or glitter at all and vowed never to tour again, unless I was put up in a five star hotel accommodation and had a salary equal to that of a movie star. But I was young and keen, and the happy smiling faces of our noisy young audiences soon woke us up and made it all worthwhile in the end. Did I really think like that back then?!

However, there was one incident later in the tour which I found quite pitiful. We had arrived in a remote coastal village in the north west of Scotland to perform the first of our three plays to an audience of infants. Instead of putting our set up in the school hall in preparation for all the young pupils to attend, which had been the norm everywhere else so far, we were told we would be performing in a small classroom, as there would be an audience of only a few youngsters. When we enquired where the rest of our audience were, the headmistress informed us that the minister of the local church had warned from his pulpit on the Sunday before we arrived, that theatre was un-Godly and it would be a mortal sin to let children watch it.

In the circumstances I was all for cancelling altogether believing that it was an all or nothing thing and that it would be ethically wrong to continue. But I was overruled by that stupid aggravating phrase 'the show must go on." Consequently the few non church-going kids had a great time, whilst their many pals watched with forlorn faces from the playground, through the classroom window.

CHAPTER SIX

SEASON OF GOODWILL AND EMPLOYMENT

1971 and the season of goodwill to all men (and women I hoped) was approaching, which meant pantomimes and Christmas shows for the jobbing actor. When my call came I jumped at the chance to play Judge Gaffney in a production of *Harvey*, a lovely, funny play about a man who believed he was a rabbit. It had been made into quite a famous film with Jimmy Stewart playing the lead. Though at the time I had never heard of the piece, I was more than pleased to be back in legitimate theatre again.

Rehearsals went extremely well, until the dress rehearsal that is. I made my first entrance and managed to spout forth only a few lines, before I was halted in my tracks by the director's voice, as it boomed out from the back of the auditorium.

"STOP!"

We stopped. The cast all looked at me as I had been the last to speak and they naturally presumed therefore that it was something I had said or done, or didn't say or do, which caused the director to blow a fuse. They weren't wrong.

I'M CLEAR, WHAT'S IT LIKE UP YOUR END?

"Tom, why have you got a f--g Christmas cake on your head?"

I was flummoxed that the director had actually sworn at me, but in the years to come I was to hear quite a few more expletives showered around rehearsal rooms, television studios and on film locations. Of course I didn't have an effin' Christmas cake on my head, but in truth I simply hadn't yet mastered the art of stage makeup when it came to the hairdo department. After all, I was still relatively new to the business and at twenty-one, the youngest member of the *Harvey* cast. I also happened to be playing the oldest character in the play and so had, naturally, whitened my hair. This was absolutely the right thing to do. But what was absolutely the wrong thing to do was to have covered my hair in diamond white shoe cream, the type used to whiten tennis shoes in these days. Under the lights of my dressing room I thought it had looked ok, but obviously under the brighter stage lights it obviously hadn't. Every follicle seemed to house its very own electrical power station and my head looked as if it had sprouted a fibre optic lamp. None of the more experienced cast had bothered to tell me that it would look utterly ridiculous when on stage, so I had been left to take the flak. It's always a bit of a worry when one is pushed to the fore as the spokesman, only to find that those who had sworn allegiance beforehand are nowhere to be seen when you turn around for their reassurance. To be fair though, at that point in rehearsals everyone is somewhat honed in to their own individual performances and lack peripheral vision for anything else, so I fully understand why my hair passed muster with them. They simply hadn't noticed. Thanks pals.

Nevertheless despite my coiffure, the critic gave the show a rave review and I got a good mention, but was slightly put out when he said that my head looked as if it had been struck by lightning. I couldn't understand his comment because I had dumped the idea of using the diamond white shoe cream on the advice of an older and I hoped wiser cast member, who suggested I use a light coloured talcum powder on my hair instead, which he sort of assured me would look much the better.

It wasn't until I was told that this critic's words were sent to the newspapers before the show opened, that it all became clear to me. Apparently in these days, it was the practise in that particular theatre that the manager always wrote the notices himself, based on what he saw during the dress rehearsal. Needless to say on paper the Christmas shows all got fantastic reviews, subsequently they were all sure fire hits at the box office. I have often wondered what would have happened had a show been cancelled between the dress rehearsal and before opening the following night.

When Harvey came to an end, I was immediately asked if I would join another theatre company. The short notice was because one of their acting lot had done a bunk, and the show was due to open in three days. They chose me based on what their assistant director had seen me do in Harvey, which I have to admit worried me slightly. I hoped he hadn't seen the dress rehearsal. That's when I thought that it must be a comedy. But I found out it wasn't really that funny - not to me anyway.

The part on offer was as a priest who came on only in the last quarter of the play, though he had quite a bit to say. The big question was could I learn it in time? I was told that if I delivered the goods I would be given a six month contract. I jumped at the chance to prove to myself, my employers as well as the audiences, that I could do it. It wasn't until I began rehearsing that I got a bit of a shock. The stage manager told me to make the tea in readiness for a break in rehearsal. It was then that I read the small print on the contract I had just signed… includes ASM duties! This was something I had sworn never to do again after my previous experience. But it was too late to do anything about that clause and with only two and a half days left to rehearse, my mind was full of getting the lines under my belt in time for the opening night. And if I had walked out, I would lose the chance of six months' work. I had only been in the business five minutes so I didn't have a gnat's whisker of any bargaining power whatsoever.

When the play's director asked how I was getting on with the line learning, I told him that I thought I was doing fine, though there was one wordy sentence I had to say, which I simply didn't understand the meaning of, therefore I was finding it a real bugger to remember.

N.B. In order to learn lines, one of the first skills you learn when training to become an actor is understanding what the lines actually mean, then you can work on the subtext e.g. why you have to say them, how does the character you are playing relate to the other characters, what is your purpose in the scene, so on and so forth etc., etc., etc. Once you have delved into all the whys and wherefores, then the lines should fall into place. But the most important thing to get on top of early on is the meaning of the lines.

This director honestly admitted he hadn't a clue what the line I was having difficulty understanding meant either, and instructed me to learn it as best I could, say it out loud with balls and conviction, and basically just to get on with it. It was a rather tall order for me in the circumstances. I am happy to say, however, that we opened without a hitch, I remembered my lines in the right order (even if I didn't understand all of them) and I was praised for doing it well. The result was that I was given a six month contract. But I'm sad to say the unwanted Assistant Stage Management clause in the contract remained.

One evening pre show, the stage manager told me he was taking a long awaited night off, so I would have to cover his stage management duties as well as my own. These included handing a banana off stage to one of the cast prior to her making her entrance.

"A banana… ? What's the matter with the woman, can't she carry a banana and walk at the same time?" I asked, dressed as I was in a priest's smock and dog collar. Extreme exhaustion had kicked in due entirely to an already ridiculous work load, ergo I was somewhat disgruntled to say the least. But my tired protests fell on his apparently deaf ears and he skipped off for his jolly, leaving me to it.

It transpired that the said actress had to say her first line to the audience from out of a turret window atop of a tower, then descend down an internal spiral staircase, before appearing from behind the turret at floor level onto the stage, complete with a banana in her hand. Along with everything I already had to do, plus so many extra duties that had been heaped on me, I felt that this banana-handing bit was just one too many duties to have to cope with.

So I made an executive decision to go back-stage and have a quiet, gentle word with the thespiana, explaining my predicament, hoping that she would empathise with me and carry her own banana. Indeed I would have done there and then had she not found me first.

"You there, priest boy, you do know you have to hand me a banana when I alight at the foot of the turret stairs don't you?"

I looked her up and down and saw that she didn't appear to have any physical handicap that would in any way prevent her from carrying a barrel load of bananas down a 500 foot vertical, slippery, rain-soaked cliff, in a gale force twelve hurricane if she so desired. So I told her she was quite capable of picking up the ruddy thing herself and left her to it. Subsequently the director was a wee bit pissed off with me, the latest addition to her troupe of nactors.

Some weeks later we were rehearsing the play *The Admirable Chrichton* about a rather well-to-do family and their manservant, called Chrichton, who get themselves shipwrecked on a desert island. Probably because my character's contribution was minimal and I had more stage management duties than acting duties to be getting on with, I wasn't enjoying the experience as much as I had hoped. Ambition was my motivation and playing yet another vicar, this time dressed mostly in a grass skirt, wasn't even a starter in my eyes. But being cast as a member of the cloth yet again got me thinking that the management may have had an ulterior motive... to get me to fall in line and get on with whichever job I was supposed to do, without question or complaint. Well... they got that more than a tad wrong.

It was a Saturday afternoon and backstage was chaos as we were preparing for the second act of the dress rehearsal, which included setting a large table for a dinner scene. I was dressed in a grass skirt, dog collar and not a lot else for my next entrance as the shipwrecked vicar. One of the kids in the show turned up backstage and told me that an old man had been mugged in the theatre car park. I shot off out of the theatre dressed as I was, to see if I could assist in any way... the elderly man and not the muggers of course! Luckily for me the bad guys had already legged it from the scene. I shudder to think what they would have done to a half-naked, grass-skirted man of the cloth had they still been there. I am happy to say that the old chap was none the worse from his experience, though he did have one hell of a bigger fright when he saw a near naked vicar running towards him looking like an escaped lunatic in a grass skirt.

Eventually I returned to the theatre, having taken some time to convince the police, who had by then appeared on the scene, that I really wasn't the one who had attacked the old chap. Convincing the police to accept my innocence wasn't easy, as by now the confused old fellow wasn't absolutely certain that it wasn't me who had attacked him. The police had begun to suspect that I had actually escaped from a lunatic asylum. Had I not been vouched for by the stage manager, I fear I would have been certified there and then.

But unbeknownst to me at the time, that wasn't to be the end of the story. It had a surprisingly happier ending as you will now be revealed.

Some years later at Dundee Rep Theatre Company, we did a terrific bawdy comedy which was an adaptation into auld Scots, of a fairly old play by a German playwright, Herman Von Kleist, called *The Broken Jug*, or as we renamed it, *The Chippit Chantie*. It was an absolute hoot. I had never heard audiences laugh so much. Our version was directed by a visiting director and would you believe it, it was the same one who wasn't over happy about my banana palaver in the play she had directed. It was a lovely surprise to me when after the curtain came down on our opening night, she rushed into my dressing room and made such a fuss of me, saying how brilliant I had been in the part and that a mime sequence I had invented was a piece of comedy genius. It was I suppose her way of saying that she was glad I had grown up at last. And would you believe it, soon after finishing my contract, her Assistant Director Davie Birch, who had originally asked me to join the company, offered me a play in Orkney. So it was all worth it in the end. Mind you, I haven't told you what happened in Orkney yet!

CHAPTER SEVEN

ORKNEY BECONS

Though it was so many years ago I remember it as if it were yesterday, racing across London on a busy Saturday morning on my way to Heathrow. I had just managed to get a seat on that morning's flight and was due to be met at Kirkwall airport by Davie and the rest of the cast who were flying up from Glasgow. It was a bonus to learn that the cast was made up of the actors Ron Bain and his wife Jeni Angus, two great pals I had worked with before. Years later Ron was to find much success as a television director. The cast also included my mate Benny from College, plus a stage manager called Sue, a terrific girl who had a handbag that hoarded everything from screw drivers to maps, from lunches to travel tickets and fly spray. How she got all that stuff in there I'll never know. There was nothing we ever asked for, that she couldn't find somewhere in that bag.

These four wise people had decided to fly up on the Monday instead, as the flights from Glasgow were suffering from a lack of seats. The weather for their journey was warm and calm so they had a lovely flight. The flight north from Heathrow for me on the Saturday was as bumpy as hell, and I was glad for the stop-over at Inverness, albeit for just enough time to disgorge most of the passengers then take on a handful more before heading skywards again.

In the early 1970s Orkney's tiny rural airport was a far cry from Heathrow. It was a strange feeling to land on an isolated runway bordered by green fields and lots of cows, with an airport terminal which to me resembled an oversized Nissan hut. I got off the aircraft, strolled across the grass and entered the arrivals lounge (the same lounge used for departures as well as collecting luggage) fully expecting to meet my fellow thesps. Instead there was no sign of anyone to greet me. The place emptied rather quickly and I was left alone wondering what to do next. Two hours passed and two further flights arrived but still no sign of any familiar faces. I began to wonder whether or not this job was a bit of a wind up. There I was in an empty Nissan hut, on a strange empty looking island, empty of trees and feeling rather empty in myself with nowhere to go. I sat down on my case and heard my plastic makeup box inside crack under my weight. Not a great start. There was nothing else for it, I would just have to take the next flight back… if there was one.

Mobile cell phones in these days were an invention the future was looking forward to having, so I was left no alternative but to call the operator from a coin slot public telephone, which I sincerely hoped was not the only one on the island, otherwise I reckoned I'd be telephoning myself. The lady who answered my plea for help had the most beautiful Orcadian accent. For me it had a magical quality to it, a sound as natural as a cool breeze caressing a field of long grass on a warm summer's evening. I really mean that.

I hoped that Davie's telephone number was registered somewhere in the system. So the conversation with the operator went something like this.

"Hello there… this is the operator… can I be of any assistance?"

"Oh yes please." I was in love already.

"So what is it you want?"

If only she really knew.

"Oh… mmmh… you see… I have arrived here at the airport in Orkney but the friend who was supposed to be meeting me hasn't turned up. This is a bit of a long shot… I was hoping maybe you could find his phone number… but I don't even know where he lives. All I have is his name… I suppose this call is a waste of your time."

"A phone call is never a waste of time here. What's your pal called?"

"David Birch," I told her. Her reply surprised me to say the least.

"Och I know Davie. He's staying at his auld mum's hoose in Stromness. He's about to do a peedie play for the St. Magnus Cathedral Appeal Fund. Now let me tell you that his mither doesn't have a phone but her neebour does. I'll tell you whit I'll dae. I'll gae her a peedie bell, it'll save you the money and I'll tell her neebour to tell his mum to tell him to come and fetch you. Just you wait there now and don't go away."

I told her I wouldn't. She seemed to giggle then the line went dead. I did as I was told, for I had nowhere else to go, though I wasn't entirely convinced the right bloke would get the message from the right mother via the right neighbour. Half an hour went by before I saw an old Ford Cortina screech to a halt outside the Nissan hut. The horn hooted and Davie shouted over to me.

"Sorry mate, I thought you were coming up with the rest of them on Monday. Their flight was full when they tried to book it."

"Ah… was it?" That would explain why I had just spent two and a half hours on me lonesome. We drove into Stromness and parked by the harbour. The weather suddenly miraculously changed, the sun shone brightly and the wind quite disappeared as if it had never blown at all.

'I could have done with this sort of weather earlier for my flight,' I thought to myself.

Davie got out of the car and I dutifully followed him, grabbing my case from the back seat.

"I won't be a minute," he said. Then he stripped off down to his shorts and proceeded to water ski around the bay.

So there I was, in a totally alien environment all prepared to do my acting bit for a worthwhile cause, watching my director in the ice cold waters of Scapa Flow, bouncing around behind a friend's speedboat on the end of a piece of rope. This wasn't acting preparation as I knew it. I remember thinking at the time that it was all a bit bizarre. Serious doubts were beginning to form in my mind as to whether I should fulfil my obligation to the contract. Needless to say these doubts were soon to be eroded and my weeks spent in Orkney turned out to be absolutely blissful, with the exception of a rather hairy car accident I got involved in on the last day of my stay, when I drove back to the airport, but more of that later.

Davie's mother was a delightful old lady who lived in a quaint cottage overlooking the harbour. Once he had dried off and changed we made our way to the island's capital Kirkwall, where he said we would meet a fellow he knew who was bound to know someone who could put me up for the duration of the play's run. A panic started to rise up inside me. Echoes of the spooky hotel I had stayed in with the old farting guest in attendance sprung to mind. I hadn't envisaged being dig less on a strange island and had taken it for granted that my digs would have already been arranged.

To say that Orcadians are hospitable is an understatement. No sooner did I meet this fellow than he produced from his larder several bottles of his own beer, home brewed from hops the natural way. It was the strongest alcoholic concoction I had ever tasted and after only a couple of glasses, any fears I had had about being without a roof over my head soon evaporated. I could have slept on a stony beach with a high incoming spring tide in a force ten gale and not have cared a jot. We eventually did saunter into the town proper which meant turning three corners and at the first door with a B&B sign that we knocked on I was welcomed like a long lost son.

On the Monday my three fellow actors and our stage manager were met at the airport, then Davie drove them straight to the Orkney Arts Centre where rehearsals started for real. I say 'rehearsals started for real' but the rest of the cast consisted of local people so we could only work on the bits they weren't in during the day, as they were still out working in the fields, on the fishing boats, in the classrooms etc. Then after their day's toil, they would join us to rehearse in the evenings. They were a very talented bunch indeed and it was a joy working with them.

As we ploughed on through the play during the daytime, it became clear to me that though we pros took on most of the workload sharing an equal amount of lines, I had far more characters to portray than any of the others. This meant a hell of a lot of costume changes for me, as well as many more entrances and exits than any of the others, which was to prove rather difficult, as the Kirkwall Arts Theatre where we were to perform had a few in-built drawbacks for us. This was probably due to our show's set design, which allowed no backstage access to the left side of the stage. In order to enter stage left you had first to enter stage right, exit stage left before coming on again from there. The alternative was to crawl on your stomach Gecko like along the back wall from upstage right to upstage left, making sure your arse did not protrude above the three foot high rostrum, which ran the width of the stage and two feet out from the wall, or 'syke' as it is known in the business.

With all these costume changes it was imperative that I pre-set them in the correct order and in the correct wing space. Thus several times during the play, I had to roll up whatever costume I was going to appear in next from stage left, and in the style of an underhand bowler, toss it from right to left behind the rostrum, but making sure it was low enough so the audience couldn't see it. Needless to say, over exuberance, caused in no small part by sheer nerves and terror, made some of these flying costumes appear up stage right then disappear off upstage left in an arc-like manoeuvre in full view of the audience. This practise was much to the consternation of my fellow players who were mightily cheesed off as they thought I was doing it deliberately for a laugh. We never ever came to blows, but more than once they quite rightly chastised me backstage later for cocking up a dramatic scene they had just played, when they heard the audience sniggering at the sight of my costume doing a parabolic flight upstage behind him.

Another problem was that there just weren't enough costumes to go round so we had to improvise as best we could. Subsequently towards the end of the play, when I had to make an appearance as a Viking King, there was bugger all left for me to wear. I managed to purloin a long flowing deep red velvet curtain which was supposed to resemble a royal cape of sorts, from which I had first to extract its curtain hooks. It really did look the business though, with its vibrant colour a striking resemblance to the dress worn by the manager of the theatre in Glasgow, though it wasn't made from squiffing sounding chiffon.

Each night after the show the curtain hooks had to be replaced and the curtain returned to the kind soul who had lent it to us for the duration of our play. Each evening before the show I would have to remove the hooks again. But according to Benny I always managed to 'miss a few of the bloody things'.

As well as the curtain, I was given a wonderful Viking helmet to wear, complete with two albatross feathers which stood proudly erect three foot high on each side. It was very dramatic and striking to look at. Without doubt the audience's attention would certainly be drawn to wherever the helmet was on stage and thence to whoever was directly underneath it. It had been sent from Shetland where it was used in the annual Valhalla Pageant, which I am told is an amazing sight, especially when a Viking longboat is set on fire offshore by locals dressed splendidly in their Viking costumes complete with helmets identical to mine. Sadly though, my appearance in our production did not have anything like the same effect. Dramatic? Yes. But amazing? No.

The helmet fitted me rather well and the highly polished shiny white metal straps which held it in place sparkled under the stage lights. It was the feathers that cocked it up for me. Or should I say, I cocked up the feathers. In a scene where I appeared as the Viking king, Ron who was playing a courtier of some sort at that point, was standing downstage facing the audience and thus the nearest actor to them, reciting some of the play's lyrical words by the eminent Orcadian George Mckay Brown, the writer of our piece. As Ron spouted his final line on cue before turning upstage to greet his king i.e. me, I made what I thought was a sublimely stunning entrance from upstage and behind him. However, what I didn't realise was that one of the hooks which I had missed removing earlier was unbeknownst to me still dangling from my costume and had managed somehow to attach itself to the stage left curtain. Consequently I made my entrance with the curtain joined at my hip like a huge black unwanted bridal veil following me on stage.

At this point matters were made worse because the curtain had also snagged one of the three foot high albatross feathers which up till then had been pointing skywards. But now, instead of the two feathers pointing majestically parallel toward the heavens, one was in fact pointing at a rakish forty-five degree angle facing the audience in the balcony. By now these magnificent feathers resembled a set of railway signals.

I knew something was up when our director Davie, who also doubled as our narrator perched at the side of the stage throughout the play, bit into his knuckles so hard I was surprised he didn't draw blood when he saw me make my grand entrance. For what he could see but I couldn't, was me attached to the stage curtain, wearing a helmet whose feathers appeared to have a life all of their own.

Innocent of what he was about to witness Ron called out something along the lines of, "And here is our magnificent…"

At that point he turned upstage in order to welcome me.

"Oh dear… oh my gawd… oh Tommy what the hell have you come as?" is what he whispered, aghast.

Benny's eyes widened in a maniacal stare, and he courageously restrained himself from laughing, having a cardiac arrest and exploding with anger simultaneously. Thus his top lip curled inwards and seemed to get stuck in his top set of teeth. Jeni, who was playing a maidservant, couldn't bear looking at me and turned away. No doubt she had tears of mirth cascading down her face though I couldn't see them. But her heaving shoulders were a bit of a giveaway.

The following day, taking no chances of a reoccurrence of the previous night's performance, my fellow actors, plus Davie and Sue, all turned up at the theatre early in order to remove every last hook from my costume before I arrived. They then securely tightened the screws which held the feathers onto the helmet. That way they ensured that I would make my entrance unaccompanied by the stage curtain, as well as making absolutely sure that my helmet's feathers stayed parallel pointing skywards. Indeed they went through the same routine every evening before curtain up for the rest of the entire run of the show.

When it eventually came to an end we were all sorry to be leaving the beautiful Orkney Islands where we had made many good friends in the too short a time we were there.

I had borrowed a car and picked up Benny from his digs and we were en route to the airport on a winding country road when the car, which had an assortment of tyre types, decided to burst one of the front ones. Everything happened in slow motion after that. The car slewed round and headed for the stone dyke. I remember thinking that I wouldn't be able to stop it in time before it hit the dyke. So with the help of the grass verge my plan was to try and get the car to leap over it. Miraculously it did and Benny and I found ourselves sitting in the car in the middle of a field. Thankfully I saw that he was all right and we unfastened our seat belts to get out. At least I tried to undo mine, but my co-ordination between hand and eye wasn't working. It was then that I noticed the red wine coloured liquid dripping onto my lap from my face. The impact of hitting the verge had indeed caused the car to take off as I had planned, but what I hadn't reckoned on was it landing momentarily on its roof onto the hard stone dyke, before somersaulting onwards. This was an unrehearsed manoeuvre, causing my head to make violent contact with the car's roof which was by now a crumpled heap of jagged metal.

For a few moments the car, Benny and I had spun upside down in mid-air, before all three of us eventually came to a stop, thankfully right way up. Without knowing it at the time, I had been knocked unconscious for some moments during its tumbling trick and was somewhat concussed, probably caused by the pit stop on the dyke half way over. We had both been very, very lucky, but the car didn't fare as well, for in those fleeting moments it had become a write-off. To this day I thank my maker that my dear friend survived with no more than a bruised ankle.

The outcome was that after getting my face stitched up in the local hospital, everyone else headed home whilst I had to stay on to recuperate. Towards the end of my extended stay I had the stitches removed from my face at the hospital then visited the surgeon who was on his day off at his house, to thank him for stitching me up in the first place. He had a particularly randy Labrador dog that unfortunately took a fancy to me. It was all I could do to stop it from humping my leg whilst the surgeon was trying to study his artwork on my face with the greatest of concentration. Not an easy feat to do as the dog caused me to wriggle a lot whilst I tried politely to discourage its advances without having to kick it hard in its bollocks.

After what I thought was a thorough examination he told me everything was healing nicely and that he would proceed to remove the stitches there and then. I had to point out to him as he approached me with his tweezers that they had already been taken out earlier that day in the hospital. A bit of advice: if ever you need stitches examined or need them removed, make sure there is no sex-crazed male Labrador anywhere in the vicinity.

It was during this spell of recuperation that I received a phone call from the BBC's radio studio in Edinburgh. They were looking for an actor for a nine-week series and asked if I would audition for the part over the phone. As it was radio it seemed perfectly natural to audition over the phone which would save me the problem of having to journey to Edinburgh on the off chance of getting the part. Though my love of listening to the radio was born in a ward in Glasgow's Yorkhill Hospital for Sick Children, I had never worked in that medium before and had only done a couple of radio lessons in Drama School. So I gave it my best shot, kidding on to be someone else on the phone to a complete stranger, who happened to be played by the producer. I am happy to report that my telephone audition was a success for I was offered the part. This was damned lucky as it took the full nine weeks duration of the contract for my facial scars to heal well enough for me to do any visual work again.

That was the way it was in the Scottish theatre scene in the seventies for me. There was lots of good work around, varied and exciting, though in my opinion the television industry in Scotland at the time didn't fare as well. And as to a Scottish film industry… it hardly existed back then.

My First and Very Last Musical (the same show)

When the radio series came to an end, Davie rang and offered me a month's work. Apparently the theatre he was working in had a bit of money left over from their annual Arts Council grant budget and he wanted to use it for a short tour, so I wouldn't actually be working in the main theatre. This fitted in nicely as I had a month to fill before joining The Royal Lyceum Company in Edinburgh. I told Davie that I would love to do it whatever it was, but only if my costume didn't include a helmet with feathers and curtains with hooks!

When the script was sent to me I gasped in astonishment. What he hadn't told me was that it was a musical. I contacted him immediately and told him that though I could sort of put over a song, I was in no way a trained singer. He said that it didn't matter because the Musical Director (MD) called John Scrimger, was the best there was, in his opinion. Apparently he could teach a horse to sing. At that time he was semi-professional, sharing his time between his gifted musical ability and a job in the town council offices.

With great trepidation I turned up for the first rehearsal. True to his word Davie's choice of MD was brilliant. The genius of the man had me singing like a linty within a few days. At least I thought I was doing all right, but I do admit to being somewhat overshadowed by the professionally trained singing voice of the actress who played my girlfriend.

The other thing Davie had failed to mention was that we would be touring local schools in the Perthshire region. At first I didn't like the idea of having to return to the nine o'clock in the morning performance ritual, but realised that even if I made a cock-up of it, no-one but the unfortunate pupils in our audiences would know. And as I was such a novice in the business surely I would gain something from the experience. Thankfully it was a local tour so we could return to base camp in Perth with every night off. I had superb digs overlooking The Inch, a stunningly lovely manicured area of grassed parkland, which banks onto the glorious River Tay. Propped up in my bed I got the benefit of the whole vista through the window. It was all very lovely. The only drawback was that the elderly housekeeper who made my evening meals, didn't realise that baked beans should be heated before serving. Unfortunately she had the same approach with all canned food. But she was a sweet lovely lady who looked after me like I was her son.

The show was *The Fantastiks*, a musical which had a great run off Broadway for decades with songs still sung today e.g. 'Deep in December', 'Soon it's Gonna Rain' and 'Love You Are Love', to name but a few. It was, I am happy to say, a great success for us all… even me… though there was one tiny incident which, though rather amusing to recall, has made me rather reticent about singing on stage again. In fact it made me adamant never to do a musical again.

In the number 'Soon It's Gonna Rain', I had a particularly high note to sing, and much as I tried, it really was hit or miss as to whether I could reach it on the day. So when I got to the line "If it never stops at all", I would surreptitiously gently nudge my partner on stage if I didn't think I was going to hit the high note on the word "all", and she, bless her, would sing it for me.

This all worked exceedingly well and without our audiences knowing, until during a performance when I noticed that one of the roguish looking teenage kids lounging in the front row next to where John was stationed at the piano, said something to his immediate neighbour, another pupil of the same variety. He had just clocked me nudging my colleague. Without so much as any show of trying to creep away unnoticed, he proceeded to get up and swagger out of the school hall. John's eyes rolled Heavenwards, but he carried on playing the piano as if nothing had happened. By the time the schoolboy returned I was halfway through a rendition of 'Love You Are Love' with the actor playing El Gallo standing on the rostrum behind, gently dropping paper leaves onto me and the actress playing my love interest. It was a very romantic scene and very touching to watch apparently, or so I had presumed. As the youth slumped back down into his seat, John, without pausing in his piano playing, leaned over to him and said something I couldn't quite hear. The lad's face immediately reddened with embarrassment. I supposed at the time, that John had quite rightly admonished the pest for buggering off during my song. Indeed he had, but not quite in the way I had expected.

Afterwards when we were travelling back to Perth, I asked him what had happened.

This is what John told me the little sod had said to his friend:

"Och f--k this, I'm awa' furra wank," were his exact words.

When he returned to his seat John chipped in, "I'm surprised you could find it, son."

Needless to say, I have kept my promise never to appear in a musical since and I am happy to say that John has remained a lifelong friend. I also permit myself a modicum of smugness in that I was later highly responsible for him becoming a full-time professional musician, who was to go on to get an MBE for his services to the theatre. For his part he introduced me to my future wife Cookie Weymouth, an English actress who, unlike me, was a professionally trained singer and actress who had starred in a West End musical.

The Good, the Bad, and the Inept

In the theatre it is the Artistic Director who is the boss, and usually the most experienced actors play the more substantial roles and so on downwards until you reach the general dogsbodies or ASMs. But it doesn't always pan out that way. My priority was and remains to this day, simply to do quality work as often as lady luck will allow, whatever the size of part offered. So I was more than happy when cast as one of the mechanicals (yet again) this time in a rock 'n' roll version of *A Midsummer Night's Dream*. There are no small parts only small actors... allegedly. Subsequently I like to think that my portrayal of the role was one of the highlights of the production and so did much to contribute towards the show being a rip-roaring success.

The foreign director's usually excellent command of the English language appeared to totally desert him if he didn't know the answer to a question, which I found quite amusing. Which particular country he originated from remains a mystery to me to this day.

We mechanicals were left to our own devices for most of the rehearsal period. I suggested to my fellow players that it would be a good idea to make our first entrance as the mechanicals en mass from various parts of the auditorium whilst singing the 'Hi Ho' song from Walt Disney's *Snow White and the Seven Dwarves*. And so we did. (We probably owe the Disney Corporation massive amounts of royalties for using one of their songs!) It was a wow of an entrance for us and each one of us got a round of applause as we appeared.

However one week before we opened, the costume department were pulling what was left of their hair out because they still hadn't a clue as to what the director wanted regarding costumes for the Mechanicals. In truth, I don't think he did either. In answer he told us all to meet with him and the costume department to discuss it. Instead of getting on with rehearsals, we all had to sit through everyone else's diatribe about what costume they thought they should wear.

By this time you will have gathered that I had had enough of the co-operative approach. When it was my turn I stated quite succinctly that I wanted a white boiler suit with an 'L' plate pinned on the back, a pair of wellington boots and a woollen benny hat… the type worn by a character called Benny in *Crossroads*… N.B. Not my mate Benny!

Not waiting for any further discussion on the subject I retired a la pub. My contribution had lasted about twenty seconds.

The reason for my choice of outfit was quite simple:

A white boiler suit lit from the arc lights above would attract attention.

The benny hat stuck on top of my head gave me an immature gauche look.

The wellies gave me an awkward gait.

The 'L' plate would get me an extra laugh if I happened to turn my back on the audience.

And that is exactly what happened as I slowly descended down the fireman's pole onto the stage on my first entrance. The lights lit up my white overalls brilliantly. I looked like a character from a soap powder commercial. The rubber wellies screeched like an anguished fart against the metal fireman's pole, and by the time I had got half way down it, my appearance was complimented by the silly looking hat. Furthermore, when I twirled around on landing, the 'L' plate got an uproarious reception.

The director's last words to me when the show ended were, "I leek yoo Tom. Yoo are, how you say eet?... very crood weeth thee point... it makes me laugh." He was a likeable chap and I really hope he meant it when he said that he liked me too.

Next job for me was in a rather larger theatre in a play about soldiers. The part offered was as a Regimental Military Policeman. I was replacing another actor at very short notice as he had gone off to do another play elsewhere.

The show was already up and running and the original cast had been trained for weeks beforehand by an army drill sergeant to get them all up to military standard marching. But because of the swift cast re-shuffle I was given only a mere four days to rehearse. I had to learn to present arms, march perfectly etc., basically to appear to all intents and purposes as the real McCoy. Quite simply as a RMP I had to march better than my fellow actor soldiers. After all we were performing in a garrison town and the real McCoy would be out there in the audience, critically watching my every move.

I think I did ok as I wasn't attacked by any irate squaddies in the street afterwards, though the director didn't bother his arse to come backstage and thank me for busting a gut with such a short rehearsal time to get it right on the night. Another good thing for me about the show was that I was taught the game of poker backstage, which the predominately male cast used to play during the interval, much to the annoyance of the stage management who had to harry us to get back on stage after half time.

The show was a success and as a bonus I had the delight of working with the late and great Rikki Fulton. My apologies for the name drop but he was special and although he was a big name in Scotland he wasn't nearly as well known south of the border.

One evening in the wings a fellow actor and I gave Rikki a rendition of my alternative version of the Stan Getz song Girl From Ipanema, made famous by the sultry sexy voice of Astrud Gilberto. Rikki doubled up and laughed so much he nearly missed his entrance.

I learned a lot from working with Rikki. He was a fine actor and a comic genius, so it gave me much pleasure to see him thoroughly amused at one of my gags... albeit a rather naughty one.

As this book is about actors' mishaps, all the many good directors I have had the pleasure to work with - which the vast majority were - will naturally hardly ever get a mention, unless it is to pick them out for special praise, or their presence is an integral part of the story at the time.

Occasionally as in all work places, a few inept bosses manage to slip in under the radar. The world of theatre is no exception.

One such director I had the misfortune to work with had the loathsome habit of rising noisily from his chair mid-rehearsal if he didn't like what he was watching, then proceed to make himself a coffee, keeping his back turned towards the rehearsing thesps, who were giving their all. After some minutes he would return, call a stop to rehearsal, pick on the actor whose work offended him and give him a right bollocking. For some reason he never did it to me. Whether it was because he thought that no amount of bollocking would make me "nact better" or that he just couldn't be arsed, I will never know nor will I ever care.

When the curtain comes down after a successful opening night it is customary for the director to go back-stage and thank the cast for their work, maybe tactfully give out a few acting notes to tighten the show before buying the chosen few, or all, a drink in the bar. But this character didn't bother. Instead he headed straight for the bar, drunk his fill on his own, and sent a typed sheet to be displayed backstage on the notice board for all to see. What he had written wasn't even in his own words. It was instead the full quote from Hamlet's 'Speak the speech I pray you trippingly on the tongue...' etc, and signed it William Shakespeare. The cast, who had worked their bollocks off, had been deeply hurt by the impersonal, curt way he had behaved during rehearsals, so this was really the final straw.

Somebody took the liberty of adding a PS at the foot of his rude missive which read, 'Bollocks to you!' Then signed it 'Francis f--g Bacon.'

Quite right too!

CHAPTER EIGHT

MORE THAN A WINDY CITY

Bear in mind dear reader that I am not writing in any chronological time scale, thus I am taking this opportunity to turn the clock back somewhat far for this next bit, to a time that was very, very, very early on in my career.

When another panto season came around, I found myself domiciled in Edinburgh for my very first time and therefore wasn't due for any touring allowance should any theatre manager in the immediate vicinity have an urge to employ me. In other words I was cheaper than having to employ some other thesp who happened to live more than twenty-five odd miles or so away from Auld Reekie. I was therefore in the eyes of any Edinburgh-based theatre accountant, highly castable material because I was cheaper. Whether or not I had a wife and fifteen children to support which should merit extra subsistence was not taken into account. But luckily I had neither a wife or any children at the time.

Therefore it came to pass, that I was cast to play many parts (cheaper by the minute) in a production of *Jack and the Beanstalk* starring the late and great Wally Carr. Wally was quite a magnificent Dame and I have since used some of his comedy material when performing the occasional stint of stand-up - a harrowing experience and the main cause of much whimpering by me when I ever have to recall them.

When I received the script I noticed that there was a character named OMNES, who seemed to be played by different actors including myself each time I entered. In my ignorance I didn't know that OMNES meant 'everyone' or 'all'. To be fair I hadn't done any Latin at school.

As well as the Omnes parts I was cast as Chocolate Soldier # 2 along with three other actors, none of whom, including me, could tap dance, which was rather unfortunate as very soon into rehearsals we were told that, among other duties, we would also be performing a tap dance routine. I am in awe at the magic of Fred Astaire, Gene Kelly and the like, and wished that I had been taught to dance with such skill. In my defence my three compatriots shared this lack of skill, if their pathetic attempts at tap dancing, was anything to go by.

However the outcome of our corporate attempt to apply in unison a well-choreographed, rhythmical foot tapping routine was not as you would expect. For we created our own mish-mashed, cobbled up version of time-steps, stemming from a genuine desire to emulate what the choreographer had shown us in rehearsals but by doing it our way. Somehow, by adopting this unorthodox approach we did manage to achieve a passable sort of physical coherence, and became a joined-up job lot in the eyes of our audiences. This interesting, eye-catching, eye-watering result was actually achieved by not so much as managing to do what the choreographer had tried in vain to teach us, but by each one of us copying what the next in line was doing and so on. Eventually we all looked as if we were doing damn near the same routine, which indeed we damned near were. The fact that it had nothing to do with professional dancing and proper tap dancing in particular, didn't matter a jot to us. And so we got away with it.

Where it came unstuck was when Chocolate Soldier # 3 was cast in another show and was replaced by a trained dancer who was also a talented musician, drama teacher and actor. Within a few minutes he had learned our routine from the choreographer, the same routine which we had previously taken two weeks to cock up. The problem was that he had never done this routine with us other three Chocolates. Therefore on the night, we three confidently went into our botched up routine, whilst he was doing the proper stuff, with style, flair, panache etc. He would have looked fantastic had he been on his own, instead he stood out as being the one who appeared to be doing all the wrong moves compared to us daft three who were all jumping around in unison.

The director decided that he wanted Wally as the Dame to make his first entrance on Daisy the cow's back and as I was the only omnes free off-stage at that time, I was given the dubious honour of donning the costume for Daisy's rear end and carrying Wally onstage, albeit with the greatest reluctance on my part. Wally was no light-weight and after a few performances my back ached so much that I refused point blank to carry him anymore. The director was really pissed off with me, but dear Wally was on my side and so I got my way. But to my dismay, I remained as Daisy's rear end throughout the run whenever she appeared, as well as having to play all the other parts I had to do.

As young, inexperienced actors at the time, the front end of the cow and me just got on with it, making sure we had a good few laughs during the run of the show. I want to point out that he remained very professional in his approach and I am more than happy to say managed to avoid disgracing himself... until, that is, the final matinee came along.

To fully comprehend my predicament in the ensuing debacle, the reader has to visualise the following i.e. me bent over from the waist inside the costume for the cow's rear end, where my face was inches away from the front end actor's rear end, around which was tied a leather strap which I held onto for stability. And boy oh boy it turned out that I really needed that strap to help keep me stable.

As is the way with the last matinee of a panto's run, there are all sorts of tricks going on on-stage to which the audience should be blissfully unaware. Thankfully ours was no exception. The tired, underpaid stage management team, who for weeks had worked their socks off running two shows a day, six days a week for weeks on end, had mischievously removed Daisy the cow's cloth teats and had somehow managed to sew uncooked, jumbo-sized real sausages onto her udders instead. When there were squeals from the actress playing the milkmaid, the front end actor from his vantage point inside the cow's head up front, turned around to see what all the commotion was about. It was then that he witnessed the said pink coloured teats disintegrating in the milkmaids hands. The vision of the mushed up raw meat was too much for him. His hitherto professional approach underwent a sea change re his promise not to disgrace himself and as he bellowed with laughter he also broke wind… big time.

It is a well-known fact that the passing of wind is something everyone does, even I am no exception. In fact I usually find the whole exercise very amusing, though it has to be said that one's own rear end emissions are somewhat bearable. But to put this blast of unwanted air into some sort of perspective, it has also to be realised that when one is a captive audience literally facing someone else's outburst at such close quarters, I can assure you there are few more awful experiences known to man.

Needless to say, the rear end i.e. me on this occasion, buckled at the knees, gasped for clean, unadulterated air, swore loudly and often, and was half-dragged around the set by the front end for the rest of the scene, which included a cow dance routine. The laughter from inside the cow's head could be heard in the rear stalls of the theatre next door.

Though deeply apologetic afterwards, he admitted that at the height of his mirth, he damned near wet himself as well. Enough said!

CHAPTER NINE
DUNDEE: I'M A NACTA AT LAST

One New Year's Eve in Edinburgh once again, I was invited to a party after the show we were doing, thrown by a fellow cast member Martin Heller, whom I was to work with in many plays at Dundee Repertory Theatre Company. An absolutely charming actor of the old school, he played the part of dotty winsome old characters to a tee, and would have me in fits at his antics on stage. Some years later he was to direct me as Billy, in the renowned play *Billy Liar*.

The dear fellow once actually fell asleep on stage during a play he was in. The plan was that as the curtain rose for the second half, he would be seen lying on a sofa presumably sleeping and was due to wake up some ten minutes into the action. But he really did fall asleep. So when a telephone rang on stage he really did wake up with a start believing it to be his alarm clock. So nonplussed was he that he tried in vain to turn the telephone off, before realising where he was and what he should have been doing. Oh the delights of a live audience.

At the New Year's Eve party I happened to meet a kindred spirit, a personable fellow called Stephen MacDonald. For the first time in my career I found myself at the right place at the right time although I wasn't aware of it at that time. It was Stephen who was to change the course of my career, quite dramatically and so very much for the better.

We talked into the wee small hours. He had just been appointed caretaker Artistic Director at Dundee Repertory Theatre following the tragic death of its previous Artistic Director, Jimmy Lovell. It was only after Jimmy had died did I learn that he had wanted me to join his company some time before, but at that time I was recovering from that nasty wee car accident in Orkney and I never received his message until it was too late. In Stephen, I was offered a second chance.

He had just finished a highly successful spell at the Phoenix Theatre in Leicester as its Artistic Director, and was of Scottish descent with bags of experience of the Scottish theatre scene. I too had copious theatre experience north of the border, having worked with farting cows etc., so we had a lot to talk about!

A week after the party, I received a call from my agent at the time who told me a 'Stephen somebody from England wanted me to come into the office for an interview'. This agent, though highly successful, had a penchant for occasionally getting names and messages a bit screwed up e. g. allegedly she once mistook the name of the play *Night of The Iguana* for 'Igoo Agoo'.

So when I arrived at her office I was delighted to see that she had got half the name right, for it was the same Stephen MacDonald whose company I had shared the New Year in with. He told me that he had a reasonable idea of what plays he was going to put on for the Dundee Rep season, though he couldn't offer me anything positive there and then. Indeed he wasn't sure how long he would be at The Rep himself. But he did ask if I could let him know if I was offered any other work in the near future.

A few days later I was invited to play Malcolm in the Scots play for a three month tour of England with a theatre company based south of the border. This was a tremendous opportunity for me to break into the English theatre scene and hopefully bring my work to the attention of the casting directors down south who had access to television and films, which was where I wanted my career to take me next. But I also really wanted to have a go at Dundee Rep., a theatre with a remarkable reputation for doing first rate work and where many cut their theatrical teeth before fame and fortune came their way.

I dutifully phoned Stephen and told him of the offer I had had. He suggested I join him at Dundee Rep immediately, offered me one play, maybe two and at a stretch perhaps three, but pointed out that an all three play contract would be a long shot. I accepted his offer of a guaranteed six weeks work only at this stage, and turned down the three month Shakespeare tour, thus letting my English audiences off the hook for some years to come. It all happened very quickly indeed. The following day I was on my way to Dundee Rep, where I am happy to say I not only did the one play, but stayed in the company for the next three years. That is one of the finer and goodly things about the business of being an actor. Good things can happen at the blink of an eye.

To be offered work in Dundee at that time was truly fantastic. Here was a theatre where some of the greats had worked, but my pleasure when arriving to start work in one of the most prestigious theatre companies in Scotland was somewhat dampened when I saw my digs for the first time. I had inherited a two room with kitchen ground floor flat with an outside toilet from a fellow thesp, whom I had been at Drama School with. Not only was it situated on a bend in the busy Lochee Road, which was a major bus route through the city and therefore bloody noisy, it was also damp, though these obstacles were slightly offset by the flat being only a mere few minutes' walk from the theatre. I opted to heat the front room only and close the other one off in order to save money and stay slightly warmer and slightly less damp. That left me with the problem of the outside toilet or privy. In order to get to it I either had to go out the front door directly onto the street and through the communal close to the back of the tenement building, or climb out through the window of the back bedroom which I had already closed off. If I opted for that route the wind howled in and the flat took hours to re-heat. The outcome was that I spent as little time in the flat as I needed to, and more time in pubs and mates' digs, until one morning I awoke to an almighty crash.

I honestly thought the building had fallen down around me and when I tentatively looked out of the front window, I saw that it had. The departing previous tenant actor had forgotten to mention that a demolition order had been placed on the adjoining tenement and I was witnessing its demise as a huge metal ball hanging from a crane battered it senseless. Dressed as I was in my night attire of one T-shirt, two thick woolly jerseys, an old pair of corduroy trousers and heavy-duty hiker's socks, I slipped on a pair of wellies and ventured outside onto the slushy snow covered pavement, where the shocked looking demolition blokes told me that my digs were destined for the same treatment in a few days. Apparently they had no idea I was living in the adjoining building. I went back inside my damp abode, took three seconds to decide whether to go or stay, then hastily packed my bags and hot footed it off in search of a warmer, drier, quieter and hopefully safer place to lay my head.

Luckily it didn't take long to find a garret room in a Victorian terraced house on Perth Road, overlooking the silvery River Tay. Though it was a good twenty minutes' walk from the theatre it didn't matter. From the room's little dormer window I could see the grass runway of Dundee's wee aerodrome, as well as both the road and rail bridges, the latter having been made famous by that indomitable poet, William McGonigall. At night I could see the lights of Tayport and Newport as they twinkled on the horizon. It was an ideal abode in a very poetic setting and I stayed there throughout my time at Dundee. To work at The Rep was demanding, challenging and exciting... an absolute gift for a fledgling thespian, and it was there that I truly felt I began to learn my craft. Indeed any actor worth their salt never stops learning, and I'm not talking just about lines either. With each play you do night after night, each character you portray, each audience you work with, they are all brand new experiences, and so the learning process goes on and on.

One of the parts I played at Dundee was Trofimov in Anton Pablovich Chekhov's play The Cherry Orchard. He is a terrific character to play and I was thrilled and delighted to be cast as him. I learned the lines and grew the appropriate beard, then donned the Russian garb; wire spectacles courtesy of the NHS which gave me an academic appearance for the first time in my life, leather-type jack boots, jodhpur type trousers and a wide-sleeved shirt in the Cossack style. With me striped trousers tucked into me boots and wearing a shortened kaftan as a top coat all courtesy of the wardrobe department, I might well have looked more like a swashbuckling buccaneer than a Russian intellectual, but that didn't bother me. I had studied hard and researched as best I could, and the eternal student Trofimov as I perceived him, began to emerge. It was the first time that I had immersed myself so deeply in a character I was playing... an extraordinary experience.

Such is the power of Chekhov. And such was Stephen's brilliant direction. Indeed there were moments when I simply lost myself in performance.

This remarkable feeling is akin to what one experiences when driving a car whilst in an auto pilot state. You become unaware of your past journey, only acutely aware of the moment you are in and the immediate surroundings as if looking in from the outside whilst looking out from the inside. Of course you must be aware of what is happening around you otherwise you, plus car, would end up wrapped round a tree. But, and this is where it all falls apart, when something totally untoward happens when on stage, the rude awakening from your semi-conscious, artistic, trance-like state hits you like a sledgehammer between the legs. Ooh the pain, the humiliation, the utter helplessness of your predicament. That's when you need more than a nurse to tenderly care for your every need.

It was Harold Wilson who said that a week is a long time in politics. I can assure you that when a cock-up happens during a live stage performance, though it lasts only a few moments, it feels like a bloody lifetime. Such a lifetime experience happened to me one evening during the last scene before half time, in our production of *The Cherry Orchard*. Trofimov, the eternal student as he is described and played by yours truly, was on stage making verbal love to Varya, the bird of his dreams. Immediately following my line "Light of my life, my one spring flower" another character called Yasha is supposed to enter from stage-right with billiard cue in hand, announce that his friend Yepihodov had broken a billiard cue, laugh heartily then exit, thus setting up an imaginary scene in an imaginary billiard room next door. It is a well-orchestrated dramatic moment in the piece, ruining Trofimov's chance of pulling Varya.

There is a technique to the art of laughing on stage and making it sound like the real McCoy. Whether the mirthful outburst is of the guffawing variety, or the wheezing type, or the silent doubled up version, or just the giggly one, they are not at all difficult to learn and master. They can then be reproduced to order by anyone with a desire so to do. However, the actor playing Yasha unfortunately must have missed the stage laughing lessons back in his College days, because his attempts at verbal mirth-making in our show were always a bit of a hit or miss affair, which simply was not good enough for the professional stage. People paid good money to hear his character laugh. If he couldn't do it properly then he shouldn't have been there. But to give him his due he tried. And boy did he try!

On the memorable night in question after my 'one spring flower' line the door stage-right opened. The actor playing Yasha entered, billiard cue dutifully in his hand. He delivered his line perfectly, even got a titter from the audience... so far so good. Any titter is to be welcomed in a Chekhov play especially if it has been previously advertised as a comedy to a twentieth-century English speaking audience, to many of whom a Chekhov play was a new experience altogether. They might well have been misled by that description and were expecting hilarity of the 'Carry On' kind and not a translation of the Russian version of high comedy.

And so it came to pass that Yasha paused for what seemed to us fellow nactas, a millennium of time. At this point my blissful autopilot state went straight out of the window. I was thrust mercilessly back into the reality of the here and now. Varya and I waited with mounting trepidation for him to get his act together. Where was the laugh? At the very least I knew that if his memory had done a bunk and he had forgotten that he had to laugh, then he could just bugger off sharpish. Left to our own devices we would have muddled through somehow until the interval's respite, which thankfully was not too far away.

Yasha glanced at me with a determined and maniacal look in his eyes, took a deep breath then closed his mouth tight shut. Apparently, he told me afterwards, this was to help build up maximum pressure in his diaphragm in preparation for the laugh which was supposed to have followed. Then as he opened his mouth wide, he simultaneously forced out the trapped air by pushing a clenched fist into his solar plexus - the same fist which held the billiard cue and whose tip was now dangerously heading in a thrusting fashion upwards towards his nasal passages. Neither Varya nor I had a clue at the time as to what this masochistic self-flagellation action was about, but we hung on in there, mainly because we had nowhere else to go.

In his defence the gurgling sound produced from deep inside his thorax could have been mistaken for a laughter-type noise but it wasn't very realistic. If only he had left it at that and exited hastily, but unfortunately there was an unwelcome addendum. The painful surprise of the billiard cue prodding his nose, combined with the build-up of air in the top half of his body, caused a similar build up in his lower half, to the extent that when it was released upstairs, it was also released in the basement. This resulted in his sphincter issuing a copious amount of unwanted wind.

I promise you, dear reader, that this is the last breaking wind story you will experience in this book. But as a recipient once again of the errant act, I just had to recall it. In truth there are more stories of this ilk I could tell, but I feel that two on the subject are more than enough to be getting along with.

But the story doesn't end there... unfortunately... oh no! There were two large sound speakers set at both sides of the stage facing the audience. For reasons that both the sound man and the lighting man could never fathom - they were the same bloke - this anarchic out of the arc sound system had the unfortunate habit of occasionally picking up the radio traffic between the local taxi drivers and their controller.

Another trick these electronic decibel providers played was to randomly tune into the immediate vicinity of anyone who happened to be wearing a hearing aid. They would then blast these unfortunate hard of hearing innocents with high pitched screeching decibel feedback.

I have a sneaking suspicion to this day that the technician did know how to fix the speakers so that they wouldn't spring into life at inopportune moments, but instead left them to it because he enjoyed the chaos that ensued both on stage as well as in the audience.

The show during which our Yasha farted was a Saturday matinee when the average age of our audience was very much upwards of the seven score years plus variety. The majority of these souls sported the old-fashioned type of hearing aids of the early 1970s which had wires quite visibly attached to clumsy-looking, pink-coloured devices sprouting from hairy ears.

I think it best to set out what happened as if it was a proper script with stage directions. In doing so I hope this will give you a better chance at visualising the scene as it unfolded.

Me: Light of my life, my one spring flower.

(Creak of door opening. Yasha Enters Stage Right)

Yasha: Yepihodov's broken a billiard cue.

(Sound of deep inhalation... a few beats of silence... then... thumping of chest action... billiard cue shoots into nasal area.)

Yasha: Agh! (garbled oath which sounds like for f-- 's sakes…!)

(A loud fart.) Parp!

Yasha: Oh shit!

(Yasha laughs aloud for real. For the first time ever it sounds good. Exit Yasha Stage Right. Door closes.)

The worst thing for me at this point was that as Yasha had been downstage of me when he let rip, he was thus closer to the audience than I was. Subsequently the two elderly Dundee ladies in the front row thought that I had done it, as I had been standing immediately upstage and behind him.

Lady in front row: Did you hear what he did? The dirty wee bugger.

That hurt me because I was damn near six feet tall, though I have noticed I have been consistently shrinking as the years have gone by.

Her friend: Aye! Fancy! And he's no' even married her yet.

As if that mattered! But to make matters worse, after the errant Yasha had made his exit, Varya and I could hear him backstage telling everyone he met what had happened. Luckily the audience couldn't. Of course the more he told the louder the laughter backstage became. This is when the stage speakers burst into life with a strong barely decipherable Dundee accent.

Taxi Controller: Taxi fur fave Dudhope T'race. Any wan in the area?

Driver: A'm oan ma way Bul.

Taxi Controller: Dinna hing aboot Ecky. Aye… she gaes a big tip this yin ye ken.

As the taxi controller switched off his communication with the driver, the stage speakers electronic feedback decided it was a good time to wake up and sent out high pitched squeals. These horrific sounds were received at full thwack by everyone wearing a hearing aid in the immediate vicinity, which of course meant everyone in the audience. These poor elderly eardrums were ravaged mercilessly by the awful din. Throughout the auditorium hands raced to yank these offending devices away from ears and kick them into touch. Such is the bliss and high drama of live theatre.

I'M CLEAR, WHAT'S IT LIKE UP YOUR END?

It is funny to use the phrase 'kicked into touch' because it reminds me of a great friend of mine, the late Robert Robertson, whom I first worked with when he was an actor at Dundee Rep. He was later to follow in Stephen's footsteps and become The Rep's Artistic Director there for many years, combining the role with playing the forensic expert in the Scottish Television series *Taggart*. Stephen in the meantime, had taken over as Artistic Director of Edinburgh's Royal Lyceum Theatre.

Following the final rehearsal of a play at around five o'clock before the curtain went up at half past seven on an opening night, Robert would give his cast the usual pep talk as was the custom for good directors everywhere. In these situations the norm is for them to heap praises on the shell-shocked performers about to 'go over the top', giving their all for the first time to hundreds of paying punters. Robert did this bit very well and with great aplomb, signing off with the phrase, "Grab it by the short and curlies and kick it into touch." If only the unsuspecting audiences knew what the cast had been told to do with the play they were about to see!

On one occasion at Dundee prior to his Artistic Directorship, Robert was playing the part of Dong in our Christmas show, *The Owl and the Pussycat*. The character Dong had a luminous nose. And so it was that Big Robert cursed Edward Lear every night he had to wear the damn thing.

The red flashing nose was made of half of a plastic practise golf ball and stuck onto Robert's own nose with glue. Inside the false nose was a small light bulb, attached to which was a wire connected to a battery hidden in his costume. The light was set to flicker-mode and it drove Robert crazy because of the strobe effect flickering on and off continuously throughout the play, right in front of his face. Needless to say the contraption was hideously uncomfortable for him to wear.

It is usual for Technical Rehearsals to take place the day before the opening night and they usually start directly after lunch, going on until around 11 p.m. by which time the cast, not to mention the stage management, are totally knackered. By the way, I thought I'd mention here that the stage management would have most likely already done an 'all-nighter' the previous night. That is to say, they would have worked through the night with little respite, striking (removing) the set from the previous show, then erecting the set for the new one, setting the props, doing the lighting, sound etc., etc., etc., etc.

The purpose of a 'tech rehearsal' as it is called, is to give the stage management the chance to run the technical side of things for the first time, working all the cues including scene changes, sound cues, lighting cues, special effects, cast calls as well as setting props etc., etc., etc., etc. in situ. The actors should play only a secondary role during this time and be available on stand-by to be called onto the stage at a moment's notice as and when needed, without hesitation, deviation or repetition, and in costume. What isn't needed is a diva insisting he/she spouts any speech they have from beginning to end, unless there's a timing issue re something the stage management have to accomplish during their rendition. Basically actors should be prepared to top and tail scenes and speeches in order to minimise the all too precious time allotted to the Stage Management to complete all their tasks. Subsequently there's an awful lot of hanging around for the actors.

Whilst it is normal to finish late into the night, it is not normal to finish at 5am the following morning as we did during our technical rehearsal of our production of The Owl and The Pussycat. But there were exceptional circumstances which made this exhausting nightmare necessary. The problem hinged around a set design peculiarity and a speech impediment.

On stage the set was built on a circular revolving rostrum partitioned down the middle by a large piece of stage scenery. When the lights went to blackout at the end of one scene, the Revolve was meant to spin round revealing a completely new set as the lights came up again on a new scene. At least that was the theory. Unfortunately in practice, the ability of the Revolve to start turning, as well as stop turning on cue at the appropriate times, was completely and utterly beyond its capability.

At the base of this Revolve hidden from the audience was a circular device like a cart wheel around which was wrapped a pleated steel coil. In the wings the other end of this coil was attached to a mangle of the type used by a washerwoman in Victorian times. I remember watching it all being constructed and marvelling at the simplicity of the design. Unfortunately that simplicity was in part its downfall. The mangle simply wasn't designed to do the job requested for it needed at least three stout fellows to turn its handle alone, which was supposed then to turn the damn Revolve thing around. This of course was made even more difficult with the added weight of actors standing on the rostrum about to make their entrances. Thus it was up to any member of the cast who was not on stage at the time to assist the Stage Management with the heaving on the mangle handle. As you can imagine this did not go down terrifically well with some of the thesps. But the bloody show had to go on somehow and so everyone eventually pulled their weight plus a hell of a lot more.

The other problem was that the person giving the verbal cues for those to work the revolving stage had a wee speech impediment which I mentioned earlier. The poor chap had a slightly muffled nasal verbal delivery at the best of times. To make matters worse, instead of simplifying and thus aiding the clarity of his speech by using the words 'Start the Revolve' and 'Stop the Revolve', he insisted instead on saying 'Go revolve' and 'Woe revolve'. As he was sitting the other side of the stage from those doing the heaving, he had to use the antiquated off stage intercom. The crackling delivery from the wall mounted speakers didn't help the audibility of his pronunciation either. Subsequently both his sound cues 'Woe' and 'Go' sounded exactly the same. Thus the actors waiting hidden from the audience would make a short-lived appearance as the Revolve started turning but didn't stop when the cue was misheard, and so it carried on turning. Several false starts to the scene ensued as they spun around and around in full view for a few seconds then hidden again and so on. When those heaving on the mangle became too exhausted and ceased hauling altogether, the revolving rostrum's momentum would run out of steam and it would eventually come to a noisy, grinding halt, by which time it was hoped that the actors would be facing the audience. Unfortunately on numerous occasions the lights came up on an empty Revolve, whereupon the troubled hiding actors standing on it would have to climb off and make a rather humble entrance appearing from around it.

The chap with the dodgy speech was also the same daft bugger who I found back stage during the first night having a sly puff on a cigarette. I remonstrated with him, telling him he should be in the wings on the book running the show.

He replied, "For f--'s shakes they've been rehearsing it fur free f--n' weeks maun, if they dinnae know it noo they never f--n' wull." His limited expertise of what was the norm re: accepted vernacular English, also limited those trying extremely hard to understand him as they had to put up with more than a modicum of vulgar expletives, whatever the occasion or company.

But dear Robert kept our spirits up in the dressing room well into the wee small hours by regaling us with some of the dirtiest songs I have ever heard - songs that he had learned during his National Service days, the lyrics of which I dare not put on paper. Suffice it to say that the last line of one of them was, "I stamped on it until its colour turned to beige"... and that was one of the milder renditions.

He always seemed to play characters which required much physical discomfort e.g. Dong as described. On another occasion when he was playing the part of Long John Silver in Treasure Island, he had to have one of his ankles strapped up into a sling. It was horrendously uncomfortable for him. But to his credit he played the part for weeks on end without any complaint. Unlike the parrot he had to use.

Much as I am a bird lover, I grew to hate that bastard of a parrot. We all did. To be fair though, the theatre is no place for a parrot. Indeed I would ban keeping any bird indoors as a pet. Though I don't have any axe to grind, I believe that birds are born to fly wherever and whenever they want. They should therefore be allowed to do so without any interference from humans. The very idea of taking them from their natural habitat and putting them in a small cage for the rest of their sorry lives is totally beyond me. Having said that, the bloody bird we had to work with was not of the friendly pet variety and I would have quite happily caged it myself. Pretty Polly it was most definitely not. In fact it had a right bitch of a temper.

We three who shared a dressing room with the parrot, did try to do our best to get along with it. But in the end I do admit that we all failed miserably. The impertinent stubborn sod would just sit there looking at us disdainfully as we put on our makeup for the show, waiting for a moment when deep in concentration our guard was down, so that it could attack us. After it got bored with violence, it began to pass the time by eating our highly expensive sticks of Leichner makeup. Then to top it all it would crap on what was left. That was the final straw. Either it went back to its owner and we got a stuffed one instead for Robert to wear on his shoulder... or... we were lining up with our various recipes for parrot stew. But Robert insisted on persevering. So that parrot sat on his shoulder night after night during the shows, day after day during the matinees, to the delight of the audiences who came to see it, with the exception of us actors, of course. A real pro was Robert.

I last saw him in the late nineteen nineties when we both worked on an episode of the Scottish television detective series called *Taggart*. During filming we were billeted in a hotel overlooking the Fourth Road Bridge. On our last night we adjourned to the hotel bar and stayed there well into the wee small hours, reminiscing about our time at Dundee Rep together some twenty-five years before. Needless to say a lot of stories were told as we downed more than a few largish drams of whiskey. Being in the company of the man who used to call me 'Big Tam King of Scotland' was an absolute joy.

Occasionally when the frustrations of this careless business do just about get the better of me, I look to the Heavens and hope that Robert Robertson can be bothered to stop what he is enjoying long enough, to regale me with some common sense.

Nactors and the Three Necessities

Booze... Food... and Sex. Of course you can have one without the others, but try telling that to an alcohol-appreciating, hungry, randy actor. Because of the precarious nature of their employment status, there has never been an actor born that I have met who would turn down a free meal, free booze, or free sex, though admittedly the latter is true with most people whatever their occupation.

If you invite a group of thespians to your party... beware. The first thing they will do is hone in on the food, whilst other partygoers form a mannerly queue waiting for a signal from the host or hostess to proceed. I know this to be true because I did it. I arrived at a party once with a fellow actor, and without a by your leave we went straight to the culinary delights on offer. We then unceremoniously filled our paper plates then our stomachs, not realising that everyone else was waiting politely to be invited to help themselves. Ergo, it is a wise host who previously warns their guests if actors have also been invited to their soiree. One such group I heard of had been invited to an after show knees up. When word got round that the actors in the play had also been invited, the guests didn't bother waiting for the curtain call, instead they nipped out early hot footing it to get there first, thus ensuring that they could at least sample some of the food and drink on offer before the cast could get at it. The sex would have to wait till later but wasn't compulsory.

Once fed actors will usually head en masse for the kitchen area, for this is where the alcoholic liquid refreshment is usually to be found at most parties. Be not alarmed. It is just because the booze on offer is free. But please do not judge actors too harshly, for I have also noticed that those in the journalistic profession are past masters of the art of demolishing copious amounts of alcohol when it is offered free also, and are more than capable of beating actors to the bar every time. Similar too are members of the medical profession... not to mention those in the armed forces, even politicians, and police, as well as navvies, artists, barristers, musicians, university dons, etc., etc., etc., which means all of us really. So it could be said that actors are just copying the masses, which is what their job is all about!

When the actors' food and booze appetites have been assuaged, or if there is simply no more left to shovel or slosh down their gullets, and if they can still just about focus through an alcoholic haze whilst standing upright without the help of a supporting friend or wall, a few diehards then move into the next phase. For in this challenged state, when it is highly dubious as to whether these larger than life characters could raise even a smile, the urge to get lucky kicks in. Hopefully without the success of an additional member of their blood line turning up nine months later. After all, the show they were in has been a great success, they have all been well fed and watered, so in their eyes it is party time.

Like anyone else who has had more than a few, whoever or whatever the object of their desire is will be approached with the bravado of alcohol blocking out common sense.

N.B. I read somewhere of someone (not an actor thank gawd) being physically attracted to their Austin Mini car... takes all sorts eh!

However, should the object of their desire be an unwilling receptor of the actor's advances, in order to let them down gently, may I offer the following advice... unless of course you are an Austin Mini. Tell them how absolutely wizard you thought they were in the play, even though unfortunately you didn't manage to see it to the bitter end because you wanted to assuage your hunger and left the theatre early in order to beat the cast to the free food. Although I would strongly suggest that it is best not to mention that last bit, especially if your exit from the theatre coincided with the actor's big dying scene.

This tactic, though simple, is guaranteed fail safe. For thesps on the receiving end of a compliment re their performance in the play of which you may only have seen half, will be putty in your hands. Ergo they will easily be dissuadable of any advances whatsoever, for they will listen intently to any praises being heaped upon them, soak up the adoration and hang on to your every complimentary word. Thus you will then be in the ascendant and in total control of the situation.

CHAPTER 10

WORKING OVERSEAS

I thoroughly enjoy travelling, even more so if I'm getting paid to do a job of work when I arrive at my destination. The adventure of setting foot in far flung corners of the planet, especially if they have been hitherto unknown to me is just too damned enticing to miss. Citizens of the USA, Central America, The Hebrides, Ireland, Holland, Denmark, France, England, India, Orkney etc., have all had the opportunity of seeing me perform, though I did take note that on occasion some preferred to stay at home.

Sometimes, however, the journeys to these far flung climes ain't always that enjoyable. Take for example my experience on board an aircraft circa 1981, when as one of a merry troupe of players, though some were a wee bit grumpy due to a tiring work schedule, much travelling and a rather late night, we were about to take off from one foreign city and fly to another, where we had been booked to ply our trade. I can assure you that the following is actually what happened.

Our flight had been delayed somewhat which we had found to be the norm for flying anywhere in that country. Eventually our plane did idly taxi towards the runway in preparation for take-off. The calm voice of the pilot issued the order 'Manual to Automatic'. His words hung in the air momentarily. Then for some unknown reason he put his foot hard down on the gas pedal. It seemed to me that he was trying to make his aircraft break the sound barrier whilst still on terra firma. A silent panic pervaded the cabin as the engines roared at full throttle. Passengers' faces quite suddenly became etched with terror. The stewardesses gave up trying to hand round curry flavoured sweets and scampered to the back of the aisles, where they sat on the floor huddling together as if for comfort... absolutely true.

The costume designer lady sitting beside me whispered in a quivering voice that there was no in-flight safety card where it should have been i.e. tucked into the appropriate seat pocket in front of her. I had hoped I would reassure her when I said amusingly that they wouldn't be much help if we crashed anyway. But my witty remark didn't help apparently. I tried another tack.

"I'm sure we'll be fine," I proffered. But she didn't believe me, which wasn't surprising because I didn't believe myself either. On checking the seat pocket in front of me however, I noticed that there were no less than five identical safety cards. Gallantly I leant her four of mine, which calmed her down a little.

Moments later the tables were turned when we checked to see if our life jackets were in position under our seats. Indeed they were, but mine had a patch stuck on it, which bore a remarkable resemblance to the type found in a bicycle tyre repair kit, except that this one was the size of my hand. I wisely decided that blind terror was out of the question as it would have been pointless. Also because the flight was an internal one, if we were to have the misfortune of hitting the deck prematurely, there was bugger all water down there to land on anyway. Thus I concluded that my patched life jacket was not an issue to worry about.

The plane slewed around on the hot sticky tarmac, its tail swinging first to the left, then to the right, then to the left again, and once more to the right before taking a sharp ninety-degree left hander onto the runway and lining up for take-off. Unlike any other flight I had ever been on or since, there was no pause at this point followed by the inevitable build-up of engine noise, before breaks were released and off it went. Oh no, that was not what happened. Instead the plane leapt forward as if it had received a hefty kick up its arse, and shot off down that runway at full pelt. It seemed to me that it was going faster on its take off than any aircraft had ever done before, or has ever done since. Concorde my aunt fanny… this thing went faster than a supersonic speeding bullet along the runway. We took to the air, resembling a rocket in what seemed like a near vertical ascent, reaching its thirty five thousand feet cruising altitude in record time, which felt like about three seconds.

During the ensuing flight I concentrated on reading the safety card to distract my mind from thinking of the worst. Then I proceeded to read the other four I had lent to my fellow passenger. Although this was a rather repetitive exercise, it did keep my mind off the turbulence. When at last our destination approached at lightning speed, we began our descent. I believe to this day that our pilot had never been taught the art of gradual descent as is the norm. Instead he had perfected the nose dive technique in preparation for landing.

Another quirky thing I noticed early on when boarding, was that the spare loo roll was lodged in the rear off-side emergency door handle. I thought at the time that one of our lot had placed it there for a laugh. But, and it was disconcerting to find this out, throughout the tour, on every internal flight we suffered, the spare loo roll was always in the same place. How embarrassing it would have been if anyone had to shuffle out of the loo into the cabin area to retrieve it.

During my sojourn to Asia, my new wife (we had only been married three months) flew out to join me. She told me that she had been horrified to see tea towels drying on a piece of string tied between the pilot's and co-pilot's seats on one of her flights. I mentioned that as we were now married, I was so very glad she was taking such an interest in domestic chores, which of course wasn't the reply she expected from her newish husband and subsequently it didn't go down at all well. It is true that I had observed similar sorts of domestic drying arrangements on other flights across the sub-continent, and I suppose I had come to accept them as the norm by then. I might even have been disappointed not to have seen clean dhotis drying in the cockpit had they not been there.

My initial reaction was one of mild disbelief when I first heard that the plays chosen to take to India were Shakespeare's Scottish play and *Who's Life is it Anyway*; after all, the former was about political assassination, whilst the latter dealt with euthanasia. It is well documented that Indian politics has been tainted with more than its fair share of assassinations throughout history. It is also widely known that there are more than a few disenfranchised people living on the streets of Indian cities, barely having enough to survive on. So why choose these plays I wondered? Surely they were totally absurd choices for the country we were visiting.

I couldn't have been proved more wrong. In *Whose Life is it Anyway*, when after a long silence the judge decides that the patient should be allowed to take his own life, there were ovations practically every night.

As for the Scots play, not only did they love it, they knew the play extremely well indeed and some even sat with the Shakespeare text on their laps, following us all the way, even finding a few laughs where we hadn't realised there were any. At first I thought they were taking the piss, but later back in my hotel room when I studied the bits that had got them chortling, I found that there was humour in there after all. Good old Willie Shakespeare. Just when you think you have a handle on what it's all about, a new revelation exposes itself.

There were, however, a few really dodgy moments during the tour. Within two days arrival in the capital Bombay - or Mumbai as someone decided it should now be called - I began to have a wee toothache problem. The theatre organiser kindly fixed me up with a visit to a highly respected dentist. And so with the surgery address scribbled on a piece of paper clutched in my left hand, I ventured into the myriad of that noisy city's busy back streets. After much searching and copious offers of help from many eager locals, I found myself ascending two flights up a rickety old staircase within a darkened passageway, similar to a dark dank close you would find in an old Glasgow tenement.

I do admit that at this stage I was seriously contemplating turning around and heading back to the hotel, making use of oil of cloves to temporarily ease the pain until our return home. The stairwell's ambience was doing nothing for my confidence, but the throbbing pain in my tooth kept me heading upwards and onwards. After all, we had a further seven and a half weeks of touring to go, so I decided to soldier on.

The waiting room was pleasant enough, extremely clean and displayed a tropical fish tank bubbling away in a corner, which I found quite comforting. But when I was called into the surgery, my heart sank. A young boy of about ten was sweeping the floor of dollops of blood-stained cotton wool with a bundle of reeds tied together like a miniature witch's broom stick. However I was somewhat put at my ease by the dentist, who greeted me warmly. He was a very convivial chap with a huge girth, sporting a permanent grin. I must still have looked more than a tad apprehensive because he then proceeded to show me written credentials as proof of his qualification to practise dentistry, and explained to me that he had trained in the UK. I think he thought this would put my mind at rest. In fact I couldn't give a damn had he been trained on another planet just as long as he knew what he was doing, which is all that mattered to me. It turned out I needed only a temporary filling around a bridge which had been fitted only recently at great expense back in London. I wish this Indian dentist had fitted the bridge in the first place then I most likely wouldn't have had to have it bloody re fixed at all. So I can report a happy ending there. It was of course the fear of the unknown that had worried me most. After seeing blood soaked detritus from a previous patient being swept up by the dentist's little helper, I defy anyone not to have felt at least a wee bit apprehensive.

An incident occurred when we were visited by a VIP. It had all the makings of a wee insurmountable diplomatic problem. When the Prime Minister of the day, Mrs Ghandi came to see our show, the security was extremely thorough and quite right too. Big burly security types thoroughly checked our costumes before we put them on, then they waited around backstage and in the dimly lit wings for the show's duration.

N.B. The wing space is a sacrosanct area of the theatre for the use of those actors and stage management and crew who are directly connected with the production only. No one else is ever allowed to be there. It is even frowned upon if a show's Director makes an appearance backstage during a performance. Unless of course there is a crisis of some sort which needs direct intervention etc., etc., etc.

So when Mrs Ghandi's armed minders turned up backstage it was a bit disconcerting to say the least. Consequently my fellow players looked somewhat more nervous than was usual. Also during that particular performance, some got quite rightly really peeved off. The reason for this was that not only were many of the audience taking photographs but quite a few were using flash photography, a practise which was absolutely disallowed back home. Performances in Blighty have been stopped for less. The problem was that one happy snapper was photographing us from the orchestra pit, which was of course directly in front and below us. Though I found this quite amusing, I was aware of the mounting tension backstage. But as there was nothing we could do there and then about him, we just got on with it. I remember wondering if the photographer had got a good shot of me.

During the interval it was decided that an announcement would have to be made to stop any more photographs from being taken, especially by the chap in the orchestra pit. There was a wee problem though, because the chap in question was none other than Rajiv Ghandi, the Prime Minister's son. But when the request was diplomatically made by our Company Manager, the audience applauded and Mr Ghandi complied without complaint and so all was well again.

It was very sad to hear years later that not only had Mrs Ghandi been assassinated, but her son Rajiv had also died when the plane he was piloting crashed. I had previously thought that had I ever gone back to India, I would have called on him and asked where in his house he had displayed my photo.

And then there's the evening we opened *Whose Life is it Anyway* in Mumbai. It will remain ingrained in my memory forever. Not that it was remarkable in any other way except that a few hours before curtain up, I succumbed to a dreadful fever of the sort that would have pole-axed Goliath, killed off lesser mortals and was having a damn good try at finishing me off there and then. But we actors are a hardy bunch, and short of actually breaking or losing a lower limb in a horrific accident, we are expected to carry on regardless.

A few of us in the cast had enjoyed the hospitality of our hotel's swimming pool in the early afternoon, before sauntering the mile to the Pritvi Theatre for a final rehearsal. At about the half way mark I began to feel dizzy, then my body temperature dropped dramatically and I started to shiver. This was extremely odd as the air temperature was above the three figure mark. By the time we arrived at the theatre all colour had apparently drained from my face, which was by then bathed in a damp, cold sweat.

Needless to say I opted for missing the pre-show rehearsal, instead I lay on my dressing room floor with as many bits of clothing and rugs that I could find draped over me in order to try and warm me up. But even with their help they didn't stop my teeth from chattering. I honestly believed I had galloping Malaria. Occasionally I would hear or see diabolical looking primeval insects scurry across the floor inches from my face, but I was in no fit state to even consider getting out of their way. I just lay there on my back like a dying Meerkat looking up at hovering vultures, trying not to look unwell whilst the little creatures ran around and over me.

About this time the stage manager came to see how I was doing. I realised that we were talking at cross purposes when I told her that I didn't think I was going to make it, meaning that I didn't think I could do the show that evening, so she'd better warn my understudy to get ready. She thought I meant I was about to snuff it. My imitation of a dying Meerkat must have been damned good. But I was in no state to argue the case. Instead of offering me solace and comfort, she was less than courteous to say the least, and left me in no doubt that she certainly wasn't going to let me expire in that hot stuffy dressing room. At least not until the show was over and I had done my bit of acting, for which I had been flown all the way to India and being paid to do. It was a lesson in tough love for me.

"You simply have to go on Tom!"

"I doooo? Whyyyy?" I asked, my teeth feeling as though they were about to fall out any moment with the amount of clattering together they were still doing.

"Cos we've just rehearsed your understudy… enough said?" Half an hour later and beginning to feel that maybe the stage manager had been right first time, that I was not long for this life, I was piled into my costume and half carried into the wings. At the appropriate time I was gently pushed onto the stage. Somehow I miraculously got through it all without any mishaps and didn't die. Such is the power of Dr Theatre as it is known in the business. No matter how diabolical you feel, providing you can stand upright, Dr Theatre will get you through the show. Luckily it was the weekend, so when I got back to my hotel I stayed in bed for the next two and a half days. Thank you Lord that it wasn't Malaria but God alone knows what it actually was. It took a week to fully recover by which time my energy levels, which had already been sapped by the heavy heat, were at an all-time low.

I'M CLEAR, WHAT'S IT LIKE UP YOUR END?

Our tour took us to Hyderabad, whose neighbour Secunderabad was joined by an invisible demarcation line. On one blissful morning, my wife Cookie and I hired a scooter taxi, which we christened a Buzz Bomb, in order that we could see as much of the two towns as possible in the few short hours I had off. This mode of transport can be found in any Indian city and is probably the quickest way to get around the traffic jammed streets. It is also a way of being scared shitless. Every other vehicle on the road beside, ahead and in front of you looks larger, more powerful and noisier, which indeed they all are. They also appeared to be driven by lunatics with a penchant for banger racing. I had a sneaking suspicion that as some taxi drivers had the belief that their next life would be much better they were trying to hurry it along. The one we had appeared to be of that belief, if his suicidal style of driving was anything to go by. It was to our great surprise that we made it to our final destination, the Secunderabad Sailing Club. It was here that Cookie's parents had spent some of their leisure time before the war years, as her father had served in the Indian Army as a Major in the Gurkhas.

Cookie, armed with a small black and white photo of the club from that bygone era, enquired if we could have a look around. We were introduced to the Vice Chairman, a delightful chap who was absolutely thrilled to see the photo. After a hearty lunch on the house, he and his wife took us on a conducted tour of the two towns in his Morris Minor, which he had lovingly restored to its former glory.

I am happy to say that back in Blighty some months later, we had the opportunity to return their kindness and hospitality when they came on a visit to the UK. However I'm afraid that my car, though old, was not of the classic variety, but I do hope they enjoyed their guided tour we gave them of Southall... their choice of venue.

Prior to us touring India with both plays, we toured England with the Scots play only. One of our dates was Poole in Dorset. In the adjoining theatre to us was that well known comic genius of stage, screen and television, the one and only Billy Connolly. He and I come from the same city, and in our formative years, both worked in the Glasgow shipyards. I felt I knew him even though we had never met.

During the second half of our show I had about twenty minutes between scenes I was in. So I seized the opportunity to work my way through the myriad of corridors until I found myself in the wings of the neighbouring theatre watching the great man weave his comic spell. I peeked through a hole in the wing drapes and looked out at a cavernous huge black hole full to the brim with the sound of hysterical laughter. On stage was Billy Connolly dressed in a black T-shirt with tails, black tights and yellow banana shaped booties. Behind him on two floor-stands leaned a guitar and a banjo. And that was it... nothing more... just the man himself, a silly outfit, and a couple of musical instruments. Our lot next door, whose cast numbered in the teens, were fully kitted out in Shakespearean garb, including thigh length made to measure leather boots, plus all the necessary accompaniment of the period, big swords hanging from big buckled belts etc. etc. etc. Mr Connolly was playing to a full house and so were we. Oh the joys of live theatre.

I have since done stand-up routines a couple of times and was reasonably successful, but the terror I experienced before going on stage far outweighed the desire to jump up and do that sort of thing again in a hurry, unless there was a lot of money being offered. And that wasn't going to be offered to me as a comic.

Watching him from the wings that night, I suddenly had an awful thought. What would happen if he had glanced into the wings and saw me dressed as I was in the doublet and hose routine, with my longish hair combed to look in the style of the period (but somehow I looked more like Sandy Shaw) and sporting a goatee beard of sorts. To all intents and purposes I must have looked like the theatre ghost. It is quite possible that he could have had heart failure at the shock. To this day I'm glad his concentration was fully on his audience.

Mine wasn't, for I was so engrossed in watching what he was doing that I nearly paid the price by missing my next entrance back in the other theatre, where I was very soon supposed to be by then. I realised I had overstayed my welcome, hastily legged it at full pelt and arrived in the wings with seconds to spare. What a difference there was in the atmosphere... not a sound from our audience... the only thing I could hear was the sound of much wailing on stage bemoaning the fact that some blighter had murdered someone else. Alas and alack all is woe around here I thought to myself... and pondered whether I was I in the wrong theatre.

CHAPTER ELEVEN

HURRICANES AND BUM BITERS IN CA

Sometime around circa 1978 I jumped at the chance of playing a Harrier Jump Jet fighter pilot, and jumped even higher when I heard I would be filming in Belize. Of course I hadn't a bloody clue as to where on the planet Belize was, but it sounded exotic enough to me. And so I found myself in one of the hottest places on earth i.e. inside the cockpit of a Harrier jump jet parked on the tarmac at Belize airport in Central America, kitted out in full flying gear including a borrowed Bandam (flying helmet) from one of the real pilots, which was painfully a tad too small for me. The constant pressure on my temples made my head feel as if I was going to implode at any second. Outside, where the crew were filming me from, the temperature was well into three figures, so you can imagine how hot it was in the cockpit. As quick as I took in liquid it literally poured out of my pores as if I were a sieve. I didn't carry an ounce of extra weight in these days, unlike now sadly, and I had more hair, unlike now sadly. I must have been barely recognisable when I returned to Blighty some weeks later, suntanned and looking even trimmer than before.

Our cast and crew numbered nine, five crew and four actors. We were billeted in a hotel which was literally thirty yards from the sea known as the Caribbean. I gained little comfort from knowing that there was only a three foot high perimeter sea wall separating us from a watery end. Do I have any phobias that I'm aware of? Lifts don't bother me, heights I have had to contend with, speed I enjoy providing I am in reasonable control etc., but I suppose I do shamefully admit to being on the side of terrified at the thought of a tsunami paying us a visit, especially as my bedroom happened to be on the ground floor i.e. sea level and therefore too bloody close. Needless to say on any night when the wind got up, I sat in the lobby with my meagre possessions packed and ready to beat a hasty retreat at the first sound of heavily lapping water. After all, this was the place that was hit by Hurricane Hattie in 1962 and flattened by huge tidal waves. Consequently a new town/city was built about fifty kilometres inland named Belmopan. I have never been able to comprehend why Belize was rebuilt once again within a few feet of that mighty and unpredictable sea, which is the home of some of the fiercest and deadliest creatures on earth. But who am I to complain? I am merely an actor who at the time was being paid a nice whack in a rather scrumptiously hot climate, doing a job which required me simply to kid on that I was someone else. What a magnificent job to be doing.

Apart from the fear of Mother Nature conspiring to drown me, I had to get used to the local wild life which included Land Crabs, whose antics would have been amusing had they not looked so horrendous. These damn things would pop their heads out from drains etc. and if they thought the coast was clear, they'd scurry at lightning speed off to their next destination, which was usually another drain. Our squadron leader swore blind that one of the buggers made an appearance in the bog just as he was sitting himself down, nipping him on the bum. As none of us were interested in seeing his apparently lacerated arse, and to be fair he was extremely reluctant to show us it anyway, his tale went down in RAF folklore, but I had a sneaking suspicion that he was telling the truth. Needless to say from then on, no-one wasted any time in answering the call of nature when it came. There were even side bets to see who could get the job done and get out of the bog again quickest, without the fabled bum biter scoring another direct hit.

The night we arrived in Belize there was a power cut. This was one of many and we got used to them, but we never got used to the cockroaches, which we could hear clattering around our tiled bedroom floors. They were bloody huge, about the size of an extra-large middle finger and the width of an extra-large thumb, brownish maroon in colour. Every night before turning in I would find at least two in my room. Only after I had battered them to death, checked that every perceivable nook and cranny was free of them and that there were no hurricanes forecast, would I then attempt to sleep, leaving the noisy air conditioning fan on to drown out the sounds of scuttling insects or the lashing of waves outside. The worst times were when I couldn't find any cockroaches at all. Just because I couldn't find them didn't mean they weren't around. There was a hole in my bathroom ceiling which was big enough to allow a herd of the buggers access. It was difficult to sleep with that thought in my mind.

One morning at breakfast while we watched the sunlight dance on the turquoise dappled Caribbean, one of our lot informed the hotel management that he had a problem with cockroaches in his bedroom, which was situated on the floor above mine. Though he was stating the obvious, his story was a little more extreme to say the least.

In the early hours of the morning when all the hotel guests had already done the cockroach exterminating game and were fast asleep, he was wakened by one of these horrendous creatures strolling over his chest. It was immediately followed by another, then its pal, and so on.

"An army of the bastards went on manoeuvres over me!" he exclaimed to the laid back hotel manager, who had probably seen and heard those sort of complaints many times before. The actor went on to say that when he pulled back the mattress he found to his horror a whole precinct full of them in the base of his bed. I was beginning to realise that filming on location was not all that it was cracked up to be and was very nearly tempted to cancel eating breakfast there and then. But as the hotel food was all paid for by the film company, my actor instincts kicked in and I felt I couldn't let this freebie meal go to waste and so I duly carried on eating.

That evening when we returned to the hotel after a heavy day's filming in blistering heat, we were told that the upper floor was out of bounds as it had been fumigated because of complaints about cockroaches. My room had a spare bed and so I kindly offered it to one of the other thesps, whose room was one of those upstairs in the anti-cockroach firing line. Nothing wrong with that, it was a matey thing for me to do in the circumstances. What wasn't too matey a thing to do was to forget that I had a roommate when I got up the following morning, donning nothing more than a pair of rubber soled flying boots. I then proceeded to bend over the wash basin and wash my face, my bare arse pointing in the direction of his shocked face. In my defence I told him that I wore the boots in order to earth myself, therefore avoiding the electric shocks I got every time the tap water made contact with my hands. At first my roommate thought that there was a strong possibility that I was lying, suggesting that I actually enjoyed displaying my nether regions to relative strangers at first light. But I managed to convince him otherwise when, bare footed, he plunged his hands under the running tap water and got the electric shock I had warned him to expect.

I had never realised before how noisy it was to travel aboard a helicopter until I experienced a tree-hopping flight over the jungle with its side doors open. Earlier whilst still on the runway, I had signed the usual disclaimer before flying i.e. if there's a cock-up and we crash then I won't put in an insurance claim. Not that there would have been much left of me anyway.

After pre-flight checks the pilot asked if anyone wanted to join him up front in the cockpit. When there were no takers he pointed out that if someone sat in the co-pilot's seat it would really help him to balance the helicopter when in flight. The result was a stampede to sit beside him, which I made sure I won. With the camera mounted by the open starboard doorway behind me, the idea was to film the Harrier jets screaming past as they overtook us. All very thrilling, until the pilot asked if I would warn him when a Harrier Jump Jet was approaching, because he didn't want to hit one by accident. Suddenly the thrill and utter enjoyment I was experiencing in being airborne at two thousand feet above mother earth in a Puma helicopter left me. It was instead replaced by a gnawing fear of what would happen if I missed seeing the approach of a Harrier Jump Jet thwacking along past us like shit off a fan. My trepidation was confounded when the pilot added that I had to tell him in clock language where the planes were coming from e.g. Harrier at two o'clock… Harrier at five past three etc. I was just about to ask him whether I should imagine the clock to be horizontal or on the vertical, when the first Harrier screamed past doing 300 bloody knots.

"Yes! Bloody hell! I saw one! About four past… something!" was all I could get out before the next one was on and past us. These fly pasts lasted about fifteen minutes in all, and sadly I think I managed only one correct, "Bandits at seven o'clock" shout before we broke off from the sortie.

Our next 'mission' was to film the jungle below us as we flew over it at tree top level, so we plummeted out of the sky to a level where leaves and branches brushed at our wheels. Our pilot quite wisely judged that as it was a rather delicate balancing act to fly at this low level, it would be wiser to lighten the load. Thus we landed and we four nactas were given roughly ten seconds to disembark in a clearing, before the Puma flew off on its 120 knots tree-shaving, hair-raising exercise elsewhere. The clearing we were dumped in was roughly the size of a shrunken five a side football pitch covered in long grass, which looked as if it hadn't been cut for ten years. It was about five foot high in places. As the clatter from the rotor blades faded, the din of the surrounding jungle inhabitants took over. This collective vocal effort of menacing calls from millions of unseen biting, scratching, munching, stinging creatures seemed to be saying;

"Let'ssss get the thespssssss!"

And so I began to stamp my feet.

"Not the best of times to be having a tantrum Tom," someone quipped. He had been enjoying the flight and was pissed off at finding himself in the back of beyond with nowhere to go. We all agreed with him.

"I'm not. Just trying to scare off any snakes that are bound to be in the immediate vicinity," I replied, pointedly looking down at the thick undergrowth, which I swear I could actually see growing. The other three made a unanimous decision there and then to join in with my tantrum dance, which we practised as a group until we were sure that the only snake with the guts to come anywhere near the stomping quartet would have to be the size of an anaconda. At the thought of one of these wrapping itself around us, we legged it away from the tall grass and into the jungle proper, where we found ourselves by a rather murky looking stream, over hung with heavily laden branches of highly coloured flowers casting dappled shadows on the water's surface. What was actually swimming underneath that surface we dared not even try to imagine.

With time on our hands, and feeling that there wasn't much of it left before we would be visited by undesirable countless terrors that had a penchant for killing humans, we began to ponder what would happen if,

God forbid, for any reason the helicopter didn't come back for us. We anxiously scanned each other's facial features for a sign that maybe one of us held the answer to our salvation. On the contrary, apart from the odd whimper or two, no-one uttered a sound relating to any sort of constructive escape plan.

Had outsiders been in our company however, we highly testosterone-fuelled actors would have fed our egos with faces showing more than a hint of impassive coolness in the face of such adversity. We would have vied with each other to be the one with an aura of centred calmness when it was obvious that all around us wasn't. After all, that is the very essence of an actor's craft... to be able to con a crowd into believing that what they are seeing is actually for real. Of course an audience will be taken in because they want to believe in the illusion presented, and because they have paid good money. It's really a piece of piss when you break it down.

However, in the absence of any paying audience, looks of abject horror were imprinted on my companions faces at the thought of being left in that terrifying jungle without the ability to contact their agents (there were no mobile phones in these days) in order that the said agents could arrange to get them the hell out of there... smartish.

It was then that an apparition appeared out of the foggy jungle ether as if levitating. It stopped a few yards in front of us. Two men and a youth on horseback, the latter bigger and stronger than the poor horse he was astride. The three amigos sat motionless looking down at us from above. It must have been a weird sight from their perspective too, dressed as we were in our flying suits like extras from Thunderbirds. They in turn were clothed like extras from a Huckleberry Finn movie. The two men sported beards without moustaches, giving the impression they had put their heads on upside down by mistake.

"What you guysh doin'?" one of the moustachless enquired in a shishful, drawling accent with a predominant sibilant S.

I remember thinking that the scenario was straight out of a bad sci-fi B movie of the worst kind. It then crossed my mind that maybe my full English breakfast Caribbean style, which I had scoffed heartily a few hours earlier, had been doctored with magic mushroom dust by some wag back at the hotel, and that all this was just a dream. But my theory went out of the window when something very sharp and painful penetrated my neck and I realised unfortunately that all was really as it seemed. I howled, thwacked at the insect, missed, and howled a second time as my hand connected with the wound.

"Hosh fly. Peshky ain't they? They been followin' ush shince the farm ten mile back heh heh heh!" the youngest offered in the identical shishling way of his elder.

"I'll give you peshky ya fat bastard," I wanted to say. But instead I replied, "Yesh. A wee bit shore too."

These three strange looking individuals stayed just long enough to find out what it was we were doing this far away from any military base. We quickly allayed their fears that we were about to start a war or lay a claim to the clearing we had just run away from. They told us that they were part of some sort of religious sect farming in the Guatemala region for five dollars an acre. 'Inshtead of five hundred dollarsh an acre back home'. They carried no weapons and had a quiet knowledgeable air, a bit like Yoda in Star Wars. The three wise Yodas left as they had arrived, so silently in fact that I genuinely thought their horses' hooves were wearing some sort of cushioned slippers. It was as if they were riding some kind of horse lookalike hovercrafts. The jungle mist swallowed them up and they disappeared back into the shadows they had appeared from. I felt that I had been in the presence of men who were doing something a bit more worthwhile with their lives than I was. But as I gave more thought at having to share the shame habitat as the peshky hosh fly, my desire to be one of them soon gave way to thankfulness that I wasn't. Eventually, and much to the relief of all four of us, the chopper did return and we were whisked off back to Belize airport.

As we flew over the tree tops thinking that we would soon be back in the bar relating how brave we all had been to survive the jungle ordeal without the help of our respective agents, we had no idea of what we were about to experience.

The chopper circled the runway then flew on for a further mile before hovering over a dirt road, which ran around the airport perimeter. From our vantage point beside the open side doors we saw that our hired film unit car, a big white coloured American job, which was supposed to be back at the airport waiting for our return, was nose down in a deep ditch. The pilot parked up close by and we all gingerly leapt on to terra firma and raced off to investigate.

The film crew member, whom we had left in charge of the vehicle, had decided to see how fast it would go along the dirt road before it would right itself off. Luckily for him, an army patrol had spotted the wreckage soon afterwards. He wasn't too badly hurt and was whisked off by medics and spent a few days recovering in the military unit hospital in a room assigned for stupid twats. In the meantime we slithered down the embankment to inspect the damage. The car's front end was caved in, the windscreen was no more, and it looked like our bloke had had a very lucky escape. As I stood in the ditch watching the army winch the car back up onto the track, someone pointed out that the car's boot or trunk as they say in Belize had been forced open, and we were informed that a friend's briefcase containing passport etc. was gone. Someone had been seen legging it into the jungle with said briefcase under his arm and was thus judged without trial to be the culprit. The missing briefcase and passport weren't as important to its owner as was the etcetera in the shape of coral jewellery, which he had bought for his wife back home. Furious, he set off alone along a jungle path in the direction the thief had taken. He went at such a pace we didn't have time to talk him out of it, and fearing for his safety, we four actors went tramping after him. This was a bit of a relief in a way, because the large biting ants which had their home in the ditch close to our wrecked vehicle were beginning to make their presence felt, in their many thousands. Any excuse to get away from the immediate area was to be welcomed. It struck me that what we actors were doing we hadn't had any training for. Namely navigating our way safely through a jungle, chock full of species of insects, reptiles and animals, which were hell bent on killing us. I reckoned on our survival rate being less than a few minutes.

Nevertheless, undaunted we intrepid inexperienced innocents high tailed it after our buddy, and soon came to a clearing in the centre of which stood about half a dozen straw roofed huts perched on stilts. Whilst pondering which hut to investigate first, the decision was suddenly made for us. Out of the corner of my eye I clocked at the far end of the clearing, a particularly nasty, bad-tempered looking, black, hairy, pig-like grizzly beast with an anger management problem. Its two sharp pointed tusks pointed skywards, its head swayed from side to side and its hooves pawed menacingly at the ground. Its horrible gaze was fixed on us. My gaze immediately became fixed on it.

I'M CLEAR, WHAT'S IT LIKE UP YOUR END?

"Chaps... I don't think yonder piggy-wiggy is too enamoured with our presence in his back yard... in fact he looks positively bloody furious... what do you reckon?... chaps?... pals... anybody?" I turned around to see that my so called pals had already begun their swift exits to safer climes, for they were running at full pelt across the clearing towards the steps of the nearest mud hut.

"Thanks a bunch you lot... !"

The pig thing, on seeing our herd stampede, decided at that moment to attack the straggler... me! In my panic to catch up with the others I felt as if I was running on the spot for a few precious seconds trying my damnedest to get forward momentum... a bit like a *Tom and Jerry* cartoon... only this was for real. Then like an Exocet I took off, arriving at the foot of the steps with one hundredth of a second to spare. I literally shot up them and threw myself into the open doorway tumbling into the other runaways. Subsequently we all ended up in a heap. Sitting in the middle of the hut floor in front of us was the most beautiful vision; a half-naked young native woman cradling a young baby asleep in her arms. With a smile that could break the hardest of hearts she looked at us unselfconsciously. We melted, apologised profusely for our ridiculous uninvited appearance, untangled ourselves, stood up and backed away.

She giggled and said quietly, "Be careful of boar, he no like strangers." We thanked her for the warning, and suitably humbled, we left.

Once outside reality kicked in once again and the vision of that mesmeric girl quickly vanished to be replaced by the sight of our four legged hairy psychotic adversary. It had trotted away back to its post, no doubt preparing itself for a further charge knowing that we would at some time have to exit the hut. I swear it was grinning menacingly up at us as we very slowly and carefully began to creep back down the steps. We kept up this snail's pace until we reached the edge of the clearing. With the comparative safety of the jungle in such close proximity, the actor out in front suddenly took off into the jungle at a rate of knots, which instigated a collective panic from us hastily following in his wake. Piggy followed suit. To anyone watching our ignominious retreat at full pelt along the narrow winding jungle path it must have seemed that we were being chased by a battalion of heavily armed trigger happy dervishers and not just one small animal with a bad attitude.

I am happy to report that it never did catch up with us, and by the time we were safely ensconced back in the hotel bar, its size had quadrupled. As to the girl's beauty there was no need to exaggerate. The problem was finding the words to describe her.

We were allowed Sundays off for a bit of R & R and were taken by launch or flown out by chopper to the various islands called quays… pronounced 'keys'. These are the stuff of the Bounty commercials. Some are no more than a few palm trees sprouting from golden sand dunes with reefs so close you could step onto them at low tide. On arrival we would open the beers, Bar-B-Q the food, and generally laze around. All very blissful for me whose previous experience of location filming was at that time limited to a disused police station in Hamilton on a cold wet day in February.

One Sunday we were taken by boat to an island I can only describe as a tropical paradise. It was the largest of all the islands we had visited up to then, and had its very own sandy street running its length. On either side of this street were pretty sun washed houses like pastel coloured beach huts on stilts with coconut matting roofs. A little jetty poked out into the turquoise Caribbean, which sparkled like crystal under the equatorial sun.

About half a mile off shore was a reef, where we were told some of the most magnificent coloured and varied species of sea creatures lived. We had little hesitation about donning masks, snorkels, goggles and flippers, as we prepared to swim out to see for ourselves these wondrous creatures. But being Scottish, and though usually tending to err on the side of impulsiveness, the canny facet to my character crept to the fore. As my companions began the swim, I tentatively asked one of the locals what the chances were of us meeting any sharks face to face en route to the reef, assuming that he would reassuringly answer me in the negative. Instead he explained with a cheeky twinkle in his dark eyes, that indeed there were sharks in these waters, some of which he took pleasure in assuring me were 'damn bloody huge man'. Seeing my fearfulness at the thought of meeting one of the 'damn bloody huge man' things, he thought to reassure me by adding that they tended not to come inshore of the reef before nightfall, when they would arrive in droves right up to the jetty, on which I was at that moment near pissing myself with fear. It was the phrase, 'tended not to come inshore' that did it for me. Tended wasn't good enough as far as I was concerned. Though the water out to the reef was no more than about ten feet at its deepest, I knew that it was more than enough for any man eating shark to have bags of room to manoeuvre in for the kill. Nevertheless I sallied forth after my troupe and got about two hundred yards before the reality of what I was doing sunk in. Thankfully the decision to carry on or bottle out was made for me. The strap on one of my flippers started playing up and kept loosening itself. It became apparent that this physically challenged flipper was going to make it difficult for me to catch up let alone keep up with the others. Also, and this was the major reason behind my reluctance to carry on, it would no doubt hinder me if I had to head for shore fast with a dark triangular fin cutting through the water behind me. I called out that I had a wee paddling problem and watched as my companions swam off towards the horizon without me. So I was left to amuse myself snorkelling on my own.

Because of the dodgy flipper I tended to swim in circles, which at first I found quite amusing but it did get tedious having to cover the same tiny wee bit of ocean time and time again. As I was inshore from the reef the sea bed was flat and sandy with very few fish to see apart from the occasional flounder similar to the ones I had seen many times in Scottish waters back home. I considered the idea of parting with the flippers altogether and heading out to the reef again, but immediately rejected the idea believing that I was much safer circling around where I was and carried on doing so for a further ten minutes or so. But as I gained in confidence I convinced myself that I was perfectly safe after all and that the flippers had to go and that I absolutely needed to venture on to pastures new. I treaded water until I managed to take them both off and tie one to each wrist. This I found to be much better as I could now travel in a straight line while the flippers dangled alongside me like dead fins. And so off I went, swimming a couple of feet below the surface watching the seabed change character, and coming up at intervals for lungfuls of air as I slowly but determinately headed out to the reef.

Though it was still sandy a few rocks began to appear, along with even more flounders as well as an assortment of different coloured fish that happily entered the fray, somewhat larger in size than the flounders though still small enough I judged not to be a threat. It was a feast for my eyes and I was chuffed to bits that I had taken the decision to join my mates, albeit that my progress was much slower than theirs had been. This was what nacting was all about. Swimming in the Caribbean and getting paid well for it. Who the hell needed dingy cold rehearsal rooms, drinking lukewarm weak coffee with iffy milk, whilst struggling to try and understand then remember seemingly indecipherable long winded texts? Certainly not me, and I couldn't have been happier. It was then that something untoward happened. I became aware that I was not the only large swimming being around.

Up to that time in my life I didn't think fish could convey or express any sort of emotion by the use of facial expression. However, once again I was to be proved wrong. As far as the fish was concerned, which appeared in front of me from out of nowhere, I must have looked like no other swimming thing it had ever encountered before, if the look of outright surprise on its elongated flat face was anything to go by. As far as I was concerned, the sight of it conveying any emotion at all was absolutely astonishing, and I was momentarily struck dumb, resulting in a total breakdown in communication between my brain and my limbs. I was rooted to the spot, which was somewhere between eight feet up from the sea bed and two down from the surface and I couldn't budge an inch. Nor could I breathe underwater. Not that it seemed to matter for I had forgotten how to breathe anyway.

The bugger was like a gigantic plaice at least six feet wide, with a long narrow slit of a mouth to match, measuring only a few inches shorter. Its body was absolutely flat. Its eyes seemed to begin to bulge as it stared me out. I had the sneaky suspicion that having recovered from its initial shock at seeing me, it was now expressing its indignation at my audacity for venturing into its personal space. Its wing-like fins undulated gracefully, hovering mid ocean a mere twenty feet or so away. Its expression seemed to change yet again, this time to what I can only describe as a sort of menacing joy, so I presumed that it was now deciding which part of me to eat first. The dingy rehearsal rooms didn't look so unappealing after all.

In terrifying situations when primal fear kicks in leaving you utterly helpless with the prospect that you are facing your last moments, I had always held the belief that if there was nothing you could do to reverse the inevitable predetermined consequences of your fate, then your mind and body would go into virtual collapse mode. You would probably crap yourself at that point, which is what I fully expected to do there and then.

I've heard it said that your life rushes past you and you remember all of it in a few last agonising moments, before the gnashing jaws close around you and the great sleep taps you on the shoulder and finally relieves you of the uncomfortable feeling inside the buttock area of your wet suit (which I wasn't wearing at the time).

How the hell does anyone know that your life rushes past you? If they're still here on this planet then they have no right to spout forth their theory, so it is literally a load of bollocks, and the following two reasons will verify my point:

a) I know for a fact that there is simply not the time to crap yourself.

b) Nothing of my past came at me, only the future, which at that moment didn't look like lasting long. Having said that… I am still here!

There are few options left open to a human being when faced with a seemingly unbeatable adversary, which could give any chance of a way out of the shit you find yourself in. In my case, though I knew I could have fought back, I also instinctively knew that against Big Face it would have been utterly useless to even attempt to try, as I only had two flippers to slap him on the face with and one of them was dodgy. Another option was to turn and run, or in my case swim, but I would have needed someone to set off a diversionary tactic like a nuclear explosion, to allow enough time for me to put at least 500 hundred yards between me and it, as a head start. Then again, I could have just rolled over and signalled capitulation (the Meerkat impersonation again) and that would have been end of story. All three options were thought about and discarded in a fraction of a millisecond. So I asked myself; if I couldn't beat it into submission, and I didn't have any plutonium handy for the diversionary tactic, and I certainly didn't want to give in and die, what was left for me to do? It came as a bloody huge surprise to both of us that I did something entirely different.

What did I do? I smiled at it! This was no mean feat as I had my snorkel in my mouth at the time. I then gave it the thumbs up and tried to laugh, again no mean feat when under water. To this day I still don't know why I did these things but suffice it to say I did. Next, my brain-to-body-signal-device kicked back in, and managed to tell my limbs to very slowly back-paddle. By waving my arms gently up and down as if I was auditioning for *Swan Lake*, I was hopefully simulating the creature's movements, which was part of my ill thought out master plan. I'm not entirely sure, but I probably did that in the hope it might see me as one of its own species, smile back at me, laugh heartily, then just sod off elsewhere. Instead Big Face simply looked confused. I suppose from its perspective, he or she could be thinking that they were being confronted by a portion of food which seemed to be signalling, if the smile on my face was anything to go by, that I was actually happy to be eaten.

The gap between us widened at an excruciatingly agonising slow pace for me. I began to believe that there might just be the slimmest of slimmest chances that I could possibly get away with it, if only I could keep my cool, not panic and glide away gracefully back to the shore where there would be plenty of opportunity to crap myself in my own time and not whilst under the threat of being devoured alive. But my body decided on a different course of action. Totally ignoring the messages being sent from my brain to play it cool, in an uncontrollable twisting motion my body with a mind of its own, suddenly threw itself around, surfaced, then headed off in the direction of the shore at a hell of a rate of knots, the flippers belting my face with every paddle my arms made, which I can assure you were very many. I hadn't a clue if Big Face was following me. I so very much wanted to shout out to my body to stay calm, but I needed every ounce of air I had left in my lungs and the bugger wouldn't have listened anyway. So I carried on thrashing through the water at one hell of a rate like a torpedo homing in on its target. In this case the target in question was the comparative safety of the jetty area. When I eventually got there, a journey which seemed to me to take five lifetimes, I was literally heaving with the exertion of my ordeal. Exhausted I hung on grimly to a dangling rope and chanced to look up at all the faces looking down at me in seeming wonderment and shouting wildly. Thinking that they had witnessed my magnificent escape and they thus were cheering me, I tried with great effort to wave up at them in appreciation. But I had misunderstood their exuberance, for I heard above the shouting, someone swear at me telling me to get out of the water if I didn't want to be killed. I looked around with mounting panic expecting to see Big Face rushing in for the kill. But there was no sign of it. Someone pointed at the water beside me and shouted excitedly, 'There it is! Get out now!' I thought the wag was trying to wind me up until I realised that the object of their interest was a dappled brown fish with a spiky body swimming around and between my legs. When it became clear to me what it actually was, I shot out of the water as if a wad of semtex wedged between my buttocks had just self ignited. Standing shakily on the jetty I looked down at the roundly shaped creature which was none other than a Stone Fish, one of the deadliest poisonous creatures to be found in these delightful warm waters of the Caribbean. I now knew I had plenty of time to crap myself… which I didn't you'll be pleased to know.

CHAPTER TWELVE

JOB HUNTING ROUTES TO AVOID

If some of the casting errors are to be observed as sheer misjudgements, then there is no rhyme, nor reason why any actor should take it personally and feel pissed off that they weren't the one chosen to play a particular part they felt they were tailor made for. It should result in not much more than a bruised ego. Also there isn't any predetermined destiny of a sure hit waiting for you at the stage door when you turn up for the first day of rehearsals, just because the piece has been written by a hitherto highly successful playwright, the director is known for his ability to turn out hits every time, and the cast is of the stellar variety.

Getting seen for a part can be a bit of a trial in itself. Of course the situation can be helped along if someone has pulled a few strings for you to allow you into the club called 'flavour of the month'. I like to think these scenarios are a rarity. After all, it's not lap dancing we're talking about here. There are other ways to get the attention of producers, directors and casting directors, but they usually depend largely on a bountiful amount of arse licking, which I have been an abject failure at doing throughout my career... thank goodness.

I'M CLEAR, WHAT'S IT LIKE UP YOUR END?

On one occasion, an actress of the middle ranking celebrity status I had previously worked with in the theatre, kindly suggested I write to a particular big noise producer saying that she would have a word in his ear and suggest me for a part in his television series. Not only did I not get it, I wasn't even asked in for an interview. It was much later that I found out the said producer couldn't abide the actress who had so kindly lent her name for my, hoped for, career advancement.

Another time when I hadn't been in London long, I was invited to an agent's party where I was told quite a few famous names from the world of television would be, including a few important movers and shakers. Around that time I was trying to stay, or should I say 'get' into shape, and a couple of times a week I practised the stupid exercise of running some six and a half miles on Wimbledon common. I say 'stupid' because not only was it the summer of '76, which had been the hottest on record for yonks and made the ground rock hard, but I couldn't afford proper running shoes with cushioned soles. Instead I wore the old type of tennis shoes with non-cushioned soles. Thus I aggravated a back problem I was having at the time - the same back problem which originated by carrying Wally Carr on my back when I was playing the cow's rear end in panto many, many years previously in a previous life, and which thankfully occurs no more.

On the night in question however, I had swallowed a couple of prescribed extra, extra mega strong pain killers to ease the discomfort brought on earlier in the day by my running routine, before meeting my brother-in-law for a pint prior to the ordeal of the party. I find these sort of theatrical get-togethers mind-bogglingly nerve-racking and need a bucketful of Dutch courage just to get me through the doorway. I am just so damned shy at gatherings of more than two people, unless they are in the audience and I am on stage hiding behind a character I have rehearsed for weeks. My brother-in-law was in a generous mood that night as he always is, and we downed quite a few pints in our shared local hostelry the Olive Branch in Marleybone, before I reluctantly bid him farewell and went off on my lonesome to the dreaded 'do'.

The truth is I hadn't watched much television as I had been consistently working nights in the theatre for years previously, so I was hard pressed to recognise any of the so-called famous stars of the small screen. As for the important movers and shakers, to this day I don't know if there were any, because I was never introduced to anybody who danced in that way. But what I did find was the makeshift free bar set up in the corner of the lounge. No-one made the slightest effort to speak to me as I wasn't moving or shaking and I hadn't been on the box enough to be recognised as anyone worth knowing. I was therefore left on my own to amuse myself, which I did with gusto courtesy of the free alcohol on offer. Not only are copious glasses of wine mixed with an earlier consumption of a barrel of beer an unhealthy concoction, add a couple of extra, extra mega strong painkillers and the result is an alcoholic liquid stupifier, followed by a memory blotter outer. I do, however, remember one immaculately dressed chap approaching me late on in the evening and kindly asking who I was and if I was all right. Though I was by this time quite wasted and had trouble focussing, I thought I still had enough wits about me to reply courteously and sensibly.

"I....? Who am I? I am not entirely sure. Anyway... who the f--k are you, pal?" Obviously my wits weren't in attendance.

Not surprisingly he didn't tell me who he was either, or if he did I can't remember, nor did I ever find out, but I'm bloody sure he majored in moving and shaking somewhere high up in the business.

To this day I studiously avoid using recommendations and try to avoid going to the 'right' parties, or any form of arse licking as it is called. I'm just bloody hopeless at it. However sometimes at these get-togethers if you are very, very lucky, you might just meet a sports personality, who might just supply you with a freebie ticket to a fitba' match. So it's always worth turning up just in case you do get lucky in the freebie ticket department, not to mention the food, booze and sex routine as previously mentioned.

When I first landed in London, it was because a big name London agent had been told of my work by an English television casting director who had seen my work in Scotland when she did her rounds of the Scottish theatre scene and spotted me at Dundee Rep. She flew up to see the show and afterwards offered to take me on her books there and then, on the proviso that I move south. That was a big decision for me. At the time I was moving from one acting job to the next without any gaps, and the standard of work in Scotland, my home country, was extremely high. But I thought that maybe here was a chance to break into working on the screen, because

London was where it was at as regards film and television, which at that time was not very prevalent in Scotland, and what there was of it was less than impressive. So I decided to give it a go.

Up to then, apart from the north of England, I had lived and worked in many of Scotland's towns and cities. So I was certainly used to living out of a suitcase, quickly adapting to new surroundings, finding it easy to make new friends and generally fit in for the duration of the jobs I had been contracted to do. But London was different. It was huge and unfriendly. In a Glasgow pub you are practically expected to start up a conversation with the stranger standing next to you. In London I found it to be the exact opposite. People were wary of your possible motives. To me, the place was to a great extent a gigantic over populated mass with no heart; an unfriendly character with no soul. I felt I just couldn't hack it.

Soon after arriving I was shunted from one casting director to another, from one producer to another, basically doing the rounds. Why I did this I wasn't sure because I remember that none of them were actually casting at the time. It was, I was told later, just to get my name and face around the scene. They were nevertheless apparently delighted to meet me and I was treated very courteously by them all. I remember trying extremely hard throughout one of the earlier interviews with a television casting director to speak in RP i.e. Received Pronunciation, which we had been told as students in Scotland we would have to master if we were going to work south of the border. Basically it is a non-dialect, non-accent type of sound, as close as you can get to the Royal delivery of English, without the mouth full of marbles routine. When the interview drew to its inevitable close, the casting director said that he was very impressed with how much I had achieved in the five or so years I had been in the business. He was sure we would work together someday soon, but was truly sorry he couldn't offer me any work at that moment. This was the usual way these meetings went so I wasn't at all surprised. We shook hands and I was in good spirits until I reached the door when he called out to me.

"Oh… by the way Tom?"

"Yes?" Maybe he had suddenly thought of a part for me?

"Is it possible for you to lose the Scottish accent at all?"

Bollocks! I thought I had. Somehow I had to change my strategy. From then on the trick I found is to go into an interview being yourself. You must sell you as yourself. If you are asked if you can do a particular accent or other and if you believe you can, pick up the nearest newspaper or magazine, or if there is one, a script, and give them what they want by reading cold. That approach never fails to impress. The only drawback is if you are dyslexic, in which case just improvise a conversation in the accent requested and as close to the way you think the character might speak.

If however, whether dyslexic or not, you are uncomfortable working in a particular accent, then you have to admit it. There's nothing worse than saying you can do something when on the day that the cameras roll, it is patently obvious you can't. The movers and shakers in the business admire gutsy people who are willing to have a go, even if they do admit to needing a few lessons in a particular expertise e.g. juggling, fire eating, bareback riding, belly dancing, accent training or whatever it is that is required. What is not appreciated is being conned. That route inevitably costs money because a bit of swift recasting may well be required and the reputations of those who cast the dodgy actor are up for grabs.

Here's an example I witnessed:

In 1980 I had a rather splendid part in a television comedy series called *Flickers* about British cinema's early years. But before I carry on with this story I am going to go off-piste a tad as I transgress in order to tell you a story about the stars of the series, Bob Hoskins and Frances de La Tour.

One day during our lunchtime break from rehearsing, word got to Bob and Frances that the rest of the cast weren't being paid until each episode was done and dusted and in the can. In other words as the series was being filmed in a multi episodic way, it could take many weeks before each episode was completed. This was tough for jobbing actors because many may not have worked for some time prior, and would be relying on the money in order to pay rents etc., etc., etc. When we returned to work after lunch, Bob and Frances announced to the director Cyril Coke that they wouldn't film in the studio that week until they had reassurance that the cast would be paid on a weekly basis. Cyril agreed with them and immediately in front of the cast, phoned through from the rehearsal room to the production office that not only would Bob and Frances not film that week, but neither would he until the actors were all paid up to date for the work they had already done. Within two hours our agents had our cheques on their desks delivered by couriers. Bob and Frances didn't need to put their heads on the block for us, indeed neither did our director Cyril, but they did. Thanks guys.

Back to the story. Granville Saxton (one of the other cast members) and I were having a cuppa during a break in filming. It was a hot summer's day as we stood in the middle of a field, enjoying the view of the beautiful Hertfordshire countryside which stretched as far as our eyes could see. We were exchanging the usual 'Did you hear the one about…!' stories, and idly watched a rehearsal for the next scene.

It should have been reasonably straight forward. A horse canters into shot over the crest of a hill. The rider gently reins in the horse and looks around. Then horse and rider canter on downhill, past the camera and out of shot. Apparently, in order to get the part, the actor on the horse had sworn blind in the interview that he could ride. This proved to be a disastrous lie.

When the director called 'Action' what we should have heard was the pleasant rhythmical sound of a cantering horse and the encouraging sounds of a rider in total control of his steed as they came into view atop the hill. Instead what we heard was the sound of galloping, thundering hoofs and the actor's squeals of abject fear. When horse and rider did appear we were more than a little concerned, for the rider was hanging on for dear life with his arms wrapped around the horse's neck as it clattered into view going along at a fair lick. With nostrils flaring, ears pegged back and the white of fearful eyes in full view, the actor looked absolutely terrified - and the horse looked much the same! Granville and I deduced that the horse didn't like the idea of its rider trying to strangle it.

Our now mirthful concern turned to uproarious laughter as we watched the horse make a bee line directly towards a group of extras (walk-on artistes) who happened to be standing around having an innocent natter further down the hill.

Admittedly the extras should not have panicked and bolted in all directions at the sight of the charging animal, because as everyone knows, a horse will always avoid stationery objects if it can. It isn't so good at avoiding moving objects, especially if the said objects run hither and thither like a bunch of old drama queens who have just come into season. But it's only fair to say in the extras' defence that an out of control, stampeding, fully grown stallion racing towards you at full throttle with a look conveying confusion as to which scurrying obstacle it should trample to death first, can be a bloody terrifying thing to stand your ground against.

Having said that, time is money when filming. The time it took to recover the frightened animal, placate the astonished petrified angry extras, give a sound bollocking to the shaken actor, and re-shoot the scene probably cost thousands. Producers don't like that.

One sunny evening I wended my way down London's Kingsway approaching The Aldwych, minding my own business having sunk a glass or two in a nearby wine bar. My thoughts were honed in on how to change my status as an unknown actor into a rather well known successful one. At that time I hadn't even had a sniff of work since arriving in London. I had left Scotland where I had never had a day's unemployment in five years, to doing sod all in bugger-all-land as I called London back then. It was the first low point in my acting career and it hurt deep. I consoled myself in the knowledge that I wasn't alone, as by that time I had met more than a few English actors who were in the same boat, and they were in their own home town.

Though the traffic was light at that time of night it was also bloody swift and I made several false starts at crossing the four lanes at the Aldwych before I heard a snarling voice shouting obscenities from about ten yards away from where I was trying in vain to cross the road. Standing beside this piece of noisy low life was his girlfriend, whom I can only describe here as a coarse-looking, tarty bird. For reasons I couldn't fathom at the time she was egging him on with her own brand of delightful phrases, which did no favours to her fairer sex.

I surmised from the occasional words of understandable English dispersed at random amongst their growing volume of expletives that they had mistakenly thought I had been trying to hail the taxi, which had paused briefly by me before quickly driving off again at a rate of knots, after I told the driver I was simply trying to get across the road. He in his turn called me a Scotch tosser. Oh how I just loved London so much more when he said these endearing words you can only imagine!

As the two Neanderthals had been waiting for a taxi they thought I had jumped the non-existent queue. What they didn't know was that I had

I'M CLEAR, WHAT'S IT LIKE UP YOUR END?

barely enough money for a train home let alone a taxi. And so it came to pass that they started towards me threatening with all sorts of horrible physical nasty things, which apparently they were about to do to my person. My immediate reaction was to leg it out of there a s a p, but I was never a fast runner and knew that the bloke, who had an athletic build to say the least, would catch me easily. I thought about fighting him, but knew that to do so would have been ridiculous, as I would have been absolutely mollocated. Anyway, how could I turn up at my next interview, if I had survived the onslaught that was about to befall me, with a face coloured with black and blue bruises and somewhat fewer teeth? Mind you, there weren't any auditions for me to go to.

And so they arrived, he inches from my face, she beside him pulling his jacket off and egging him on to doing me in etc., etc., etc.

When I opened my mouth to speak something quite astonishing happened. My fear had somehow evaporated the saliva and constricted my vocal chords. Consequently my voice not only lowered a couple of octaves, but took on a quality not unlike rough gravel being crushed into an empty beer can. For the first time in my life I sounded bloody hard. Instead of apologising profusely and begging forgiveness for their misunderstanding, I decided on a different course of action.

Cashing in on my new found hard man voice, I heard myself quietly growl some expletives in the strongest, thickest-sounding accent of my home town that I could muster. It quickly dawned on them which part of the world I came from. They hadn't a clue as to what I was actually saying, nor for that matter did I, but it didn't seem to matter. My performance had the desired effect. She started to haul him away. He put out his hand and offered to shake mine, apologising saying that he hadn't realised I was from Glasgow.

"And wat the f--'s wrong wi' Glasgow, pal?"

"Nuffink... sorry mate... Oi really em." That's what he sounded like to me anyway.

Though my legs felt like jelly I brazened on with my act and less than politely ordered them to leave the immediate vicinity, decorating my prose with a few further made up unintelligible Glaswegian sounding expletives that didn't really exist. I then attempted a swagger and headed slowly off, like Big John from my shipyard days. Once out of sight genuine panic set in, and I ran all the way to Waterloo. The following morning I joined a karate club. That was one of the better decisions I have made in my life. The episode was also one of my best performances to date. If only I had been filmed and been paid for it !

Weeks went by and money was running out fast, so being a pragmatic Scot I found a job to keep me going. This was a new experience for me as I had never had to work outside the business back home in God's sweet country. But needs must and I found myself driving a big laundry delivery van around the metropolis. The fact that I hadn't a clue where I was going didn't matter because I had purchased this wonderful little map book called an *A to Z*. Sat navs weren't in existence then. But even equipped with such a wonderful wee book of maps, I still frequently got lost, and quite often didn't have enough time to complete my deliveries.

The person in the Brixton laundry who sent me out on my travels each day in the summer of 1976 was a delightful lady called Ruby Boyce. She was like a mother hen to all the drivers. Twenty two years later I received a letter wishing me well playing Captain Hook in Peter Pan. It was from Ruby. She had seen my name advertised on her local theatre's posters. Sadly she wasn't well enough to come to the show. She was such a lovely special person, so kind and so very, very good to me.

It was nearing Christmas and there was a backlog of clean laundry to be delivered, so I was hard at it from morning till night, occasionally phoning the agent to see if anything had turned up for me, but there never was. No such thing as a mobile phone in 1976. The experience of sod all happening after years of such a good run of work back home hit hard. But I was determined not to give in. It was a tough and could have been a soul destroying time for me. I had to learn the hard lesson in life; basically how to survive it, instead of simply enjoying it.

The day before Christmas Eve, though I didn't know it at the time, would be my last ever as a laundry delivery man, as I was off to Scotland for Christmas and would end up being offered a season back at The Royal Lyceum in Edinburgh with the same Artistic Director who had taken me on at Dundee, Stephen MacDonald. But on that wild wet wintry late afternoon, I was parked up in the van somewhere in Chelsea. The rain was pouring down and there was no one home at the house I had just called at. As I started up the van's engine a rather well to do looking middle aged woman battered the van door with her brolly. When I opened it I was nearly asphyxiated by the stench of her presumably expensive perfume.

"You there… are you the dirty laundry man?"

"No missus, I'm the clean one. I expect the dirty one got sacked for using too much cologne… not unlike that one you -!"

Luckily she interrupted me. "Don't be facetious, young man. I can see that box there has my name on it. Why haven't you delivered it?"

"Call me old fashioned missus but as you weren't home I thought it prudent to take it back to the depot for safe keeping."

"Be that as it may, I'm here now so you can deliver it… now."

I hadn't intended bursting her bubble but she had left me no alternative. "Look here ya snotty wee cow, I am not a laundry delivery man… I happen to be a nacta and a very fine one at that…"

It was her turn to interrupt me. "Then why are you doing this job I wonder?"

She did have a point there, but I didn't want to throw in the towel just yet. "Because… things… ain't going… according… to plan at the moment. D'ye get my meaning ya daft…!" I gave up at that point.

The rest I left to her imagination. I know that my reaction was really quite churlish, and I regret it a wee bit to this day, but I hope you will understand that I was mightily pissed off. And so having made my point I lifted the box onto my lap in preparation of thrusting it into her arms. But I wasn't expecting the next bit.

"Well young man… I am a casting director… let's look forward to the next time we meet at a casting session shall we?!" she exclaimed.

I knew she was for real because she had used the words 'casting session'. Only people in the business would have said it that way. She then grabbed the laundry box and strode away like Mussolini with piles. We never did meet again thank goodness, which was just as well because I don't think I would have got any part she was casting.

CHAPTER THIRTEEN

VIVE LA FRENCH? I DON'T THINK SO

I have always been of the notion that one cannot plan a career in the acting business, one can only guide it. Therefore it came as no surprise that simply because of a chance meeting with a stills-cameraman called Ian Williams on a film shoot I was doing in London, I would end up in a candid camera type film shoot in the South of France... and I certainly hadn't planned that.

The cameraman in question had other irons in his fire, namely a small film production company of his own. He also had a big American 4X4 truck-like station wagon which he was driving back to his home in Brighton after we finished filming, the town in which I happened to live also. And so we shared our home-bound journey together in his gas guzzling eye catching mobile house on wheels. We got on great and agreed that we should meet up for a pint in the not too distant future.

A few weeks later when he called me I thought it was to arrange that pint or two we had talked about having. Instead he offered me a job, which included a dip into writing, something I already had a bit of a penchant for. But it all came in the form of a challenge... nothing has ever been straightforward in my sluggish race to international stardom. He asked me to come up with a madcap hysterically funny scenario for a video, which I would perform in and he would secretly film. He would then present this video to one of the world's leading motor manufacturers, who had commissioned his film company to aid in the launch of their latest car. In other words, he was to be the producer, director, camera and sound man, and I was to be the nacta and ideas man.

Comedy for the screen is not necessarily a funny business to write. A clown dropping his kegs is funny in a slapstick way, but Othello's tights heading south mid speech would be hysterically funny because it wasn't supposed to happen. To put it bluntly we humans are pretty basic when it comes to laughter. Basically we laugh heartily at others misfortunes. So I concluded that I would have to put together a scenario which showed someone having some sort of mishap, which would in turn make those watching howl with laughter, thus helping the car giant in question to add many more millions of pounds to their coffers. How that was all going to join up I do not know. Gawd… where was I supposed to begin?

To explain:

In the early 1980s, a car manufacturer launched their latest set of wheels, a magnificent, state-of-the-art, luxurious vehicle retailing upwards from goodness knows how many tens of thousands of pounds. They wanted to do something out of the ordinary for the enjoyment of the motoring journalists who would be writing their critiques of the car in their glossy, well-read motoring magazines. It was an extremely costly exercise to herald their latest creation, a triumphant show-case of mechanical machinery on which many millions of pounds had already been spent in developing it. For the event they had hired a wonderful hotel situated deep in the heart of France's southern region to where the journalists would be flown, thence wined and dined and entertained. For 'something out of the ordinary' in the entertainment department they hired Ian William's film company, who in turned hired me. Between us we were expected to create a sensational evening for all on which the success of the car's launch ultimately depended.

And so it came to pass that fourteen journalists were flown daily to the south of France by private jet. On arrival at the airport, which was set in backwoods many miles from any civilisation, seven of these aforementioned brand new cars were lined up beside the runway waiting for them. In pairs, these journos drove off on a predetermined route which took them on a grand tour via the Alps. They arrived sometime later at the hotel, which boasted swimming pool, terrace bar, a cordon bleu menu to salivate over as you read it, a superb wine list etc. etc. etc. and all of this situated atop a hill heralding the most spectacular view of the valley below.

An evening of merriment was had by all, culminating in the viewing of the aforementioned video. The following morning the happy band of now rather fatter journos with rather heavy duty hangovers would retrace their route in the same cars back to the airport. The jet would disgorge the next batch of fourteen eager beavers before flying the previous lot back home to England. It was to be hoped that the departing lot when they got back to their offices, would write glowing reports on the new car and reminisce on the hysterical video for many years to come.

Well... that was the plan.

To be absolutely frank, based on Ian's first reaction to the ideas I presented, the prognosis for the video's success was not good. I have read that the best movies started out as ideas scribbled on napkins during exotic lunches, watered down with copious amounts of out of this world priced wines, by a couple of movie makers, whilst enjoying the delights of overlooking a beach laden with exotic semi-nude ladies sunning themselves on sun kissed beaches against a backdrop of multimillion dollar yachts sailing by. For Ian and I it was a somewhat different scenario. Instead, over a few pints drunk on the patio of my then wee two bedroom terraced house, this is what I came up with, as the high alcoholic content from my home brewed beer concoction kicked in.

"How's about... if... as the journalists arrive at the hotel... they are welcomed by the Maître d'... while his assistant... let's call him... Henri... will park the cars... and the waitress... let's call her Fifi... can offer them wine and cheese... you can be ensconced in a room overlooking the car park working the hidden video camera and film the journalists reactions. What do you think Ian?" When I realised that Ian wasn't exactly rolling in the aisles with mirth, I went on. "Of course the journalists will be shocked to see Henri throwing these brand new very expensive cars around on the gravel as I try to park 'em."

"You? You will be Henri?"

"Yes. A couple of handbrake turns, a few stalls followed by a dodgy looking emergency stop should do it."

"Can you drive like that?"

"Trust me... I've been driving like that for years."

"And that's funny? Thirty plus thousand pounds worth of new car being tossed around?"

"Absolutely hysterical. Remember that these journalists are responsible for the safe return of the vehicles. If they think there is the least chance I'll crunch one they'll be having kittens. Your job is to focus in on their faces and record their reactions."

"Can you speak French?"

"Luckily I won't have to. I'll just take their keys, park the cars badly then sod off."

"Uh huh... So what's with offering them cheese and wine? Not exactly rib-tickling, is it?"

"It will be after we've doctored the vino with a modicum of vinegar etc., and given the cheese a couple of extra flavours. Hee hee hee! Oh, and by the way, my wife Cookie will be Fifi the sexy French waitress dressed in an outfit accordingly."

"Can she speak French?"

"Probably, but to be honest I'm not entirely sure. I know she can read Russian pretty well. Anyway she just needs to look sexy, smile shyly and say extremely little. Believe me, saying extremely little will be the hardest bit for her."

"Ok... what about the Maître d'? What's the gag there and who's it going to be?"

This was the most important bit of casting of them all and it was fraught with potential hazards, so I knew I had to get it right. Also, there were very few actors out there I knew personally who would even consider an unscripted role which was dependant on totally believable improvisation. On top of all that, it was absolutely imperative for the character to look like a born and bred Frenchman, as the actor playing him would be the one welcoming the journalists face to face in the manner of an authentic Maître d'. Combining aloofness, authority and kindness in an improvised scenario in a foreign language and in a foreign country, was indeed a tall order for any actor to undertake, so it would be a hell of a job for me to find one who could play the part fantastically well and totally convincingly.

"I've got the very bloke. His name is Granville Saxton. We did a series on telly together. Great sense of humour. He and I were filming on location once when we saw a horse near trample to death ten extras. We pissed ourselves laughing watching it."

"Seems like an ok guy."

"Yep he certainly is. An immense talent. Tall… about six foot three, dark haired… can look like anything from Count Dracula, General De Gaulle, Captain Hook etc. if you ask him nicely. As for improvisation? He can do it standing on his head. Absolutely perfect for the role. In fact I'd go as far as to say he's the only one I know who could pull it off. Let's just hope the bugger's available."

"Ok… you've convinced me… if he is available he's hired. Let's get started."

Tracking Granville down and finding out if he was available was the easy part. Talking him into saying 'yes' would require a great deal of tact, for Granville is no fool. It would I thought require a good meal, and a bottle or two of damned good wine to soften him up as well as a fool proof sales pitch. I knew I had to make it all sound irresistible. I was helped a little by the wonderful travel brochures I produced of the French province we would be working in.

Granville is a lover of the finer things in life and the prospect of experiencing fabulous French cuisine, wonderful wine of the region, countryside bathed in delicate colours, and with the possibility of visiting a few local art galleries thrown in for good measure, was I hoped to prove too much of a temptation for him to turn down.

"And all for a few hours of work a day in a place that is closer to the Equator than Surrey," I pointed out to him. Amazingly I talked him into doing it. Even more amazingly, because of concentrating all my efforts to get him to sign on the dotted line, I forgot to ask him if he could speak French. As it turned out he couldn't!

What I omitted to tell him, simply because at the time I was myself unaware, was that the cast and crew would not be staying in the exquisite hotel with the journalists. Of course not... *Sacre Bleu*! We couldn't possibly take the risk of being spotted between the filming in the afternoon and the viewing in the evening when our true selves would be revealed. I admit I was a little apprehensive about the sort of hostelry we cast and crew would end up in but kept this concern to myself. Indeed my fears were realised when we found ourselves billeted miles away in a one horse village somewhere deep in the French countryside. Cast and crew consisted of my wife Cookie as Fifi the maid, Granville as the Maître d', me as writer and daft Henri, Ian as producer/cameraman/ sound man, and a liaison lady from the car company who had been hired to watch over us throughout the week's filming. Thankfully she could speak perfect French. She was terrific and helped us whenever we needed an extra pair of hands. Basically we all chipped in as and when needed.

Our hotel turned out to be a run-down dilapidated affair without a bar. Not unlike a French version of Faulty Towers without Basil, Sybil, Manuel and the rest, and whose owner was more than upset that we hadn't arrived on time. Eventually and very reluctantly he opened up for us after much cajoling and I suspect the crossing of palm with the rustle of Francs from Ian. We were made only tepidly welcome and the owner stated in no uncertain terms that his hotel would be locked by eleven o'clock every night. This wasn't a tremendous problem to us as we would all probably be thoroughly knackered by that time anyway, having been up early every morning, ferrying film gear, costumes etc., filming the scam, presenting it to the journalists in the evenings, before heading off into the night hunting for friendly restaurants that might still be open.

Unbeknownst to us, the hotel owner had failed to inform a group of ten cycling guests about the imposed curfew. They had previously booked an overnight stay but turned up at midnight without telling him in advance that they, like us, would be late arriving. Having already been paid in advance the owner had locked up and buggered off to bed, not caring a whit where his other ten guests had got to.

Failing to get in the normal way i.e. through the front door, the cyclists found a ground floor room window slightly ajar at the rear of the hotel, with a dim light shining from within. It happened to be Granville's room. He had a small light on by his bed side table as he sat reading, wearing a dark red and black velvet dressing gown, very Noel Coward like and smoking a cigarette. I said earlier that Granville could present himself as General De Gaulle, Captain Hook or even Count Dracula to great acclaim. By this I mean that these were just three of the countless characters he could play, or at the very least, lookalike without too much trouble. In other words he is an accomplished character actor of fine repute who, like a chameleon, can adapt his personage to suit whatever role he has been hired to play, providing he is paid so to do.

On the evening in question when the late arriving cyclists were locked out, they climbed with their bikes through the window and into Granville's bedroom, where they saw to their horror, someone sitting in bed apparently in the personage of Count Dracula, the dim light spillage from the bedside lamp serving to accentuate his sharp dark features. Consequently we were awakened in our upstairs bedrooms by screams of terror.

What we heard didn't come from Granville on seeing the army of scantily clad health freaks, looking like huge insects of the Praying Mantis variety invading his privacy. But from the cyclists themselves, who thought the last vestiges of their energy would be sucked dry from their bodies by the smoking grinning Count in the bed. One of the cyclists had a strong Australian accent and when he shrieked, "Fuck me look at the Count on the bed!" it sounded like, "Fuck me look at the cunt in the bed!" Granville told them in no uncertain terms that he wasn't enamoured of being called that by total strangers who had arrived in his boudoir uninvited. Apparently he then bared his teeth at them. Many apologies ensued from them for their misunderstanding and they hurried out of his room into the hotel proper, dragging their bikes along behind them.

On our first filming day in France Ian had set up another scenario for us to try out for the journalists' arrival. The petite, private-type airport was stuck in the back of beyond with not a soul in sight except for two inquisitive local coppers who arrived to snoop around at what we were up to. We were ill prepared for what was about to happen.

Cookie and I were dressed as Douane i.e. French customs officers, and we were to find some dodgy magazines and naughty female underwear previously planted in one of the journalist's luggage back in the UK. Ho ho ho? I don't think so! Thankfully this was not my idea but as we were under contract we had to give it a go. In the customs area we had erected a workman's tent, like the red and white striped ones used by telephone engineers to have their cups of tea in when they are supposed to be fixing telephone lines. The difference was that our tent was black. Inside it Ian had the camera set up to ready to film, with the lens peeking through a small tear in the cloth. Granville, crouched beside him, was working the sound.

I complained that I didn't think a stick-on Terry Thomas-like moustache and customs hat was enough to disguise me from being seen as Henri later at the hotel, but as there was no one else available, I had to do it. When it was explained to the coppers what we were up to, they thought it all highly amusing and suggested that they too could get in on the act by arresting the poor unsuspecting journalist when we found the planted goodies in his bags. But happily our liaison lady who spoke excellent French managed to dissuade them from their acting debuts.

All went roughly according to plan until the plane touched down, then all hell broke loose. Unbeknownst to us, this little scenario we were about to play out hadn't been presented to the bureaucratically burdened French authorities and therefore hadn't received the go-ahead from them. Subsequently, just as the plane's wheels screeched along the runway, a big official looking black car screeched to a halt outside. Three burly plain clothes heavies got out along with a small Gestapo-like creature who was a dead ringer for Goebbels but without the club foot. They entered the arrivals lounge, which was not much larger than the airport Nissan hut in Orkney, and made straight for us. I didn't have a bloody clue as to what the one that resembled Goebbels was saying as he babbled away in a heavy guttural accent at my wife Cookie. When he began wagging his finger at her name tag which displayed the name Douane on it (French for customs) I had had enough. I stepped between them and started with the diplomatic Glasgow way of getting your wife out of a tight spot routine. Looking down at him I spat out roughly the following.

"What's up wi' you pal? She's only kidding on to be a customs official," I informed him in the Glasgow shipyard style. Suddenly I was aware that the previously friendly local coppers had changed sides and had begun to unfasten their leather holster covers, displaying fully loaded handguns. It was then that I recalled that France had given in some forty years earlier to their neighbours... the German lot. Just my luck, I thought, to have a run-in with pals of the Vichy French, those lovely creeps that became pals with Adolf. If only I could have had a pill like that little shit Himmler swallowed before he could be dealt with at Nuremburg, because I would have stuffed it down the throat of the bad tempered and ill-mannered creep who I was now facing.

At this point and without warning, Ian and Granville sprang from the tent to offer their assistance and nearly gave us all, including the French, a communal heart attack. To avoid being seen by the journalists earlier, they were camouflaged from head to toe in long cloaks made from the same black material as the tent, looking like two rather odd Islamic ladies one tall and rather slim, t'other short and rather stout. So when they spoke in their deep male voices, they confused the French even more. In the French eyes they were terrorists, especially when they saw Granville hold in his hand what looked like a homemade bomb. It was of course the microphone he had been working which he had gaffa-taped onto a battery pack. In typical French courageous style the Douane official and his mates as well as the two coppers all dived for cover.

Heaven sent, the liaison lady stepped into the fray and proceeded to calm the whole stramash down. The result was that we had to scrap the idea of the customs scenario thank goodness, pack up and move out quickly before the journalists appeared. We then had to hot foot it the twenty odd miles in our hired people carrier which lacked air conditioning, back to the hotel. Once there, we then proceeded to set up the camera hidden behind curtains in an upstairs bedroom window overlooking the hotel car park. Then we wired ourselves up to the sound equipment, doctored the wine and cheese, change into our other outfits, and re-appear as Maître d', Henri and Fifi for the arriving journalists. Against all the odds we did it.

And so it began. One day followed another surprisingly without mishap. The car manufacturer bods were delighted with the video capers and the journalists all took it in good spirits as they watched themselves in the evenings on screen, quaffing vinegar flavoured wine and devour the hotel speciality… chocolate covered battered goats cheese. Cookie was stunning as Fifi the maid and I looked the part of the idiot assistant with my hair shorn. The previous week I had been filming in a movie circa late 1930s and had my hair cut in the style of the period. The result was that I looked very close to being one of the Three Stooges… the really stupid one. The worrying thing was that I found it incredibly easy to fall into the role.

Granville was outstanding as the hotel's Maître d'. His lack of knowledge of the French language was more than compensated for by his heavily guttural accented delivery and dominating presence, dressed as he was in an outfit consisting of the ubiquitous striped trousers and tails etc. A warm welcoming French type smile could be quickly replaced with a cold heartless French type stare of the kind I thought belonged only to Charles De Gaulle and his cronies, until Granville's Maître d' came on the scene.

Usually the cars arrived at roughly ten minute intervals over an hour long period. By the fourth day we had got used to the routine of Granville welcoming the visitors in the hotel's gravel forecourt, then apologising profusely for his assistant Henri's 'Horeefeec bid dreeving'. We would then watch aghast as one after another motoring journalist would genuinely compliment Fifi on the rancid tasting wine and doctored goat's cheese she served them with. However, on the penultimate day we nearly blew it.

Partly due to a bloody funny and thankfully un politically correct and very rude joke Granville and I shared, which started us off in a giggly mood, and partly due also to my portrayal of Henri, who quite suddenly and without any prior planning by me, decided to lose the powers of speech and hearing, the car launch teetered on the brink of disaster. It didn't help either when Henri, for no apparent reason, had become obsessed with a penchant for journalists' ties.

The day had started well. The late morning sun bathed the forecourt in a rich warm welcoming amber coloured hue. We had arrived at the appointed time, set up our stall of wines and cheeses, changed into our appropriate gear, then welcomed the first couple of cars as they arrived over the following twenty minutes, whilst Ian filmed the whole saga. When the journalists had sampled the wine and cheese they tottered off contentedly into the hotel. Granville and I started telling each other jokes to pass the time as we hung about the hotel's driveway waiting for the call that the third car was on its way. Granville came out with a cracker about two dogs and a Red Indian chief which had us both in fits of giggles, when Ian's voice suddenly crackled into our hidden ear pieces.

"Car coming," he warned, watching it approach from the bottom of the mile long drive up a dodgy dusty track to the hotel. He then went on to warn us that the woman journo in the passenger seat had spent the last year studying French at night school and wanted to try it out as soon as she arrived.

Granville commented, "Isn't it bloody typical... there's always one who wants to bugger it up for everyone else, isn't there!" At that very moment one of the journalists re appeared from the hotel, sidled up to Granville and gave him a nudge and asked surreptitiously with a mouth still masticating chocolate-flavoured goats' cheese, if Granville could snaffle a case of the wine he had just been given by Fifi to sample, and slip it into the boot of car number two for him to smuggle back to Blighty. On top of this request, a little taster of francs was stuffed into Granville's hand.

Granville reacted superbly in character and gave the bloke such a condescending look that the poor bugger immediately changed the subject, grabbed the dosh back and proffered pictures of his family, before making off in a humble fashion, quite rightly chastised for his impertinence. Granville whispered to me that if we had a mind to do it, we could make quite a killing on the side by selling the doctored wine at a cut price to all the journalists, who we deduced didn't know the difference between a bottle Chateux Rothschild and a bucket of Giraffe's piss. But we were professional actors, and as such, loyal employees to our pay masters to whom we were contracted, and therefore desisted from such a playful ploy.

Next up another journalist appeared from the hotel. Having already downed more than a modicum of our wine, he had witnessed his friend's unseemly behaviour and turned up to apologise on his behalf. Granville graciously accepted his sentiments and the man was satisfied that his journalist professional honour had been reinstated. At which point I intervened. To this day I don't know why I did... but I did. Homing my attention in on the bloke's tie, I said in very poor pidgin English, "I veeeery mich leek yoor tee."

"My tee?"

"Henri means your tie monsieur." Granville smiled ingratiatingly at him before throwing me one of his, 'I'm going to kill you later you bastard' looks. He then explained to the concerned journalist that I was registered on the grey-matter challenged list and as such should be ignored. Unfortunately for Granville, this well-meaning bloke was the sort who wanted to help anyone he perceived as less fortunate than himself. On top of which he was already slightly pissed. And so he courteously took off his tie and graciously presented me with it. We were speechless. He waddled off, no doubt feeling a sense of pride that he had helped a less fortunate mortal. We noted that his chin was decorated with a small dollop of brown coloured chocolate. Granville and I now awaited with mounting apprehension the arrival of our next hurdle, the French speaking English journalist. Then a third bloody journalist appeared from the hotel.

"Excoosi missuar, but can I ask what part of the goat the cheese comes from?" asked the driver of the first car, who with glass of wine in hand had managed in the time since his arrival to change into a pair of pink-coloured shorts which closely matched the colour of his legs. I expected Granville to give the obvious answer that goats' cheese came from goats' milk of course. But oh no! Not him! Granville was so astounded by the ridiculous question that he couldn't resist from going into an improvised routine.

"Thee goats' cheeseseesees? Eet cims from the throte of thee goat... they squeeze oot thee leequeed for thee cheeeeseesees thet way... *comprenez vous, monsieur*?" He finished by raising his hands in a typical French gesture and curling his lips to give that Latin air of *Je ne sais quoi*. Why he did that I don't know, because he had just explained that he did know!

"Thanks mate, I've always wanted to know that."

"Ees that so?" Granville was well into his stride by now. "Hiv you seen any wild boar yit?"

"Wild boar? You get 'em 'ere?"

"Sure we git 'em 'ere. There ees one now. Queek look over theeer." He pointed over the bloke's shoulder, and when he turned to look for the wild boar, Granville looked at me and winked.

"You are too sloo. Yoo meesed eet!" he exclaimed dramatically.

"I wasn't looking for eet," I replied.

"I wasn't speaking to yoo," Granville snarled at me.

I was praying that he would leave it at that, but he went on.

"Have you heerd of thee dince of thee moths?"

"The dince of the wots?" asked the bloke.

"Thee moths. Eet ees a verrry faimoos ritual heeer. Eet ees called thee 'neet of thee moth dince'. Eef you look at thee stars later, thee moths, they weel dince fir yoo."

Granville glanced at me again. By now I had tears streaming down my face and my shoulders were heaving. He looked over at Cookie who had overheard the story of the moth dancers. She in turn swiftly left the immediate vicinity and concentrated her attention on the beauty of a nearby flower bed. The journalist was oblivious to all this and remained entranced by the idea of an evening of watching moths dancing. How he was taken in by all this nonsense I'll never know, but I can honestly assure you he was. Through our ear pieces we could hear Ian wheeze with laughter. I think that is what really did it for Granville. It suddenly all became too much for him and he bellowed out loud, pretended it was a sneeze then walked majestically away from the now bewildered journalist. I heard Granville muffle into his hidden microphone as he stifled another mirthful outburst, "I've gone… I can't go on any more… get me out of here."

With tears now streaming from his eyes as well, he couldn't see where he was going and wandered into one of the parked cars, his shin bearing the brunt of the collision.

"Oh my f--g leg," he moaned in perfect sounding English! "That wasn't very polite," mumbled the bloke.

"Nor was it very French," I whispered to Granville.

"Car coming," Ian warned.

The confused journalist sauntered back into the hotel, Cookie walked briskly to her station by the table of wine and cheese, Granville wiped his eyes and rubbed his leg, and I took a deep breath wondering if I could make it through to the finish that day without being carted off in a strait jacket whilst laughing in an uncontrollable and hysterical manic way.

The car drew up and Granville bent down to the open passenger window.

"*Bonjour, madame et monsieur*, velcum tozee lonsh of thee new fibuloos kir. Pleese if yoo weel step oot of thee fibuloos kir and Henri here, he weel perk eet fir yoo."

"*Merci beaucoup Monsieur. Mais je parle Francais*," the woman replied, then turned away for a moment to undo her seat belt. Granville stood up to his full height, looked over the car's roof to the far side where I was getting ready for the hand-over of the keys, and pointed his finger downwards at the passenger seat. In a silent voice he mouthed the words, "French speaker. We're in the shit!"

I'M CLEAR, WHAT'S IT LIKE UP YOUR END?

I replied, mouthing the words, "I'm not... you are... I've lost me voice." I then proceeded to make short grunting sounds as if I really had lost my voice. At the same time I held my throat indicating that I was in some pain. Granville's face was a picture.

"What?!" he whispered angrily.

"Voice... s'gone, matey!" I hissed.

"You'll be bloody gone in a minute if it doesn't return this instant... matey," he said, his stage whisper becoming somewhat dangerously close to being overheard.

The woman climbed out of the car and babbled something to Granville in French. He looked at me but I just shrugged my shoulders and remained silent. My French was on a par with his in that it was non-existent. She babbled again at Granville, this time quicker and louder as if he was deaf. I thought that if he doesn't say something soon and make some go at speaking French then the game's up and we might as well go home. This was a great worry as we hadn't yet been paid. Actors always get paid last, and this job was no exception. We had to get to the finishing line before the game was up.

"Madame!" he exclaimed.

I breathed a sigh of relief.

"I heer whit yoo are sayeeng. But I must eenseest yoo speak een Eengleesh."

"But I've been studying your lovely French language and I am desperate to try it out."

"I appreesheeate that madame, but I too am despeeerate. Very despeeerate I cin assoore yoo."

"He *certainment* ees," I managed to squeak.

The woman turned her attention to me. Granville give me the two finger salute from behind her back.

She turned to face him again. "You were saying that you were desperate?"

"Yeees... for I also haf been studying a forain langooage, and eet ees yours. Yes, I am lerneeng the Eeengleesh, so I too wint to try eet oot on yoo."

That genius impromtu answer saved both our bacons. The lady complied and we eventually got through to the final day without any more accidents, ordeals or mishaps. Our employers were more than happy with our work. Ian was happy too and we were paid eventually.

CHAPTER FOURTEEN

DUTCH CLAPS

The next sojourn beyond our shores which I will regale you with took me to Holland not long after my arrival in London second time around circa '78-ish. It was a three week tour playing in all the major towns and cities that have survived to this day because each have their fair share of big dykes. The company was a tie up between British actors and an American director, and we rehearsed two one act plays for a fortnight. Our rehearsal room was in a community centre farm somewhere in north London.

When I first arrived I thought it an odd though quaint place for us theatricals to be working, and my gut reaction was one of mild concern. This was confounded when a group of mothers with toddlers turned up on our first morning's rehearsal and dumped their noisy little treasures in a crèche, which was a padded room adjoining our rehearsal room. A sinking feeling set in, which wasn't helped when at coffee break I noticed some local tearaways running riot around the building, whilst their parents were getting some sort of educational training elsewhere. If it had been up to me their children would have been the ones getting educated and I'd have sent their parents off for a well-earned holiday.

The place was run in a very co-operative type way which was a great idea but chaotic in its delivery. They can work really well and did so in the past when my mum used to collect her divvy from the local co-operative shop, but it certainly wasn't working for us actors in that community centre.

Next I was informed that umpteen goats, sheep, dogs, cats, chickens and various other animals had free range of anywhere they fancied. We were told in no uncertain terms, that these animals were on a par with us humans and must be treated with the utmost respect. No problem there as I am an animal lover as I have already said. But we were also told that one of the goats, the one who happened to be sporting the biggest ruddy great horns I have ever seen on a goat, wasn't too enamoured at having to share what he saw as his space with us humans. Had it not been for the fact that I had a terrific part in one of the plays, which was an extremely well written two hander, then I would have torn up the contract and legged it out of there fast.

You will notice that I have only mentioned one of the plays so far. That is because the other one, when rehearsals began, was still being written by the director. This was not a good sign. But I was told that I only hopped on, made a one line appearance as a soldier in this second play then hopped off again, so I wasn't unduly bothered. Looking back, I should have been. By the way, I would like to mention at this point that this same director, as well as directing and writing, cooked the lunches on a rota system in the communal kitchen for all the workers in the centre. Thus the reason for my indifference to co-operatives today, but I am willing to be swayed.

Rehearsals for the first piece went well except that the director wasn't there because when he wasn't in his office writing, he was making lunches. And so we were more or less left to get on with it, which I think turned out for the best in the circumstances. You see Tommy, a co-operative approach can work after all. Yup I'm convinced now.

At the start of the second week we were handed the new play hot from the director's typewriter. I noticed my copy was marked here and there with detritus stains from his culinary lunch time creations. Unfortunately my worst fears re this play were proved right. It was bloody awful. Basically the story line was about an Irish Priest hiding a terrorist. In the first play the actor playing the Irish Priest played a Rabbi, so he had a hell of a job to do in this second offering to convince the same audience he was someone else and had a completely new religion. I have to say though that he turned in

I'M CLEAR, WHAT'S IT LIKE UP YOUR END?

two magnificent performances each time he took to the stage.

Back to play # 2. As it happens the Priest had hidden the said terrorist behind a false door in a confessional box. The dialogue was full of Irish 'begorras'. To this day I have never heard any Irish person say 'begorra'; and the soldier characters we had to portray were caricatures as well. But with only my one line of "Doesn't look like she's in 'ere sarge," I thought I could handle it.

Regarding stage props for the show: all through rehearsals I had been promised a real rifle to carry, but to this day (nigh on thirty-seven years later) it never did arrive, and so I had to go on stage with a piece of wood in the basic shape of a rifle tied at the nozzle and butt by a piece of rope type webbing.

Our first performance was in a theatre in Amsterdam our base for the show's duration. Adjoining the theatre was a bohemian cafe bar where Dutch actors would sit around most of each day reading the freebie newspapers. They were a friendly, laid back lot without a care in the world. I found out that whether or not the Dutch actors were working, the state would pay them some sort of earnings related benefit so they could live a stress free if not frugal existence for as long as they wanted to believe they were in the business. The same system apparently applied to French actors living in France at the time. But us Brits back home had to fill in a myriad of forms just to become eligible for a meagre hand-out that only lasted a short time before it was cut off and we were forced at gun point to change occupations. An actress I know even joined the ranks of the department of employment as a member of staff, which is a bizarre thing to do because as an employee she was paid by the state. Same thing isn't it? If she 'signed on' or worked for them, doesn't the state pay in the end anyway? Me? I didn't bother with all that, back then I just delivered laundry instead when I was 'resting'.

As the lights dimmed, signalling the end of the first of our two plays, my fellow player and I were greeted with rapturous applause, which culminated in a standing ovation. The Dutch really know how to turn on the charm when they like something so we were delighted with their appreciative response.

Backstage, adrenaline still pumping, I changed costume and prepared myself for the following piece of theatrical skulduggery, namely the crap play. I felt truly sorry for the other actors who had pulled the short straw and were now dreading the prospect of what they were about to show to a live audience for the first time. I tried to lift their spirits.

"I watched most of the dress rehearsal and it honestly looked… ok-ish. Believe me."

The expressions on their faces showed that they didn't believe me, and thus my honesty was highly questionable. I tried another tack.

"It doesn't matter what we do here in Holland. No-one back home will know."

When that didn't work either I blurted out, "Oh for Heaven's sake, I'm in this load of shit too, remember?"

That cheered them up a bit. But the show got off to a bad start on its first outing when the false door in the confessional box didn't close properly, even though the Priest tried his best to shut it. Behind this door hid the actress playing the terrorist. Though she and the Priest were more than aware that the door was ajar, neither me nor the army sergeant waiting in the wings to come on had a clue what was happening. But the audience were aware of it and started to fidget with apprehension and mirth.

N.B. It struck me that had two of the Wise Men who brought Jesus Frankincense and Myrrh, brought instead Apprehension and Mirth, then he might have got off to a better start in life… reality being a great leveller. Gold was an ok gift though.

Anyway… the door problem in the confessional only served to add to the mounting fearful atmosphere already being experienced on stage by the Priest and the half hidden terrorist as they waded through the turgid dialogue, talking to each other through the door's gap.

The ensuing scene went something along these lines :

(The Irish sounding priest talks loudly to himself)

Priest: She'll be safe in there now to be sure.

(He fails to close the false door properly. A bit more chat between the terrorist and the Priest ensues as they battle with the door. On cue, the sergeant followed by me, both of us dressed in full army uniform, plod onto the stage.)

Sergeant: Have a gander around 'ere, see if you can find the terrorist wot is on the loose.

(This next line is delivered in my version of a cockney accent)

Me: It doesn't look like she's in 'ere sarge.

Sergeant: Just do it private, that's an order.

Priest: Begorra, there's no terrorist hidin' in these parts to be sure.

There was a dull thud on the stage behind me. A titter started in the audience. The sergeant looked at me then he rolled his eyes Heavenwards. I looked at the priest. He focused on a spot on the floor directly behind me and nodded surreptitiously at it. I looked round and saw my rifle dangling from the end of the rope, the nozzle end scraping the stage. Quickly I yanked it up over my shoulders and into my arms in one swift movement as if presenting arms. If you remember, I had learned to do that in a play I was in earlier. It now looked to all intents and purposes as if I was about to mount a bayonet charge armed with a branch of a tree in the direction of the audience, and would have done if I could have spotted where the bloody director/writer was sitting. The sergeant looked at the wooden type rifle I was holding, coughed into his cupped hand and muttered to me:

Sergeant: Tom dear boy, you must be barkin' mad.

(That got me started. I felt the titters well up inside me. Then in a loud voice he commanded)

Sergeant: Carry on soldier.

(Instead of keeping schtum, I replied through gritted teeth)

Me: I'll try sir!

He threw me a look. It wasn't a nice one. As rehearsed I proceeded to wander around the stage. Apart from in the audience to whom I gave the majority of my attention to, there was nowhere for her to hide except in the confessional box which was slap bang in the upstage centre position facing the audience. I wandered up to it and stuck the tree branch through the curtain, just like the Wermacht did in the movies when they were looking for escaped allied POWs hiding in hay wagons and such like. Satisfied she wasn't there, I walked on down to the front of the stage and looked out at the audience again as if scanning them for any sign of someone in a beret and trench coat holding a device with the words 'This is a bomb' printed on it. I remember thinking that it may not be a bad idea to be blown to smithereens there and then. At least it would end our nightmare of doing the show and the audience from having to watch it. By this time they must have been debating as to whether they were watching a bad drama or an equally bad comedy.

It was at this moment that the false door in the confessional chose to spring noisily open and reveal the sought after terrorist dressed in a trench coat and beret and sporting a helpless look of deep seated anguish. At first I didn't see what had happened. It was the audience who enlightened me by pointing and giggling at what was going on behind my back. I turned around and watched as she slowly pulled the false door closed. Quickly looking the other way, I locked eyes with the priest, who by the look on his face was about to pass out. The sergeant saved the day by carrying on courageously with the dialogue, totally ignoring the fact that we had been rumbled and that it was pointless going on. But go on we did. Or I should say they did.

Sergeant: Look 'ere Mr Priest sir. We've been on the trail of a terrorist for some months and we know she's 'ere somewhere. So if I woz you I'd spill the beans and then me and the lad 'ere can go back to our cosy billet and put our feet...

He sat down mid speech on a three legged stool which should have had four. Needless to say it collapsed under him. The audience roared. The priest held onto the side of the confessional box for support, and I damn near disgraced myself. I simply couldn't take any more. Turning away from my distressed colleagues, I marched off stage as best I could in the circumstances, in what I hoped would look like true soldier fashion, sat down on the floor in the wings and howled with silent laughter. I couldn't stop and had to be dragged away by the stage management to my dressing room, in order that those poor buggers left with the carnage on stage could carry on with the rest of the play, without the added problem of seeing me rolling about on the floor in the wings.

Some might read this and believe that I have embellished that story in order to squeeze as much mirth as possible from it. I can assure those of you who think that are wrong. All of it is true. For those wishing to go on the stage as a career, let it be a dire warning of things to come. Hee hee hee!

What I haven't mentioned is that only three days into rehearsals, one of the actors went off to shoot a pilot for a new television comedy series and had to pull out of our show. Subsequently he was duly replaced. That comedy series went on to be one of the most successful ever on British television. It made huge household stars of all concerned. Absolutely fantastic for our actor I say. Of course I would have been delighted had it been me instead and I could have said goodbye to the mad goat etc., but in reality I was just so genuinely pleased that at last someone had got a break in this crazy business and that their dreams were coming true.

When the play I was in at the Edinburgh Festival was chosen to transfer to a New York off Broadway Theatre I was chuffed to bits. The Big Apple was a city that I had always wanted to re visit, having seen most of it in American films and TV series over the years. My first sojourn there was literally a flying visit when my youngest son was only ten years old and we filmed a promotional film for a national airline. There was literally no time to sightsee. We just flew in one day, filmed the next and flew back later that same day. So with this theatre job, I was looking forward to seeing somewhat more of that exciting city that never sleeps.

The flight from Heathrow was a bit of a trial for me because the bloke in front had put his seat into the laid back position as soon as were airborne. It remained that way for the duration of the whole seven-hour flight, which meant that the television screen on the back of his chair facing me was literally inches from my face. When I asked him if he could please push his seat back up I was told that it was broken and he couldn't move it. I believed him until I noticed that it worked fine when we were preparing to land. 'Welcome to the USA Tom.'

Clearing immigration took bloody ages, even after we had filled in mountains of paperwork weeks before back in the UK. Eventually we got through and with two of the other actors I was to share a billet with, managed to hail a taxi. Our producer came too as she was the only one who knew the address of our digs. Or at least we thought she did.

Whilst the theatre was in uptown Manhattan, our digs were in

Brooklyn's Williamsburg district. To get to work involved a forty-five minute train journey including one change. There was not much point in returning to the digs for a rest before the show during the day, as the journeys took just too damn long. I think I walked every numbered street there is in New York during my month's stay just to kill time. And as it was midwinter, it was also bloody freezing.

The taxi took us to Williamsburg ok, but the producer had lost the address of where we were to billet. So we drove around darkened streets in areas that our cab driver was rather reluctant to visit, until she eventually recognised our temporary abode from when she had booked it some weeks before. It was a tenement style building about five stories high. The sign on the communal entrance hall door read 'If you see anyone suspicious in this building call Sgt Kavinsky at Precinct blah blah blah… etc!'

'This is just f--g brilliant,' I thought. 'Staying in a place that's on a tenants beware list.'

The hallway sported well-worn lino on the floor. The first door on the left was our gaff. But much as we tried we simply could not get the damned thing to open. Eventually we had a go with the same key in the second door. It opened perfectly and we went in to a rather small three bedroom apartment with a tiny lounge, a ginormous television, a sofa, two chairs and a dining table. The telly screen was so big that it gave me blurred vision when I tried to watch it for the first and only time. The sofa backed onto a door. It was the one which wouldn't open earlier. I noticed that the lock had been bolted over and sealed on the inside. Our bedrooms were off the lounge.

Mine was ok-ish with a three quarter size double bed and a huge wardrobe. The window had a blind which let everyone on the street outside see in when I put the light on. Consequently I had to rig up a curtain type thing which involved a large towel, a sweeping brush and four books. And they say show business is all tinsel and glitter.

The one saving grace of the place was that it was immaculately clean. It was, however, absolutely roastingly warm. That didn't bother me much as the heater in my bedroom didn't work. I was happy with that as the heat from the lounge was more than enough to heat the whole tenement. We regrouped having checked out the various nooks and crannies including a kitchen which bordered on the side of pantry size.

I'M CLEAR, WHAT'S IT LIKE UP YOUR END?

"Everybody ok?" the producer asked, hoping for a positive response.

"It's shit," I said.

"Oh!"

Though I pride myself in being a man of few words, I listed my complaints which consisted of many words.

Over the following weeks when I ventured further afield I found Williamsburg to be quite a fascinating place, if more than a tad bohemian. Great coffee shops, quirky restaurants all in all generally a good place to hang out. The problem I had was that our digs were in a very, very run down area. It was where part of the car chasing sequence in *The French Connection* was filmed. The nearest train station was a five-minute walk, which I had to endure every night on my return. There were always suspicious-looking individuals in the shadowed doorways. The streets were dark and foreboding, and I was very much aware of an atmosphere of grim hopelessness about the place.

As my complaints list eventually ended, a horrendous banging noise began to resonate around the building followed by some gruesome shouting. The producer phoned the proprietor. The banging continued unabated, while she shouted down the phone that someone was trying to break into the place with a sledgehammer. I happened to notice on the table a folder with 'Welcome Pack' written in bold capitals. On opening the first page I saw a picture of the smiling proprietor sitting on a sofa with four bikini clad beauties draped around him. I got the message loud and clear. It was time to let the producer get the message too.

"That kind of sums it all up… find me decent digs or I walk," was my parting shot. Needless to say there wasn't enough dosh in the kitty for a better place for us to lay our heads, and so I spent the duration of the play's run living in that damned apartment.

Eventually the banging noise ceased and so she left. Then we three housemates went for a late evening stroll. My heart sank as I observed the surroundings I had found myself in. We returned shortly after downing a couple of beers and I turned in early. It was only about 9.30 p.m. but it had been a long day; early flight, jet lag and disappointment all added up to me be being extremely knackered and we hadn't even opened the bloody show yet. I fell asleep as soon as my head hit the pillow, hoping that the morrow might bring better results… like new digs Uptown for starters.

Not long after arriving in the land of nod, I awoke from my deep sleep when my ears picked up sounds of mumbled foreign voices coming from the lounge. Opening my bedroom door I was faced with four Hispanic chaps. I took note that they were short in stature, but they certainly made up for their lack of height by being built like brick shithouses… in other words they were about as wide as they were tall. Their vast widths were well accentuated by the puffer jackets they sported. One held a canvas tool bag of some sort which clanked with the sound of metal on metal when he moved it. My over active imagination thought that it was the sound of weapons I could hear clanking.

To this day I do not know who was more shocked, me or my unwelcome visitors, who to their horror saw a middle-aged, sleep-riddled, grumpy, startled Glaswegian wearing nothing more than his shorts and speaking in an incoherent-sounding language.

"Who the f--k are you ya bastas… and what the f--k are youse doin' in ma hoose if it is not too impolite a f--g question to ask?"

In reply they spoke in an incoherent Spanish-type language so we were neither of us any the wiser. I surreptitiously tapped on the bedroom door behind me. When I opened it my fellow thesp sat bolt upright in bed looking rather guilty for some reason. I said that it might be to all our advantages if he could drag his arse out of his pit and give me some much needed help. But instead of gallantly coming to my assistance, he dived back under his duvet from whence I had startled him, and proceeded to stay there. I closed his bedroom door quietly behind me and found myself smiling at my uninvited visitors. It is possible I was trying to dissuade them from killing me by using the same trick with them that I had done many years before with the big fish I came face to face with in the Caribbean. I really can't remember.

They took a collective tentative step towards me.

'That's that then,' I thought to myself. 'Bysie bysie world… I'm aff tae a better place… hopefully there'll be better digs when I get there!'

At this very moment the other bedroom door opened, and out strolled my other flatmate. He looked our visitors up and down calmly. They looked him up and down awkwardly, clad as he was like me, in only his shorts. He was also a hell of a lot shorter than me and was slight in stature, so to them he was not a threat of any sort, whereas I probably resembled a threatening, snarling beast of an unknown species who hadn't visited any gym for many, many years.

"Tom, I think it was an air lock and someone was hitting it with a hammer or something... that's what the noise was earlier." He turned around and went back to his bed as if nothing was untoward. The four guys' faces immediately broke into broad grins. For some reason they had understood him ok. Maybe it was because he spoke more understandable English than me.

Slowly and for my sole benefit - for I was the only one left to speak to - in over-pronounced heavily accented English their leader explained that the proprietor had sent them round to deal with the break-in, which our producer had screamed down the phone to him about. They were here to do battle with who they had been told was a maniac with a bad attitude and a sledgehammer. What they found was a maniac with a bad attitude, dressed only in his shorts trying to communicate in what sounded to them like Neanderthal speak. The bloke carrying the canvas bag closed it and we all shook hands. Thus World War Three, and my demise, were thankfully averted. They started laughing and chatting to each other, pointing at my shorts as they made their way out into the corridor. I went back to bed. My whole day had been surreal. What the next four weeks had in store for me I didn't dare to imagine.

Well I survived, the run went well and I do want to revisit that vibrant city. But only on the proviso that my digs are within walking distance of where I'm working, hopefully in the lovely, colourful, exciting Upper Manhattan district and I won't demand bikini clad birds to keep me amused during my stay.

Whilst you have read that I have had a real downer about where I was forced to stay, I want to state that the New Yorkers I met with during my months' sojourn in the height of winter, couldn't have been more friendly and helpful. Before I visited the Big Apple I was told that they would rather give wrong directions than appear to not help at all. Indeed I experienced just that. Basically they are just so damned polite and nice to strangers. And if that all sounds a bit gushy, then so be it.

After all is said and done I am a just a jobbing nacta, who is trying hard to ply his trade as best I can, and when a bit of kindness and a big dose of compliments come my way, I relish them!

Another wee incident I experienced in NY happened on a Sunday afternoon when I made my way to the theatre to prepare for an afternoon matinee. On the street corner just down from the theatre was a bank. It had big wide windows through which you could see a large open plan reception area. As I passed by I noticed two characters popping their heads up from behind a desk. They caught my attention and one waved to me ushering me over to the window. I paused wondering what the hell they were doing in the bank at that hour on a Sunday when it was supposed to be closed. I looked around but there was no one in the immediate vicinity. And so a mime act began between us.

I got the gist that they had locked themselves in. But they didn't look like bank staff to me. They were dressed in casual baggy jeans worn so low that had they turned around they would have shown off the cracks of their bare arses. On their heads they sported baseball caps jauntily worn pointing sideways, one eastwards t'other sort of westwards. As I started to move on they appeared to get quite irate with me and I realised that I may be their only salvation had they indeed locked themselves in. Then again I may be kidding myself and I didn't want to end up as an accomplice to a bank robbery had I managed to let them out.

By now the time was getting on and I really needed to get to the theatre rather soonish. I glanced up the street and saw to my relief a police car parking up. So I left the two suspicious characters, but not before I did a mime of a police car with its siren and lights blaring coming to get them. That didn't seem to please them too much. When I arrived at the car and tapped on the passenger side window it crept open extremely slowly. Both coppers were drinking coffee from large cardboard beakers and the driver had a mouth full of pastrami sandwich on rye. I knew this because most of it was visible when he chewed. The one in the passenger seat looked me up and down. If ever the film industry needed a character to play a serial killer, the cop I was looking at would fit the bill perfectly and his partner looked like he was his accomplice that buried the bodies. He grumbled more than spoke in a heavy street wise NY accent. It felt like I was in a scene from NYPD and I was the nervous witness who had just seen a neighbour's cat run over by an alien. I felt totally out of place, totally out of my comfort zone, and totally out of my tiny mind as to why in hell I had bothered to get involved.

"Yeh?" the cop drawled as if he was dying a slow death brought on by a strong dose of boredom and disinterest.

"So sorry to disturb you officer, but I've just seen a couple of likely lads who seem to be in a bit of a predicament, if you get my meaning."

"Where?"

"Down the street… in the bank… don't know why because banks shouldn't be open for business today for goodness sakes!"

I was beginning to sound like a happy evangelical clapper from the local church who was complaining about Sunday opening times.

"What they doin'?"

"Not a lot actually… just acting a tad suspicious… looks like they might have broken in… and can't break out…" I trailed off.

"Are they armed?" he asked tiredly.

"I don't know. I didn't ask. That's your job isn't it?"

His mate leant forward to get a better look at the Johnny foreigner who had spoiled his tea break. Neither of these two joyful employees of the NYPD could appear to be less arsed if they had tried. By now I was getting more than a bit pissed off, but doggedly I soldiered on, somewhat pedantically.

"Not that I want to tell you your job or anything else chaps for that matter, but it might pay dividends for your possible future advancement in your chosen careers, if you have a wee gander at what might well be ensuing in the bank don't you think? Might also be an idea not to use the blues and twos, or in your case the reds and twos, when you eventually decide to get involved, so as not to frighten the bank robbers into using their weapons… that is if they have any at all."

I hadn't a clue as to whether Cagney and Lacey had understood even a modicum of what I had just said. And as I didn't want to get involved in a shootout like the ones I had seen so many times in the huge amount of American television crime series we buy in each year from the States, I gestured to them indicating that it was now up to them to sort it out. After all, I reasoned that I had done my bit and had no further interest in pursuing the situation one iota further.

The cop car window slid closed as slowly as it had opened. Then suddenly and without warning, the car's engine roared into life, the red light started flashing on its roof and the siren wailed. Why oh why hadn't they taken my advice? Terrific! And so they sped towards the bank.

In the meantime my audiences had started to queue outside the theatre so I couldn't hang about for one moment longer. And the outcome of the bank robbery that probably wasn't? I haven't a clue to this day. But in hindsight I think it wasn't a robbery at all. Instead, it was probably just two bank cleaners winding me up for a laugh. They waited until an easily conned passerby i.e. me arrived on the scene and chose me as their patsy. I like to think that is what they were doing anyway. Or it is just possible that I had averted a major bank heist in New York, the city that doesn't sleep, but should really pay more attention to a Johnny foreigner like me.

CHAPTER FIFTEEN

PLAYING AWAY FROM HOME

As a single man, an actor working away from home, generally speaking, is onto a good thing, for he has no ties i.e. no-one to drag him out of the pub after the show before he gets so pissed that he starts to take himself too seriously, believing that super stardom will most certainly not pass him by. Indeed he has probably managed to convince himself and everyone else within earshot, that fame is just around the corner. However, and I speak from experience, it is tough for an actor who is not single, has a wife and young family to support on a rather basic salary, if the job he is doing at the time requires him to be hundreds of miles away from home for many a long week, and he is billeted in a single room on the outskirts of the city.

Take the time, for instance, when I was cast in a play in Manchester, just over three and a half hours drive in the wee small hours (in the days before speed cameras) to my home in Brighton. Nowadays it takes at least the best part of a day! After some three weeks rehearsals and a week's playing, passing a wet Sunday afternoon driving around the north moorlands for the want of something better to do was not my idea of fun. I seem to recall it never seemed to stop raining during my whole stay.

Eventually I found a phone booth in a lay-by and called home. Speaking to my wife and listening to my baby son only added to the lack of delight I was already experiencing as it reminded me how much I was missing them, but I am happy to say they were missing me too, which was I admit a very selfish thought on my part. So we three decided that they would join me.

That very afternoon I went hell for leather back to the city, pulled out all the stops and eventually found new digs in a house with a lovely lady who had two teenage boys. Luckily she didn't mind a baby around, nor did she mind my little son, and within two days my wife Cookie, our infant son Andrew, one Moses basket, one travelling cot, a couple of baby duvets, a bag of disposable nappies plus all the paraphernalia necessary for the wellbeing of a lonely young dad, got off the train at sunny Manchester's Piccadilly Station. Yes folks the sun came out!

My new landlady and her sons couldn't have been nicer. They gave Cookie and Andrew such a warm northern welcome and treated them like an extended family. So I went off to work daily a happier though much knackered man, but not for the reason I wanted to be. The problem was that my young son wasn't used to sleeping in a travelling cot, let alone a strange room in a strange house. What do you do with a baby who wakes up the moment his mum and dad go to bed and cries for attention? Normally you would work through it. Let him cry for a few minutes the first night, then a tad longer the next and so on until he got the message. But that wouldn't have been fair to our new found family who were trying to live normal lives and have an eight hour trouble free sleep.

And so it came to pass that when everyone else in the western hemisphere was tucked up in their beds fast asleep, my wife and I put our baby in his Moses basket and drove him around Manchester until the milkman started his rounds. Usually by this time both baby and wife were both fast asleep. I then had the problem of finding my way back to the new digs. After a few nights of this I began to wonder if being wet, lonely and alert was not more favourable to being a sleep starved happy dad.

During my stay in Manchester in the early eighties, word filtered down the miles that an idea was surfacing about only actors living in Scotland should be allowed to work in Scotland. I'm happy to say that the idea didn't get any further.

But what really riled me was that I wouldn't have been allowed to work in the country of my birth. I had trained as an actor in Scotland worked solidly in the Scottish theatre scene for five years and was highly instrumental in creating the Dundee Rep Action Group whose work, after two years of hard graft, toiling in whatever spare time we had whilst putting on plays on a three week turn around, succeeded in getting the proposal passed for a new repertory theatre to be built. I am told that it now proudly boasts to be one of the most successful working theatres in Scotland.

I feel a wry satisfaction that the warped prejudiced idea put forward was given the bums rush.

Re: digs. Cookie and I had more luck again when we were working in Leatherhead cast in Richard Harris's play, *Outside Edge*. We were delighted to be invited to stay with our army friends in their house in barracks deep in the heart of Surrey, which was less than a half-hour drive to the theatre. As the Major was off on manoeuvres and his wife worked during the day, we looked after their children, collecting them from school etc., and in the evenings when we went off to entertain the masses in Leatherhead, the Major's wife and her two devoted daughters would look after our little Andrew. We didn't want to go down the nanny route again having had a rather worrying experience on the one occasion we hired one. Unbeknown to us, she used to leave our son asleep in his cot while she went out to phone her boyfriend from a telephone booth in another street. So it was a great and safe arrangement living at the army barracks and it saved us loads of money in nanny fees and rent. So far so good; but why is it that the best laid plans, as Robert Burns said, gang aft aglae?

Everything was going swimmingly well until half way through the second week of our stay. A sequence of events occurred culminating in a scenario which I would only have believed possible had it been concocted for a thriller type movie with a strange twist at the end.

One morning in the mid-winter sunshine circa 1984, with the snow lying placidly on the ground offering a silent pathway into the forest of trees which hid the army barracks' married quarters from the country road that bordered it along one side, I began a journey up to a London Theatre to attend an audition for a workshop on a new play about terrorism. I have never liked the word 'workshop' when it refers to theatre. It sends me the message that I'm going to be working my arse off for sod all money on a play which stands next to no chance of seeing the light of day, but nevertheless along with a bunch of other hungry talented thesps I will spend the next three weeks or so trying in vain to make the damn thing work.

At that time I believed that terrorism was a spooky choice of subject to be doing a play about, because the IRA were rather active on mainland Britain, and they may not have taken kindly to a bunch of arty-farties out to make an intellectual killing, albeit of a theatrical nature.

Those auditioning me were condescending in their manner when they heard I was doing a comedy in Leatherhead. As far as they were concerned they gave the impression that Leatherhead was out in the sticks somewhere and probably had just got running water for the first time. I could feel the sneers when I told them I was more than happy to be working there in such a prestigious show. Nevertheless as I had travelled all the way to the smoke to meet these people, I gave it my best shot. Thankfully it couldn't have been good enough because I didn't get the job. Had I been successful I had already made up my mind that I wasn't going to do it anyway, so in the end everyone was happy with the result.

By the time I arrived back at the barracks in the afternoon, some army mates of our friends happened to call in because their car's engine had blown up en route to the West Country… nothing to do with a bomb, simply because the silly sods hadn't put enough oil in the engine. However, and this added to the rising apprehension within me, they happened to be members of the bomb disposal squad.

A couple of hours later before leaving for the theatre later when the sun began to dip behind the horizon and the wintry evening light kicked in, I checked as usual under the car for any little presents left by people who weren't too keen on the British Army's presence in Northern Ireland. It was standard procedure for anyone living in a military establishment in the eighties and a new experience for us, living as we were rent free courtesy of Her Majesty. As we drove off, I filtered the day's events through my mind and began to feel a tad uneasy, for it had been peppered with little worrying incidents for me: a play about terrorism, a bomb disposal chap's car engine blowing up, living in army barracks at a dodgy time, newspapers covering ever increasing atrocities. All pretty frightening stuff. But when we arrived at the theatre I put it all to the back of my mind, and went into nacting mode.

I'M CLEAR, WHAT'S IT LIKE UP YOUR END?

I diverse a little here but I feel it is worth mentioning. Cookie and another actress in the play shared a dressing room. After the show there was a knock on their door and a well dressed woman popped her head round and said that she had had a lovely evening watching the play, and especially liked Cookie's performance. Not the most tactful thing to say in a shared dressing room, though I have to admit that Cookie was utterly brilliant in the part of Maggie. She brought the house down nightly with her characterisation and comedy timing.

The woman effused even more and went on to say that she thought it was the best thing she had seen Cookie do. That should have been enough praise to heap on even the most celebrated demanding diva, but not for this woman.

"Really you were wonderful darling. I'll see you in the bar…?"

"Thank you, that'll be nice… but who are you?" Cookie asked.

"Who am I? I am your agent!"

In Cookie's defence she hadn't seen the woman in six months!

When the show finished we set of on our return journey to the barracks, giggling all the way about the faux pas, and realising that it was probably time for Cookie to change agents, if that hadn't already been decided for her.

Back to the story. Our car's tyres crunched over the hard packed snow as we drove along a dark country road which cut through a dense pine forest. There was not another car or soul in sight. Apart from the beauty of it all, the night had a rather surreal atmosphere, as if it was closing in on us. It was perfect to shoot an episode of the *X Files*.

An eerie glow in the trees up ahead signalled the entrance to the barracks. I slowed the car and gently turned the wheel. I could feel the tyres working hard, trying to keep some sort of grip on the rutted ice. The wheels slewed a bit then righted themselves as I turned the steering wheel into reverse lock and did a bit of cadence breaking which my father (an ex-police driver) had taught me to do. For some reason the barrier was unmanned. We drove on under the raised barrier into the barracks proper, creeping slowly along. It was worrying why the barrier had been left up but I kept that wee insecure thought to myself. A few street lights dimly lit the tall fir trees which cast long shadows on the narrowing empty road in front of us. Our friends' semi-detached house was the second but last situated at the far end of a cul-de-sac. Beyond its large rear garden the dark foreboding forest stretched unseen for miles around. Parking the car at the side of the house I locked it then we entered through the back door as pre-arranged. Once inside the well-lit kitchen we felt cosy and safe in the house's warmth, away from the chill night outside. We called out, but no-one replied. Thinking that our friend was upstairs with one of the children, we weren't concerned at that point that anything was out of the ordinary. Cookie started to fill a kettle to make a cuppa, and accidentally splashed some water on the kitchen work surface. As she began to wipe it clean she noticed that a message had been written on it in what must have been some sort of water soluble ink because there was little left of it. It read, 'Really sorry... have to... worry... all my fault!'

The rest was illegible. Before she could say anything I was off up the stairs taking them two at a time to check that the kids were ok. When I reached the landing I stopped dead in my tracks. I called out to Cookie to remain downstairs and under no circumstances was she to follow me up until I had sorted things out. She was a tad confused as she couldn't recall us having had any sort of disagreement. And anyway, had we had an argument, it was normal for me to have to stay downstairs if you get my meaning.

"But I think...!" she started to protest.

"Don't think... just wait there!" This was a dangerous thing to say to a liberated lady and could quite as easily have caused a mother of all arguments, but my choice of words thankfully went unchallenged by her.

On the floor leading from the master bedroom and running the length of the landing to the childrens' bedrooms, was a length of insulated wire plugged into a black coloured metallic looking device about the size of two cigarette packets. Taped onto it with black gaffa tape was an alarm clock. My mind raced in all directions, fed as it was by the events of the day. I hadn't been taught how to disarm a bomb at drama school, but thought that getting down on all fours and crawling towards it was a good idea. Apart from being the longest crawl of my life, it also took more time than it would have, had I had the sense to run instead the short distance to the kids' rooms, collect them and then get the hell out of there smartish. But fear doesn't always make you act in a sensible fashion. Cookie thought I had flipped when she saw my rear end followed by my feet disappear as I shuffled off down the corridor on my hands and knees. Just as I arrived at the 'bomb' there was a loud creak, which sounded like an earth shattering noise to me. Whether it came from the floorboard I was kneeling on, or my knee, I couldn't have cared less, but the disembodied voice that followed it nearly killed me there and then.

"Hello? Everything all right in there?" it rasped.

"F--g hell!" I think I replied in answer.

I then very stupidly yanked the wire out of the now 'speaking bomb'. Cookie arrived and knelt down beside me. She coolly re-attached the wire and spoke into the device.

"Sorry about my husband. He lost it for a moment there. Everything's just fine thank you."

"Oh good. Trish forgot to tell you she had a dinner bash in the mess. We can step down from babysitting duty now and get off to kip can we?"

"Yes. Goodnight to you and thank you so much."

She looked at me in the way only a wife can when her spouse has made a complete prat of himself.

"Baby alarm is it?" I asked feebly.

"You didn't think it was a...?" She laughed. She went on to explain that the wire went all the way out of the master bedroom window and through into next door's bedroom window to a receiver, which the neighbours could listen into for any noises e.g. a child crying, or a prat of an adult crawling on all fours. As for the alarm clock? The ticking insured that the baby alarm was active.

I was tempted to write to my old drama school and suggest they add baby alarm identification classes to their curriculum.

This next story finds me in a rather good play which opened at the Edinburgh Festival and went on tour from the heart of Surrey to the heart of Glasgow via Guidford and Malvern etc. It was a four hander written by Nichola McCauliffe, whom I once described as a one woman talent show. She's also a well-known actress on both the stage and television and has a remarkable singing voice. There's nowt she can't do really.

It was bit of a relief when we had a whole week's break half way through the run. This meant I could nip home for a bit of home cooking and remind myself what my wee family looked like, as well as reminding them what I looked like. Sunday was the last day of my leave and I took a stroll to the local park to watch my mates playing Sunday football, which I would also have been doing had I not been on tour. I had really been missing it since neither of the two actresses in the company wanted to play. Also, and rather more importantly, is that taking part in a sport whilst performing in a play was a no-no in our contracts, as it was deemed dangerous. No management wants any of their cast ending up in A&E and being unable to continue in the show. Quite right too. So when my mates asked me to join in with the football game because they were a man short, I had to decline for fear of getting an injury. Quite right too, again.

"Ok, so what about going in goal then Tom you woose?"

'Why not indeed,' I thought and wandered onto the pitch. Nothing ever happens to goalies. Ten minutes into the match was when I broke two fingers of my right hand trying to catch the ball, which had been struck with some considerable force. And so it came to pass that I ended up in A&E, which was the last place I wanted to be at that time. I had visions of my hand being sealed in a cumbersome plaster cast, but was more than relieved to learn that broken fingers of the type I had sustained were best left to their own devices as they would in time just mend. As bloody painful as they were, I was delighted to hear that news.

Next morning I set off on the drive to a theatre in Gloucestershire from my home in Brighton, with my left hand working perfectly, whilst my right sported two purple coloured painful fingers that really wanted to be wrapped up in a warm type bandage instead of holding onto a steering wheel.

Anyway, the point of this story is that I am happy to report I got there unscathed and walked with a nonchalant air into the theatre as if nothing was wrong with me. Then I calmly mentioned to the management that I happened to have been watching a football match the previous day (which in all honesty I had been, because as a goalie I had been more of a spectator) when an extremely hard hit ball came at me at a rate of knots, and it was all I could do to stop it from hitting me square on my face... thus these two broken fingers. I lifted them up as if they were trophies I had just won. The management were so sympathetic I was tempted to exclaim, "We would have won had I saved the f--g ball as well." But I deemed it wise to stay silent.

The next point of this story is explaining how I coped with the business of my character having to pour coffees onstage during the play with two broken fingers. I deduced that I could easily hack that because in my early years in the business, when I had to pour coffee into cups during an intimate studio theatre production, I decided that my character would pour it from the coffee jar directly into the cups. Therefore I had no need of a teaspoon which I simply couldn't hold with two broken fingers. Brilliant! Thankfully I got away with it. Pouring drinks I could do from a decanter and therefore didn't have to open a bottle. All good so far.

The biggest problem arose was when I had a quick costume change in the wings. It is never easy taking off and putting on clothes quickly especially when there is little to no light in which to see what you are doing. This was made worse for me by the fact that I simply couldn't untie my tie, undo or do up the buttons on my shirt, or fit the cufflinks on the cuffs, or clip the cummerbund around my waist, or undo the zip of the suit trousers I was about to take off, and do up the zip of the tux trousers I needed to put on.

The only person available to help in the wings at that time was an actress who needed to do her own quick change before she could even begin to help me. But somehow she managed it. First she stripped down to her basque, stockings and suspenders etc., in record time, then immediately turned her attention to my predicament. Off came my tie, then my cufflinks, followed by my shirt, which she unceremoniously hauled off my back. The next bit I will never forget.

Kneeling down facing my crotch she began to undo my fly zip. At that moment I happened to glance down at the wonderfully scantily dressed lady as she looked up at me. Our eyes met.

"If the paparazzi could see us now!" was what she said. I didn't need to reply as we both knew that the picture would have made the front page in every red top newspaper in the land, especially so as her husband worked for one of them. We didn't have time to ponder that thought as she hauled my trousers off, replaced them with another pair and zipped me up, slipped on her cocktail dress and followed me onto the stage. The actress was Nichola McAuliffe!

CHAPTER SIXTEEN

THEY'RE GONNA PUT ME IN THE MOVIES

Circa 1971-ish

I hadn't been in the business five minutes when a call came from my agent at the time (the one who thought the play *Night of The Iguana* was called *Igoo Agoo*) for me to go to a hotel somewhere in the West End of Glasgow for 6 a.m. the very next morning, where I would be given a film script, and 'could I remember to take a pair of black shoes?' She didn't know what the part was that I would be playing, but as it was my first film I was so thrilled that, 'Frankly my dear, I couldn't give a damn.' From the hotel I would be taken to the film location wherever that was, meet the director, film crew, fellow stars and we would shoot my scenes. It was all a bit of a surprise as I didn't know I had been put up for a part in a film I hadn't known existed until then.

Next morning, half an hour before I was due to arrive, I turned up in the foyer of the hotel with a pair of black shoes tucked under my arm, and waited. Nearly an hour passed and as I was still waiting I decided to nose around the adjoining rooms to see if someone was there with my script, but no-one was. Instead I was approached by one of the hotel staff who was on the point of calling the police following my suspicious snooping, when a dull grey coloured beaten up minivan screeched to a halt outside. A largish chap with oil-stained hands jumped out and rushed into the foyer calling my name. The hotel bloke was unsure whether to let me go or turn the both of us in, but decided on the former as he was about to go off duty and didn't want the hassle.

Largish chap and I climbed aboard the clapped out minivan, my first chauffeur driven car of my career, and we sped off. I didn't know whether to thank the driver for saving me from a spell behind bars or to bollock him for being late. Choosing neither I stayed schtum. He was a man of few words so I learnt very little about what the day had in store for me. I did learn, however, that I would be playing a police constable and that there was a uniform jacket, a policeman's hat and a pair of dark coloured trousers in the back of the van lying beside a greasy old alternator, which he had had to replace that very morning which was the reason for his late arrival apparently. I climbed ungainly into the back of the van. This was a rather hair raising manoeuvre to accomplish in so small a space whilst travelling at speed. As we swayed around corners, with rising difficulty I tried on my first film costume. I knew it couldn't possibly be a perfect fit because that would have been too easy and I wasn't wrong. Though the jacket did fit, the waistline of the trousers was at least two inches less than mine. As for the hat? Suffice it to say that size-wise it would have been a better fit for King Kong. The sky blue shirt necessary to complete the picture, he informed me, would be bought at C&A's in Hamilton, near where we were heading. It was not exactly the most exotic of locations, and the high I had first experienced at being cast in my first movie was fast beginning to wane. The trousers I could cope with because the jacket covered the waistline, and leaving them unbuttoned I could keep them up by using the belt from my own pair, but the hat was ridiculously too large for my head. Having said that, and providing that I didn't turn my head to right or left, it looked absolutely made to measure from the front. But if I did happen to glance swiftly in either direction, then the hat remained facing front. The only way round the problem was to refrain from turning my head at all, but that was obviously going to be restrictive when it came to nacting. The driver handed me a roll of Jeyes toilet paper (the hard stuff popular back then, though gawd knows why) which he kept in the car's glove box for reasons I didn't really want to know and so didn't ask. I stuffed some under the hat brim and providing there were no profile shots, I thought I might just get away with it.

Along with the toilet paper, the glove box also held my script. I hungrily perused the pages hunting for my scenes and was disappointed to see that I only had one, though I did have two separate entrances in it. Not much of a debut, but it was a start.

Firstly, I had to knock on the door of the police interview room, and on hearing my cue from the sergeant inside saying, "Yes?" I then had to open the door, pop my head into the room and say, "Cuppa tea Sarge?"

Some moments later into the scene I had to repeat this action, but this time my line was, "Telephone Sarge, it's important." I wondered how Steve McQueen would say these two pathetic lines and make them somehow memorable. I sadly came to the conclusion that even he couldn't, resigning myself to doing the best I could with my lack lustre character of a two lines copper.

It took us the best part of an hour to get to the location, which turned out to be a disused police station on the outskirts of Hamilton. When we arrived the film crew were having their ubiquitous tea break whilst waiting for the actor playing the copper to arrive i.e. me. I was rushed into makeup where I had a swift hair trim then a powder puff was quickly dabbed on my face. Next, wearing my own black shoes with the over-tight trousers, I was lead at a trot by a pretty production assistant into the police station, at the same time donning the jacket, hat and buttoning up the new sky blue shirt which had miraculously appeared moments earlier. In our haste I tripped over some heavy duty electric cables and would have fallen headlong through the glass door into the reception area, had it not been for the quick thinking of one of the film crew who opened the door just in time when he saw me fall towards it. He concluded quite rightly that as I was dressed as a copper then I must be the missing actor, and called to his mates that the bloke now lying on the floor was the one they all had been waiting for, so they could at last get on with the filming.

The cables that had nearly made me a 'cropper copper' ha ha ha ha! were plugged into power points in the former police house next door, in which a local council resident was living at the time. From the interior of the house they went on through its front garden, along the street and into the police station where I had just made my unfortunate entrance. They then travelled the length of a corridor via the glass door, on out of a window along a patio before finally disappearing into the interview room via its window. Inside this room were the lights, camera, sound equipment, film crew, director, as well as two other actors, one playing the sergeant, the other the suspect. As you can imagine it was all a very tight squeeze.

Up to this point I had been really laid back about appearing for the first time in front of a film camera and was in no way phased by the idea, though I was slightly annoyed with myself for arriving on set in such an undignified fashion. But I knew my meagre lines off by heart, and that ultimately was all that mattered to me, so I believed I had nothing to worry about. That was before the director appeared from the interview room. His demeanour conveyed to me that he was already having a bad day. He started by complaining that filming was behind schedule, which had not been helped by my late appearance. I was tempted to tell him that it wasn't my fault I was late, it was to do with the minivan's broken alternator, but decided to make sympathetic sounds instead and say nothing. He then said that he hoped I knew all my lines and stared long and hard at me as if daring me to say I didn't. When I assured him I did indeed know what I had to say and followed it with a quick rendition of "Cuppa tea sarge," and "Telephone sarge it's important," he put his arm around my shoulder, walked me the length of the corridor and then whispered in my ear, "What's with the bumf paper stuck in your hat son?"

I told him and he blew a fuse at the nearest person he could find, namely the pretty production assistant who I noticed followed at his heels like a lap dog whenever he appeared. He cried out that there was no alternative but he was going to have to shoot me full in the face. For a moment I thought he meant he was going to kill me. Then as quickly as he exploded he calmed down again and said, "Cut the hat."

'Christ,' I thought, he was going to go at it with a knife while I was still wearing it. What he meant was that I wasn't to wear the damn thing at all.

Then he proceeded to go into a strange routine. First he stared at his feet, frowning quizzically at them as if he had never seen them before and pondered the possibility that they belonged to someone else. Next he looked skywards, pursed his lips, shook his head and took a sharp intake of breath through gritted teeth. It was like watching a bad impersonation of Marlon Brando preparing to say a line. And I was bloody sure even Brando would have got the line out quicker. He then turned to face me, put his hands on my shoulders and said, "Tom. It is Tom isn't it?"

"Yes it is… Tom… is my name."

"Tom… there are no small parts."

"No? Oh dear. What a pity."

I thought I was being taken off the movie before I had started and warmed at the prospect.

"Only small actors!"

Realising I was not to be re-cast I tried hard not to look disappointed. He then threw his arms around me in a crushing bear hug before releasing me again and striding off back into the interview room. My earlier cool composure had evaporated by this point, and I began to feel very nervous about having to say anything to the lens of a camera with this director anywhere near me. Then I heard him shout from inside the room.

"Stand by Tom… and… roll film."

I wasn't even going to have a rehearsal! So I took a deep breath and sidled up to the door as coolly as I could muster. There was an ominous silence. I waited. Nothing! I then heard a mumbled voice say what I thought was my cue and made an executive decision to go for it. I gave the door a firm knock, opened it, popped my head into the room and said my first line ever as a budding film star.

"Cuppa tea, sarge?"

The director gave me a look of total incomprehension.

"What the f--k are you doing son?"

"My first line… about… the tea."

He rested his chin in the palms of his hands and shook his head slowly from side to side.

"Too soon Tom. You were miles too soon. You didn't wait for your cue the sergeant's line did you?

"I thought he had said it… sorry."

Deciding it would be more prudent if he gave me a separate cue himself, he winked at me, crossed his fingers then told me to do it again, hoping that this time I would get it right. I closed the door and stood in that empty corridor feeling what a right prat I had made of myself. From inside the room came his gruff voice.

"Standing by everyone?"

No-one replied so I thought I had better fill in the silent gap.

"Yes thank you," I called out somewhat meekly.

There was a pause then I heard him mumble, "For gawd's sakes." I silently prayed that all would go well for the next take. From inside the room the voice rapped out again.

"Sound?"

"With you."

"Let's do it!"

"Camera?"

"Turning."

"Let's shoot this baby!"

Then there was utter silence. Though it was only a few moments long it seemed like a week.

"Roll it!"

I knocked on the door again, opened it, popped my head round, but this time before I could get a word out the director said, "Now what the f--k are you doing son?"

"You said 'roll it' and so I thought that was my cue you gave me."

"No... you'll hear me shout ACTION after the sergeant says his line," he said and pointed to the door.

I left the room, closed the door behind me, clenched my fists and screwed up my face tight in frustration. Why oh why did I choose this as a profession?

"Are you standing by Tom?" the weary voice asked from inside the room.

"Absolutely," I replied in the most reassuring way I could, which probably wasn't very convincing at all. From inside the room the inane orders were spat out.

"Sound?"

"With you."

"Camera?"

"Turning."

"Let's roll!"

I waited. I was damn sure I wasn't going to cock up again. My lines raced through my head for the umpteenth time.

"Cuppa tea Sarge? Telephone Sarge it's important."

At that very moment the woman who lived in the house next door, which was where the film crew had plugged in all their electrics, chose to arrive on the scene. She strode purposefully up the corridor towards me. Unfortunately she didn't look too happy.

"Who's paying fur ma electricity bill?" she demanded to know.

"What?" I asked quietly. I didn't need this, not now just as I was about to make my film debut.

"The electric? Wan o you pricks has wired his fancy machine intae ma socket. So who's paying?"

"ACTION!" came from inside the room.

"Just a minute missus I promise I'll sort it out in a sec," I pleaded.

"ACTION Tom for crying out loud!"

She grabbed my arm. "You wilna get away with this do you hear?"

"ACTION TOM FOR F--'S SAKE!!!"

I shrugged her off, opened the door, popped my head round and said, "Cuppa tea, Sarge it's important... and by the way the telephone's ringing. Oops!"

You would have thought that I never would have faced another camera ever again, let alone play another copper. But I have since played countless policemen on the box, quite a few villains too and I'm happy to say, never ever again had an experience like that one... ever!

CHAPTER SEVENTEEN

WITH FRIENDS LIKE THESE

The world of the actor is really quite small. Invariably when one turns up on the first day of a new job, one will meet at least one other fellow thesp whom one has worked with before. The same thing can happen in pubs. No sooner do you settle down in a big comfy fire-side chair relishing the prospect of quaffing a pint of your favourite brew, poured by the strength of the biceps of your favourite barmaid in your favourite tavern, than someone you vaguely remember as a pain in the arse from your past, enters the scene and spoils your evening. It happened to one, once.

I had gone to ground in my favourite watering hole trying to avoid a bloke I had worked with years before, as I had heard he was looking for someone to help out with some sort of a show gig he was producing. He was known for these live events and I had been warned that they were best to be avoided. But he tracked me down and told me that he had been let down at short notice and desperately needed help. As he was known to be a bit flaky and somewhat disorganised, I really didn't want to get involved, especially in anything that wasn't kosher acting work. Apart from that, 'show gigs' just weren't my thing, whatever they were. But I heard myself saying, "Of course I'll help you out… what are fellow nactors for!"

Next thing I knew I had committed myself to meeting him at six a.m. the following morning which happened to be a Saturday. Unless you were working in theatre or filming on location, Saturdays were mostly always free. Of course the sneaky bugger had already checked that I was 'resting' therefore I couldn't use the 'Sorry pal but I'm busy' excuse. He promised me I wouldn't have to do much in the gig, just turn up and help to organise things a bit, adding that he'd see me all right… thus hinting that he'd provide me with enough dosh to make my involvement worthwhile. So I agreed to meet at his house deep in the heart of the Sussex countryside the following morning.

Following a night of a tropical type downpour, it was a particularly bright morning as I drove the twenty-odd miles over hill and down dale, my buttocks only partly protected from the sodden wet seat by my rolled up raincoat which I was perched precariously on. My old MGB's hood frame had buckled in the previous night's storm and wouldn't close properly. Normally idyllic countryside surroundings coupled with a fresh summer wind rushing through my hair would have got me in fine fettle and looking forward to plying my trade. But I had a deepening apprehension about what might be in store for me and my arse was becoming damper by the mile. Nevertheless I had promised to turn up. True to my word at the appointed hour I arrived at his house to be met by a red-faced, hellishly over-weight chap dressed apparently as Allan a Dare, one of Robin de Hood's band of merry men. If this was not off-putting enough he told me (here comes the frightening bit) that as well as the odd go at being an actor, he was also a professional part time stunt man. That's a bit like saying you are a professional part-time gynaecologist. They're just isn't any such thing not if you are going to do the job properly. Surely you either are or you are not, a professional anything. And if you are a stunt man, you are not over weight with what looked suspiciously like a high blood pressure problem. Plus you would have had years of training. Fat Allan looked as though two minutes on an exercise bike would have ended his life. He informed me that we had to go straight to the jousting field where my mate would be waiting with my costume.

"Jousting field? Costume? What costume?" I asked.

"The one you are wearing as Big Ned."

I was beginning to get seriously worried. "Big Ned? Me?" I blurted out.

Surely this Fat Allan would be better cast as him, I thought. "Who's Big Ned when he's at home pal?" I seethed.

"Oh dear. I'm sure it will all be sorted it out when we get there... shall we...?" he wheezed at me and led the way to my car.

Ten minutes later we arrived in a large field with a clubhouse, from which a fenced-in walkway led to where a few medieval market stalls with stocks, gallows and a rostrum were set out in a circle. In the centre of this circle stood a structure made up of scaffold poles built up to a height of about twenty feet. At its foot was a large pile of empty cardboard boxes. The audience, if any dared to bother to turn up, were supposed to stand and watch whatever it was that would be happening, from behind the fence.

Fat Allan complained about his arse being damp from sitting in the unprotected passenger seat. I ignored him. I had other more important issues to be getting on with.

"So what will be happening?" I asked when I caught up with the producer of this ridiculous caper. He explained that the event I had been cajoled into being part of had been advertised as a medieval jousting and battle day. But unfortunately the individual called Simon, who was to supply the jousting horses as well as play Big Ned, had reneged. He had called to say that the ground was too wet to gallop on and therefore he had to look after his horses back at the stables. I agreed that it sounded a pretty good reason for cancelling, not only for the good of the horses, but the whole damned shebang in general. However I heard later that the real reason he hadn't turned up was because he was pissed off at the money being offered him. Though the jousting, which was to be the main event, had indeed been cancelled, the producer insisted that the show must go on. I had heard that ridiculous philosophy before, but I found myself nodding sagely as if in agreement.

"Fair enough," I replied. "But I fail to see where Big Ned now fits into any of this."

"He's the major baddie. Come with me."

I followed him into the club house. Inside it was absolute chaos. There were around forty various individuals of varying sexes, all searching through a huge tangled bundle of medieval clothes lying on precariously sagging trestle tables of varying sizes. If someone happened to find any sort of costume that looked as if there was the vaguest chance it might fit them, they whooped with joy and struggled to get into it.

To this day I have never seen such a strange looking group of partly dressed people in my life. They turned out to be specimens from right across the human spectrum e.g. two bank managers, one dentist, a doctor, three giggling stockbrokers (males), a mental health nurse, (I thought we might need her later), a personal assistant, one gentleman farmer and a couple of farm hands, plus four receptionists, a pilot, pub landlord and an estate agent as well as five navvies and various other odds and sods, or I should say, odd looking sods. Just as I was about to turn and make a bolt for the exit door, the producer grabbed hold of my arm and made an announcement to all and sundry.

"Folks, listen up," he called out.

The cacophony of noise died down. Everyone paused mid dressing to listen to their leader.

"You all know that that bastard Simon the slaughterhouse operative who was going to supply us with the gee-gees and play Big Ned has let us down badly?"

A lot of boos and expletives welcomed that announcement.

"However, you remember I said that I wouldn't let you down… and that I'd find a replacement for him?"

"We remember. Did you? We didn't know that!"

He carried on regardless.

"What you don't know is that the bloke who's turned up to fill the breach vacated by the shit Simon, happens to be a real nacta… a fully-fledged, highly trained one at that… a star no less who I worked with back in my rep days."

I shuffled my feet and stared at the floor hoping that it was riddled with woodworm and that it would disintegrate and I would fall through it and disappear from sight forever, landing somewhere in the bowels of mother earth.

"Folks, he is here to lend his professional advice and play the part of Big Ned, which I know he will do better than Simon the arse could ever have done."

There then followed a lot of appreciative grunts and a few inquisitive high pitched squeals plus a "Jolly good," from the gentleman farmer.

"So where is the bugger then?" enquired a horsey looking doctor who's huge tits were bursting to make a grand entrance from behind a leather doublet, which would have suited one of the big farm hands much better.

"Well folks, he's here. Say a big hello and thank you to Tom Cotcher!"

He hauled me closer to him raising his hand in the air. As he was holding my hand it shot upwards as if in a Heil Hitler salute. There was an embarrassed silence broken eventually by one of the farm hands.

"Thought you said he was a star this mate of yours."

My producer ignored the remark.

"C'mon folks let's hear it for Tom."

That did it. There were whoops of joy. If nothing else, he had these people eating out of his hands. "You have to be joking mate," I protested, shouting to be heard over the din. He held my arm which was still pointing skywards much tighter.

"Don't let me down now Tom. I couldn't take it twice in two days."

"But if anyone recognises me I might as well say bye bye to what's left of any career I would have had."

"Nobody in the audience is going to see you."

"How? Are they all from Saint Dunstan's or something?"

"Because, my good and dear friend, you'll be wearing this." He handed me a plastic helmet with an adjustable visor. He demonstrated that when it was in the closed position it completely covered my face.

What could I do? I hated letting anybody down but this was really pushing the Good Samaritan bit to the limit.

"Ok," I heard myself sigh reluctantly.

"Cheers mate. I appreciate it."

"So what exactly is it you want me to do?"

Two hours later the field outside was packed with paying punters as I led my band of rogues out of the clubhouse. From his position on the rostrum, the part time stunt man alias Fat Allan a Dare, wheezed into a megaphone.

"Ladeees and Gentlemeeen. I give you Big Ned and his band o' rogues who are about to hang the good Friar Tuck."

The first bout of unwanted laughter came when the bloke playing Friar Tuck was recognised as the local vet. Nevertheless we carried on regardless as we walked snarling and grunting to the gallows dragging him sheepishly behind us. Dressed as he was in a brown smock tied at the waist with a piece of hemp and sporting a friar-type wig on his pate, I have to say that of all of us, he really did look the part. The gallows on the other hand didn't. It was a flimsy looking structure made up from various bits of laminate off-cuts with a noose made of heavy duty industrial string hanging from it.

"But who is that behind them? Why, it is Robin de Hood and his band o' merry men. See to them Robin," encouraged Fat Allan, barely managing to get the words out.

There then ensued a very roughly choreographed fight sequence. I hate to admit it but I was partly to blame for putting it together. The only saving grace was that I had made sure that Big Ned, the character I was playing, was the first to be slaughtered. As I lay on the ground, Fat Allan bent over me.

"Wot you doin' Tom?" he panted at me with a sword in one hand and a megaphone in the other.

"I'm dying," I said happily from inside the helmet's closed visor.

"You can't do that."

"Can't I?"

"No! You're supposed to fight me now. You chase me up the scaffold and I jump off. It's my big finish."

"Aaaaagh," I replied and died with a grin on my face until the stupid sod lifted my visor; then my expression changed.

"What are you doing you prat?" I hissed at him, terrified that somebody might just recognise me.

"So… you're really dead then?"

"Yes, and so will you be pal if you don't put the visor back down right now and f--k off smartish."

He did and I was eventually carried ceremoniously from the battlefield by the stockbrokers dressed in doublets, multi coloured tights and period wigs. Once in the clubhouse I quickly changed into my own clothes then went back and mingled with the crowd. If I thought my bit had been bad, what I saw was worse. Whilst everyone else was knocking seven bells out of each other in a maelstrom of red mist, Fat Allan was on his own, fencing shadows having no one to fight now that Big Ned was dead. Then for no apparent reason he began to climb the scaffold. The fighting below him ceased as the players stopped to watch the rare spectacle of a hugely overweight devil may care idiot, haul himself upwards. By the time he got to the top he was quite breathless, just managing to wheeze into the megaphone.

"Eeeeegh!"

Then he jumped and landed on the boxes which did little too break the fall of such a large frame as his was. He lay motionless for some moments and the crowd stopped laughing long enough for it to look like it could be serious, until some urchin threw an ice cream at him which appeared to be the food catalyst that woke him and he struggled back onto his feet.

As for me? I sneaked off back to my car and drove off after I heard one of the punters say, "That Big Ned character. I think I've seen him before somewhere."

I have since written a television comedy based loosely on my experience as Big Ned, but I'm not sure if I have truly captured the honest madness of the event, or indeed if I ever could.

CHAPTER EIGHTEEN
CELEBRITY STATUS

The fame thing was never an aim of mine, and in truth I had been happy to avoid it for years. And though while I admit it does have its uses, it also comes with a few drawbacks. For me, a mere minor celeb whose name is Tom, I had to get used to being called Bill, due to the fact that I was one of a cast of twenty-seven or so in a television series of that name. "Allo Bill aw wight?" was the usual holler from devoted punters of the cockney variety. That was really nice to hear and it happened very often indeed. I guess it made having to pay their license fees a wee bit easier if they were enjoying what was on offer. But it was disconcerting to my youngest son Ed, who had always believed that his dad's name was Tom. As he grew up he learned to take it in his stride as he and his big brother began to make up their own names for me e.g. Baldy, Sleepy etc. But in his tender years it was difficult for Ed to come to terms with a man who on the television screen had an uncanny resemblance to his own dad, but was called Alan, and who appeared to run faster than his real dad who he knew as Tom in front of punters who would call his dad Bill. I explained that the fact I was getting paid to run faster on telly whilst kidding on to be DC Alan Woods was a

I'M CLEAR, WHAT'S IT LIKE UP YOUR END?

big incentive, hoping that would suffice.

One aspect on the positive side of recognition is that occasionally you are asked to do things you would never dream of doing. Take my sojourn to Shoreham Airport for example.

It was a day full of sunshine and hope for the many disabled and underprivileged kids who had been invited to the airport for flying experience organised by that master of Master of Ceremonies, the great communicator himself, the one and only Noel Edmunds. I was delighted to be asked to attend, and was in great spirits when I arrived with my wife and boys. The event lacked for nothing and everything ran like clockwork. Both the fixed wing pilots and chopper pilots were hard at it all day, flying their young excited passengers on joy rides over the South Downs. I did my minor celeb bit whilst Cookie and our boys enjoyed the sideshows and flying displays.

As the afternoon wore on I heard a rumour that an aircraft race was being organised as a finale. When I heard this I marvelled at the marketing skills of Mr Edmunds even more, thrilled at the prospect of watching such a breathtaking spectacle. It was certainly going to be a magnificent way to end such a successful day. However, at that point I had no idea that my wife had volunteered me to be a passenger in one of the planes taking part in the race.

"Oh she did, did she?"

"She said that you'd love to do it," replied one of the lady organisers.

"Really?"

"She said that you've always fancied flying."

"Flying yes and I have had one flying lesson… but racing… in the sky… as a passenger? Isn't there anyone else?"

"Noel usually does it but he's really tied up with flying his helicopter for the kids at the moment."

Suddenly the tannoy burst into life. "Ladies gentlemen boys and girls. The aircraft race will take place shortly. The fastest plane to watch out for will be flown by the very experienced ace pilot Mr Spencer Flack."

A big cheer went up.

"Spencer's passenger will be none other than Tom Cotcher, better known to everyone as DC Alan Woods of *The Bill*."

Another cheer went up as my heart sank. I admit to enjoying the speed and thrills of high speed driving in a motor car… I even did a racing driver course at the famous Goodwood race circuit, as well as skid pad training and I am a member of the Institute of Advanced Motorists etc., so I do like driving cars a lot. But I've never been brilliant as a passenger. In fact I find sitting doing nothing whilst in a moving vehicle quite an alarming experience. Now I was not only being asked to fly in a plane, but I was also going to be a passenger in an aircraft race, with a complete stranger at the controls. I was more than aware that unlike a car, if anything went wrong with the pilot, I didn't have a clue how to take over and fly it, let alone land the bloody thing.

"Of course I'll do it."

"Thank you so much. Noel will be pleased. Not to mention all the children who have come here today. Thank you so very much."

A bit more grovelling went on then I never saw her again. My wife who had been watching me from the safety of the hospitality bar gave me the thumbs up. I wanted to give her a different hand signal in reply.

Then I was introduced to my pilot a chap called Spencer Flack, who thankfully looked the part of a cool headed pilot capable of flying anything anytime anywhere, while being shot at by a battery of surface to air missiles, playing a game of baccarat and downing a glass of Martini stirred not shaken at the same time. We climbed on board his twin-engine plane and he immediately handed me a map. I was somewhat perturbed by this as I had fully expected him to know where the hell we were supposed to be going. However he reassured me that the map was for my benefit only. Marked on it were coloured flags that plotted where the yachts were anchored in the English Channel as markers for our route. One of the ground crew then placed a large transmitting device on my lap, then a set of earphones with a microphone attached were shoved down over my ears. He explained to me that as I was linked up to a radio station broadcasting from Brighton's Palace pier, I would be heard live throughout the whole of East and West Sussex, Kent, and in certain parts of Hampshire and Dorset, basically covering most of the south east of England. It dawned on me that the many thousands of radio listeners in England's most southerly counties could soon be hearing my last screams if things didn't go according to plan and we nose-dived towards eternity in the briny.

Because it was a handicap race we were last to take off, as we were the speediest aeroplane taking part, which I can certainly vouch for! Above the marker yachts we pulled two G's banking and turning at right angles about four hundred feet above the English Channel. It was one hell of a thrill and the radio listeners certainly heard enough yelps and shouts from me, as one by one we zoomed past our competitors.

"Passing over the... jees! Alongside the cliff tops now and the turbulence... bloody hell! You'll recognise the plane I'm in... aaagh... it's the one wobbling its... Hell's teeth Spencer! How did you do that?!"

Needless to say we were the first to return, thankfully safely, some half an hour later. My pilot, Spencer Flack lived up to his pilot-sounding name. He was an absolutely terrific pilot, and after that hair-raising experience, I would fly with him again any time.

Even members of the Royal Family are not immune to having to witness my minor celebrity status. Because of the obvious connection between the television show *The Bill*, and in real life Her Majesty's Prison Service, I was volunteered to represent our lot at a publicity launch held in Wandsworth Prison, to herald the start of a new government initiative supporting victims of crime. I believed it to be a thoroughly useful project so I was more than happy to oblige by simply turning up on the appointed day and being part of the scene. That was supposed to be the sum total of my duties. Invited dignitaries included in the VIP guest line-up were the Head of the Prison Service, the then Home Secretary Michael Howard, Terry Waite, and to top it all, Her Royal Highness Princess Anne, one of my favourite Royals. Also present were about forty assorted other guests including moi, and a band of paparazzi plus television crews and their news reporters. It must have been a nightmare for the prison security people to police. I had filmed in prisons before, including Wandsworth, so I knew how strict the security was.

In fact I have never seen a television crew pack up at the end of a day's filming so quick, as when a crew from *The Bill* were told they had to be out of the prison gates by a certain time otherwise they would be locked in automatically for the night, if they weren't ready to leave before their appointed time was up. However as this event was scheduled for the early afternoon, there wouldn't be a problem about overstaying our welcome. Also I doubt very much if the prison authorities would have relished the prospect of facing an irate Princess Anne, had she had to endure an unscheduled night in the cells.

We were herded into what resembled a large unheated Nissan hut within the prison grounds, where we awaited the arrival of the VIP's. Beside the rows of neatly placed seats, the news crews and reporters vied for the best positions to set up their cameras and generally get unrestricted views of the podium area. I settled down in my seat thoroughly enjoying watching the pantomime going on around me, when out of the corner of my eye I noticed one of the organisers of the event shuffling along the row of seats heading in my direction. She had that 'Would you mind flying in an aircraft race?' look on her face. I found out I wasn't far wrong. She did indeed want something from me.

"Tom?"

"Yeeees?" I asked, not sure whether or not I really wanted to know what she was going to say next.

"I'm afraid Terry Waite's plane due in from Delhi to Heathrow has been somewhat held up."

"That's a pity. Blimey, he hasn't been kidnapped again has he?" "

"Good Lord no! Soooo… unfortunately he won't be able to get here on time."

"Oh dear, what are you going to do?"

"I was wondering… if…?"

"Yeeees?

"Would you mind awfully standing in for Terry and giving a speech on his behalf?"

"Me? In front of all these VIPs? Including Her Royal Highness Princess Anne? Giving a speech I haven't prepared about a subject I know sod all about!?"

"Absolutely. Thank you so much. Here's a few leaflets on what this is all about. Luckily the Princess has been delayed too, so you've got at least another ten minutes to put something together."

Suddenly the enjoyment I had been experiencing up to that point went out of the barred window I was left staring at, and was replaced by a deep foreboding. What a nightmare scenario to have to go through.

I recalled to myself when I was the guest speaker at a Children's Charity dinner. That was hair raising enough for me as I had never done anything like that before, but at least I had plenty of advance warning for it and had a speech all prepared. Having said that, on my arrival at the venue I was told by the organisers that they hoped my speech was full of laughs because quite a few members from the local rugby club, as well as some members from the local Round Table were in the audience and they all enjoyed a good laugh. Needless to say, within a few sentences of the speech I had prepared about the sterling work done by the charity in question, I threw caution to the wind as well as the rest of the speech, and launched into a good load of tried and tested jokes by one of my favourite comedians instead and just managed to get away with it. The comedian I borrowed the gags from was the Cornish farmer Jethro.

The occasion in the Prison, however, was somewhat different. Somehow I don't think telling jokes like, "When I made love to my wife last night she said I was taking a long time. I replied that I couldn't think of anybody," would have been fitting in front of such dignitaries including Royalty, although I do have a sneaking suspicion that the Princess would probably have enjoyed my risqué jokes more than stuffy speeches.

The ten minutes allotted to me to acquaint myself with what the hell I was going to say passed very quickly as I hurriedly perused as many leaflets and pamphlets on the subject that I could find on display. Suddenly everyone stood up as the Princess, followed by her VIP entourage, entered our hut. The lady organiser smiled at me and gave me the thumbs up, uncannily like my wife gave to me at the start of the aircraft race wishing me good luck. I tried to smile reassuringly back. Obviously my efforts to appear cool didn't ring true as her expression changed and her face took on a look of intense concern.

The three dignitaries were warmly welcomed. The first to kick off was the Head of the Prison Service. He had a pleasing delivery and like all good speakers, thankfully knew when to stop and was thus rewarded with polite applause. Next up was Michael Howard who gave us his well-researched views on the subject and once again hands were courteously clapped together. I noticed that both had their speeches well prepared on neatly typed paper. Me? I had only the first few words of mine, "Hello there Your Royal Highness…" scrawled on the front cover of a glossy magazine, which displayed some of the appalling injuries that victims of crime had suffered.

When Princess Anne finished her erudite and well delivered eloquent oratory, she was quite rightly heartily applauded. It was obvious she had been well briefed on the subject too, for she knew it well, and gave a first class display of how public speaking should be done. How very impressed I was by these three accomplished orators who delivered what they had come to say with confidence and aplomb, their knowledge of the subject unquestionable. Then it was my turn. I am happy to report that the Head of the Prison Service kindly warned the audience that I had courageously agreed to stand in for Terry Waite only at the very last minute.

Standing up I stared at the Princess with what I imagine must have looked like fearful apprehension. She folded her arms and smiled back at me reassuringly with a twinkle in her eyes. I had the distinct feeling that she was really looking forward to the possibility that I would screw up badly. If I were in her position I would have wished for exactly that… indeed I'd have put money on it that I would be embarrassingly awful. After all, with so many functions to attend, the chance of the occasional cock-up must surely come as a welcome relief for her.

In order to calm myself I inhaled a huge amount of air. Of course I had inhaled far too much and immediately felt the effects of giddiness and was aware that my eyelids had begun to flutter uncontrollably. I looked around at the assembled faces and caught sight of my reflection in a camera lens. The eye flutter in a strange way would have worked in my favour as it gave me a slightly supercilious look, but coupled with my attempts to smile, it probably gave the impression that I was under the influence of a Class A illegal substance. Luckily the moment passed and I launched into a diatribe about how it was about time that victims had a voice etc., etc., etc. By the look on the faces around me I seemed to be doing reasonably well. I polished it all off with what I hoped would be a coup de grass. Having read only recently about the Princess's son's love of rugby, I said that I was thrilled that he had chosen to play for the Scottish rugby scene, and not for the other lot south of the border. There then followed an ominous silence, during which I had visions of being dragged off to the Tower to be hung drawn and quartered. But true to the rumour that the Royal Family share a good sense of humour, the Princess smiled sagely at me, which was a cue for everyone to join in and feel free to laugh out loud, partly at my quip, but mainly out of relief that she had taken my comment so well. It also showed that she had a lovely sense of humour too.

There are cases where, as a minor celeb, you get yourself in a right pickle simply because of your own carelessness. Take for example the time I was invited to appear in my first - and to date, only - live television talk show. The venue was in Belfast. I should have known that all would not go smoothly when whoever it was who was supposed to meet me at the airport and take me to the television studios, didn't bother to turn up. It was around six o'clock on a dismally wet winter's evening as I wandered aimlessly around the concourse, and out into the rain soaked car park time and time again, in the vague hope that someone would be there waiting for me. Eventually, some forty minutes later as I sat sipping the umpteenth cup of coffee and considering catching the next plane home, the tannoy blurted out that there was a telephone call for me.

"Many, many apologies, Mr Cotcher. But there has been a cock-up," the voice said from down the line.

This I already knew.

"Please go immediately to the car park where a VIP car will take you to straight to your hotel."

Off I dutifully trotted back to the car park. Apart from a few idle taxis there was no VIP car that I could see in the darkening evening light. Unless…! In a far corner I noticed there was a saloon car with its engine running. The large driver sitting hunched over the wheel looked over at me and nodded. This didn't look VIP enough to me, but as there was no alternative I turned up my coat collar and splashed on over to it with my overnight bag clutched tightly in my wet hand.

"Are you by any chance the VIP car?"

"Get in."

Not the welcome I had been expecting. But the authority in his voice left little room for argument. I hauled myself into the front passenger seat with my overnight bag perched on my now wet trouser legs and we drove off towards the hotel where I would be staying the night. At least I hoped that was where we were going. I had been told that the hotel was a ten-minute drive from the airport, and when my silent driver approached yet another set of traffic lights I noted that I had been in the car some fourteen minutes. At this point my overactive imagination took over. What a coup for the terrorists… kidnapping a minor celeb and sending his talents back to Blighty bit by bit in packages of varying sizes. I made up my mind that the next time we had to stop at traffic lights I would do a runner and take my chances in the dark, foreboding, unfriendly-looking back streets of Belfast at the height of the troubles. But what if my driver doesn't stop at the next red light because he believed that we would be sitting ducks for a hit by unfriendly foes? I would then be leaping from a moving car! Och what the hell… in for a penny. Surreptitiously I put my hand on the door handle and was about to throw open the door and take a gamble on finding my way on my lonesome, when suddenly the car's engine roared and we shot through the lights just before they turned red. Before I knew it we had turned into the hotel driveway. Breathing a sigh of relief I thanked the driver profusely for having got me there in one piece. I think he thought I was slightly mad. He wasn't far wrong. I was mad at myself at nearly having made a right prick of myself.

The welcome in the hotel was different. Here I was treated to the double handshakes and copious offers of free drinks plus whatever I wanted to eat etc. The Northern Irish were turning out to be even friendlier than I had imagined, on a par with the people of my own home town of Glasgow.

I showered then donned a complete change of clothes. Out went the check shirt, tweed jacket and cords, and on went a spanking new shirt and tie, freshly dry-cleaned suit which had been neatly folded by my wife, new socks and… this is the most important bit which at the time I hadn't given a second thought to… a brand new pair of jockey shorts, my preferred chosen underwear attire. Because my overnight case was on the side of small, I had stuffed the shorts into a side pocket. Consequently when I took them out of the pocket they were extremely wrinkled. I did my best to straighten them but when I put them on, one leg insisted on travelling up my thigh and digging into my groin giving myself what is called these days a 'wedgie'. The other thing to note was that the gusset opening at the front seemed to have a mind of its own and tended to open and close at random as I walked up and down my hotel bedroom, trying to master the technique of getting it to stay closed and in place until I deemed it necessary to open for whatever reason. I came to the conclusion that as I only had to walk to my waiting car, and at the other end walk into the television studio, my new set of underwear wouldn't be a problem to me.

I was delighted to share a car en route to the studios with Derek Nimmo, the star guest on the show. I thought I looked smart, but that charming humorous fellow was absolutely immaculately turned out.

In the studio hospitality bar I couldn't have been made more welcome. However I insisted on drinking soft drinks only as I considered this chat show sojourn to be work, and I have this deal with myself that I never touch alcohol until after the curtain comes down on any job I have been asked to do. I dutifully promised my hosts that I would make up for it afterwards, which I most certainly did. Also on the show with me that night was a famous soap opera star who was trying to make something of his singing career. He had a smashing voice, but I have to admit I hadn't a clue as to who he was as I hardly ever watch soaps. Nevertheless he went down a wow with the Irish audience who obviously did watch soaps and consequently knew who he was rather well.

When it was my turn to appear I felt relaxed and looked forward to the new experience. That should have sent alarm bells ringing for me because whenever I feel good about what is about to happen, invariably something untoward crops up from left field and sabotages my enjoyment. I was about to be proved right once again.

Whilst standing in the wings listening to my introduction I remembered a story told to me by another an actor friend of mine when he appeared on the show. With him there was another guest who got a bit pissed beforehand and said to the show's host that he came from the Irish island of Muff where a lot of diving went on. I was determined not to make any gaffes, especially on my live television chat show debut. The host gave me a terrific intro, along the lines of, "Ladies and gentlemen, will you give a big welcome please to someone from across the water we all lovingly know as DC Alan Woods... Mr Tom Cotcher."

I took one step onto the studio floor and was immediately in full view of the audience who began applauding like mad. It was at that precise moment that one of the legs of my brand new boxer shorts decided to shoot up into my groin at an alarming rate, as it had done back in the hotel bedroom. This had the knock-on effect of opening wide the front gusset which I had begun to believe as having a mind of its own. Consequently I had the rare experience of walking across a television studio floor in front of a live audience, as well as millions of viewers watching from the comfort of their homes, whilst praying to myself that I had remembered to zip up my flies properly. If I hadn't done, I knew that not only would my career be over there and then, but I would have had to spend years at Her Majesty's pleasure for exposing myself to millions of television viewers as well as to a live audience. Though this would have been an absolute first for any actor to achieve, it was not the accolade I would have hoped to be remembered by. Thankfully no-one realised my predicament, and very luckily for me, the fly zipper was indeed closed. But I can tell you now that I believe Nelson Mandela's Long Walk was a stroll in the park compared to how long the walk across that studio floor felt like for me.

CHAPTER NINETEEN

PLAYING ANOTHER COP

Up to now, most of the stories I have related were somewhat terrifying as well horrendous to live through at the time, but looking back I kind of miss them. How crazy is that? But I would hate to think for the rest of the time I have left in this crazy business that everything was going to run like clockwork. Then where would I get the adrenaline rush from? One of my favourite comedians, the gifted genius Les Dawson said that once you have security you're finished. I know what he meant because I certainly need that feeling of unpredictability to fuel the dynamic e.g. in my case, not knowing what the hell the next job will be, or indeed if there is going to be a next job, and when I get it will I be able to hack it? Fuck it! "Bring it on," I say, with all its frightening uncertainties. That'll do for starters.

In 1992 my agent had a conversation with a casting director and they came to the conclusion that I needed some air time on the box that would raise my profile again since I hadn't been in a TV series for over a year. The way to do it they agreed was to get me on the *The Bill*, which was then a high standard prime time drama transmitted twice a week. So, on their advice I wrote to the producers at Thames Television. I sent the letter on a Friday, and on the Monday I got a call to go for an interview, which I had two days later. That went well except that the Executive Producer told me that I would have to do a screen test before they made their decision as to whether or not they wanted me for the series. I thought it a bit cheeky to be asked to do a screen test as I had already sent in a show reel of my telly work, on top of which I had starred in a series called *Making News* for Thames Television just over a year before. But being a little older and wiser than I was earlier in this book, I of course said I would love to turn up for a screen test, which I did and subsequently became a regular as DC Alan Woods.

I loved creating him. He was a good listener and a no-nonsense, straight-talking bloke you wouldn't mess with, who had a keen sense of humour when he needed it. The fact that I was playing a copper in a serious drama didn't stop me enjoying the cock-ups. And the series certainly had its own fair share of them during our twelve hour long filming days in some of the dodgiest areas of London.

A fellow actor I tuned into early on was Kevin Lloyd, who played Tosh Lines. I called him Fat Boy and he called me Double Chin so we got on famously. Provided we didn't make too much eye contact during a scene we were playing then all would be well, otherwise we would invariably end up giggling like lunatics at nothing at all. It was absolutely tragic that a few of years after I left the series he died.

My fondest memory of him was on a shoot we did that had started at seven in the morning, and by the time we set up to do our final scene at our last location it was nearing seven in the evening. Needless to say everyone was getting a little tetchy. Though it should have been straightforward, it turned out not to be. The following is what should have happened:

1) Chris Ellison (my mate and Godfather to my eldest son) who played D I Burnside, knocks on the front door of a terraced house.

2) When there's no reply, Kevin belts the door with a huge sledge hammer.

3) The door flies open.

4) Chris runs into the house followed by two other regulars from CID

5) I follow next.

6) Kevin follows me.

7) The cameraman, complete with heavy camera resting on his shoulder enters next.

8) The sound man, with all his sound paraphernalia dangling from belts around his waist and holding aloft a boom mike, brings up the rear.

5) We all run at a fair lick, on down the hallway and into the kitchen at the back of the house.

6) In the kitchen Chris arrests the leader of the four walk–on artistes, the baddies, who are sitting playing cards.

Though it required precise co-ordination of movement from all concerned, it should have been reasonably easy to shoot as one shot. After all, by then we and the crew were all tried and tested regulars on the show, so most of the time all went like clockwork. After a couple of rehearsals we should have been ready to go for the first take.

So we gave it a try. The first thing to go wrong was that when Chris tried to arrest the first baddie he met in the kitchen, the bloke lifted Chris up instead, and shook him like a leaf. Chris is a pretty big bloke himself, but the 'heavy' was being played by none other than an ex-European boxing champion.

"No mate you've got it wrong. I'm supposed to arrest you for crying out loud!" Chris protested, his feet dangling six inches off the floor.

When the rest of us piled into the kitchen and saw what was happening we fell about. It was all the director could do to get us back outside to our first positions and ready to go again.

The next problem we had was that no matter how hard Kevin whacked that door on each subsequent take, the bloody thing stubbornly decided to remain on its hinges. Normally it wouldn't merit more than a wry smile from the rest of us, but when Kevin turned around to look at us, his face was puce with the effort of wielding the heavy sledge hammer, and after the fourth attempt at braking down the door, he wheezed in his thick northern accent, "Some silly bollocks screwed t' soddin' door too bloody tight shut by 'aff!" Instead of sympathy he was met by his fellow actors doubling up in the front garden desperately trying to control their laughter.

The door was worked on by the props guys and we were on a dire warning from the director that if we cocked up again, heads would roll. As we waited in line along the front pathway with our backs to the camera lens, I caught a glimpse of Kevin's shoulders and saw that they were heaving up and down. That got me started and tears began to stream down my face to the extent that I couldn't see properly. Chris and the other two twigged what was happening and began to giggle just as the director shouted, "ACTION!"

All hell then broke loose. Kevin was taken by surprise and swung the sledge hammer so hard he not only smashed the door off its hinges, but his sweaty palms momentarily lost their grip and the hammer shot out of his hands heading half way across London. The door crashed open, Chris took off down the hallway like an Exocet and was followed hot on his heels by the two other CID blokes then me. My problem was that my vision hadn't fully recovered from crying with laughter moments earlier, and I misjudged the height of the doorstep simply because I couldn't see it properly. Just as my foot caught it, Kevin leapt into place behind me and began to gather speed. When I tripped and fell my full length through the open doorway, Kevin couldn't stop in time or avoid me, and instead ran up my legs, then my back, finally tripping over my head. I knew that the cameraman who was following Kevin wouldn't see me on the floor as he was looking through the camera lens at eye level. Sure enough, when I couldn't roll out of his way in time, both he and his camera, followed by the sound man with all his gear, all joined me on the floor. Pure bedlam ensued and I can assure you the director was not a happy bunny.

We did go for that scene one more time and I am very happy to say that it all went smoothly. But when I watched that episode on telly some six weeks later, I could see that each one of us was suffering from 'heaving shoulders syndrome', but from an audience point of view, it looked like we were breathing heavily in anticipation of the drama that was to come.

There is always the risk that if an actor stays in a series too long it will be difficult to find work afterwards as they will consistently be associated with it. Unfortunately that did happen to me, for I didn't get back on the telly for two and a half years after I finished my four year stint on *The Bill*. Although I quite happily went on to work in the theatre in the meantime, I was pleased as punch to eventually get back on the small screen again when I was cast in an episode of Dangerfield. The main reason was that I was playing a wee smelly low life character which meant that I had broken the mould of only playing the smartly dressed streetwise copper. But I wouldn't have missed the experience of being in *The Bill* for anything.

I did find that I much preferred filming small cast episodes working with one or two visiting actors, than to be in an episode with a whole lot of the regulars with everyone vying for air time. Don't get me wrong, we all got on really well. Indeed I felt much the same about not wanting to work in big cast stage productions and began to think that maybe there was something wrong with me, until I read that a highly respected knight of the theatre thinks much the same way about big cast productions. 'Well,' I thought to myself, 'He's done ok so there can't be much wrong with me after all.'

I suppose it is strange that I am comfortable in a job which requires me to stand up in front of hundreds of people and remember to spout forth copious amounts of dialogue, whilst in real life I can get nervous simply walking into a room full of people, even those I know. Nor am I good in large crowds. I don't get hot flushes or heart palpitations or anything else for that matter. It's just that, much as I like my fellow humans, I'm not good at coping with them en masse. Thus I miss out on shopping malls, religious rallies, football matches, orgies, etc. In the cinema or theatre I tend to sit in the seat next to the aisle where I know I can leave when I want, and generally avoid gatherings of more than would take to fill a pub. And I never stand in a queue unless I absolutely have to e.g. when waiting to get served in a busy pub. But there was one event which I thought would have been rude to avoid turning up for... it was a big 'do' to celebrate the transmitting of 500 *Bill* episodes.

The venue was a ballroom in London's Haymarket. I arrived on time, but instead of going straight in, I shuffled off to a pub and downed a few to give me the confidence to be able to walk into the crowd and talk sense to a friendly bunch of people I already knew. Of course the reality is that too much Dutch courage kicks sensible conversation into touch, and I had certainly done that in the past. But that night I was disciplined and had only a couple of large ones to see me through.

After leaving the pub I waited in an alleyway across the road from the venue and watched through the drizzling rain as the guests arrived. About ten minutes passed when a couple of members of the crew whom I got on particularly well with poured themselves out of a taxi. By then I felt I had spent enough time in the rain, and feeling courageous enough to enter the fray with a couple of soul mates by my side, I decided that now was the time to tag along with them. Taking a deep breath I stepped out from my hiding place and onto the wet and slippery pavement. The timing couldn't have been worse. At that very moment from around the corner came a woman running at full pelt. She was a big lass. Her full body weight hit me side on, and I went derriere over tit landing on my backside. She hardly paused in her haste to get where she was going and shouted in a disconcertingly deep-sounding Cockney accent, "Sorry mate, you aw wight?" and ran on into the night clutching a wallkie-talkie in her rather overlarge, hairy hand. She was quite a formidable character and strong as an ox. Not the best of disguises I thought for an undercover cop.

The result of our unexpected encounter was that my jacket and trousers were wet and scuffed from the fall and my left hand and wrist were grazed. I brushed myself down with my uninjured hand as best I could, but as it too was wet and dirt streaked it wasn't much use. Next thing I knew a tramp took me for one of his lot and offered me a swig from his bottle wrapped in a greasy brown paper bag. At that point I was sorely tempted to accept. Instead I thrust some dosherooni into his pocket, thanked him profusely, wiped the rain from my damp brow with the back of my bloodied hand, and marched off over the road determined to catch up with the crew. When they saw me all bedraggled and wet they burst into fits thinking that I was already as pissed as a fart. Then they became anxious believing that the blood stained smear on my face was for real and that I had been in some sort of stramash. I reassured them I hadn't been, told them what had just happened and they went off to buy the drinks whilst I went down stairs to the find the gents, where I hoped to tidy myself up enough to be presentable.

As the night was still young I found it empty. There were several washbasins along one wall and two electric hand dryers above them, one at each end. In the mirror, which ran the length of the wall, I saw that I had a dark, muddy, blood stained streak running in an L shape down my forehead and then at right angles over my nose. No wonder my friends had been concerned. Frankly my visog looked a mess, and my clothes didn't look much better. And so I got to work.

Firstly the jacket came off, and with the help of a few handfuls of bog roll, I rubbed it until the wet blotches became acceptably dry and disappeared. Then I did the same with my trousers whilst wearing them. Next I turned on the taps in order to wash my face. That did it! I'd like to meet the silly sod who designed these feckin' faucets. Instead of water coming out at a normal pace, it shot out in a jet with the force of a tsunami, hit the rim of the wash basin, leapt over it before landing with a loud whooshing sound all over the crotch of my trousers. My crotch looked even wetter than it did all these years ago in Glasgow airport when I was washing cars for a living. I now had the awful dilemma of how to dry them, and toyed with the idea of locking myself in the WC, taking them off and flapping them around a bit hoping that this action would dry them out sufficiently enough for me to make an acceptable appearance upstairs at the 'do'. But I rejected this method knowing it would be worse than useless.

It dawned on me that unless I took some sort of drastic action soon, my trousers would take the best part of the night to dry naturally. I tried rubbing the crotch using the crumpled up bog roll method, but that proved hopeless as well. Particles of damp bog paper stuck to the material giving the impression I had galloping dandruff in the crotch area. I sat down on the can feeling more than despondent. There seemed to be no way out. Then I had this brilliant idea. Of course… the electric hand drier… I would blow dry my trousers. All that entailed was for me to stand under the hot air for five minutes and Bob's your uncle (or your auntie depending which sort of parties you go to) the trousers would be as dry as a bone again.

There was one last major obstacle to overcome though. As both dryers were fitted to the wall at shoulder height, the hot air didn't reach as low as my crotch. And there was no way I was going to stand in the gents, trouserless, whilst holding them up to the dryer. Then I had an epiphany. Skipping gingerly over to the door I peeked out making sure there was no-one about to enter, rushed back and climbed onto the ledge which supported the wash basins. The dryer was on the wall was a couple of feet above the basin. In order to stay upright, I therefore had to put my left knee in the wash basin and wedge my right leg against the bog door rim a few feet along from the dryer. By this time the damp area on my crotch was noticeably spreading and reached half way down my thighs. At this rate I reckoned it would reach my ankles in no time. With one hand pressed against the mirror and the other against the door frame for support, I could quite easily move my pelvis in a circular motion. This in turn would allow the hot air, which was becoming uncomfortably much the hotter by then, to reach as low as my upper thighs.

All went well until a troupe of blokes arrived and saw what appeared to them to be me trying to have sexual intercourse with an electric hand dryer. Instead of making the expected crass comments etc., they carried on with their business in total silence until they got outside and I heard them laughing heartily. But I couldn't give a damn. Within a couple of minutes my trousers were dry, and I thought I looked presentable enough to make my entrance amongst the heaving throng upstairs. All I can say is that no one commented on my appearance so I must have looked ok, which was one hell of a relief. After all I had been through to get to this bloody 'do', I am happy to say that I did enjoy myself for most of the evening, until one of my mates sidled up to me and whispered conspiratorially in my ear.

"There is a strong rumour that you had a bit of a blow in the gents." He smiled wickedly then wandered off giggling to himself.

That roguish interpretation of events could have abolished my career there and then, had the powers that be been misled re my innocent encounter with a hand dryer.

Years later I got a hell of a surprise when I watched a scene from Rowan Atkinson's series *Mr Bean*, where he had a very similar experience with a hand dryer in a public loo. So I am not alone after all!

In *The Bill* we needed situations to look as authentic as possible, so when the script called for a mini riot on a housing estate that is exactly what was arranged with walk-on artistes playing the rioters. Though the local police authority would always be informed beforehand for permission to be granted, there had been some sort of a cock-up in this department, subsequently they hadn't been forewarned. The result was that when a resident saw a dozen yobbish types attack our kid-on police van and rolling it onto its side, they called the real police who turned up in force minutes later to quell what they genuinely believed to be a riot.

First on the scene was an unmarked police car. Out jumped a plain-clothed CID bloke.

He took one look at me then said, "Oh hi Alan. Got a call that the natives were revolting round here. Everything ok is it?"

I'M CLEAR, WHAT'S IT LIKE UP YOUR END?

"They're not revolting. It's a shoot we're on."

"A shoot? F--g hell! Better get the ARU boys down here and fast."

(ARU - The Armed Response Unit.)

He eventually realised what was happening after I kindly pointed out that we were shooting a scene from *The Bill* and was highly embarrassed at his mistaken identity. As for me, I was highly delighted that my portrayal of DC Alan Woods on the telly had been taken for the real McCoy by the real police.

Usually stunt drivers are employed when a real hairy car chase type sequence is called for, but occasionally I got to throw cars around too, which was one of the high spots for me in *The Bill*. But no matter who is behind the wheel, when there is a scene to be filmed involving a bit of fast driving, naturally one hell of a lot of preparation goes into eliminating any possible element of danger for those involved, and anyone else for that matter. But there's always the unexpected, as in the following scenario.

I had had a very dodgy car experience filming an episode of a television series many moons ago circa mid 1980s when I had to drive with the film camera and lights mounted on the car's bonnet (hood) pointing back at me, as I drove along the busy Euston Road. No-one realised until it was too late what the outcome would be, when the director told me to deviate from the previously planned route and drive through the Euston Underpass instead. In short, the darkened space caused the glare from the lights on the bonnet to flare across the windscreen, temporarily blinding me. Luckily I managed just in time to stick my head out of the driver's window and see that I was heading in a straight line towards a concrete wall, when I should have been following the bend in the road. Since then I have always been very respectful of the potential pitfalls when filming driving sequences on the open road, and in the four years I was in *The Bill*, no-one was ever hurt in any car scenes I was in or witnessed.

Scenes requiring the need for violence in the series were different. Whilst many actors revelled in being part of the rough and tumble kid on fighting stuff, I couldn't stand it. Simply because I always seemed be paired up with the overzealous fellow with a body mass similar to an oil tanker, hell bent on proving his manliness by charging at me like a souped-up juggernaut as soon as he heard the director shout "ACTION!"

Consequently I experienced many a painful encounter from them time and time again. Of course I had the option of being well protected with lots of padding, but to be honest that sort of gear was usually uncomfortable and hot to wear and got in the way by restricting movement, so I was always a tad reluctant to wear it. Unless of course I knew exactly what particular part of my anatomy was going to be thwacked and therefore it would be imperative to protect it, or them e.g. shin guards if my shins were going to be the target, or a cricket box if there was even the least chance of my bollocks bearing the brunt of an onslaught, simply because I didn't trust a hyped up actor to do the kid on stuff safely and land his kicks and punches in the right places.

But back to cars, thank goodness. In one *Bill* episode I had been directed to drive from the fifth floor of a multi storey car park to street level in as little time as possible... "And totally safely please Tom!" was the request from the somewhat nervous director. Behind me sat the cameraman and sound man, both with all their recording and filming gear in situ, so there was a lot depending on me not screwing up. Having to dip into the insurance kitty for starters would be an unwelcome result if I did have a wee shunt.

At one point on the journey, I had to do a rehearsed emergency stop when one of the film crew who had volunteered to be a shopper, stepped out in front of me at a specific point on my journey, whilst pushing a supermarket trolley which of course I had to avoid... and I had to avoid him as well! It was made absolutely safe to do because we made sure that there were acres of room between us, so that even if the brakes failed I would have missed him by a mile. But from the camera's point of view he was made to look so very, very much closer. Oh the wonders of filming!

For safety, we had cone-men at the pedestrian entrances on each floor, as well as one in charge at ground level, making sure that no public on foot or in cars could enter during the car scene. Cone men as they are called, are invaluable when it comes to traffic control. They are the ones who will cordon off a side street or even a busy main road with nothing more than a few traffic cones, a walkie-talkie, and their own physical presence, in order to ensure that no member of the public or vehicle strays into shot and gets run over or pranged. They are indeed brave souls and tend to get a lot of verbal abuse from punters. But without them the punters themselves would be in extreme danger.

I'M CLEAR, WHAT'S IT LIKE UP YOUR END?

For the car park driving scene that was about to be shot, I had taken the time to stroll the route beforehand. This was just to make sure there weren't any hidden surprises that I would have to suddenly contend with, like an oil patch I could skid on, or an obstacle that could blow a tyre, or a corner wall mirror reflecting sunlight into my line of vision.

Then I drove it at half speed to get the hang of it all. By the time 'Stand By' was announced, I was strapped in with the engine ticking over waiting to go, my right foot hovering expectantly over the accelerator pedal. I knew how Steve McQueen must have felt as he buckled up for the car chase scene in *Bullitt*. Well… I can dream can't I?

The walkie-talkie on my passenger seat was the lifeline between crew, director, cone-men and me. When everyone had asked everyone else if they were ready, the last person to give a final all clear was the most important cone man of all for this set up i.e. the one on the ground floor level holding up the traffic wanting to enter the car park. The following is what I heard over my walkie-talkie.

Director: Ok… standby everyone.

First Asst: That's a standby everyone.

Director: Over to you Jim.

First Asst: Thanks guv. Turn over.

Cameraman: Rolling.

First Asst: Sound?

Sound man: Running.

First Asst: How are we doing camera?

Cameraman: We've got speed.

First Asst: Fred? (a cone man) How are we doing?

Fred: Levels five, four, three, two and one all clear.

First Asst: Ground floor? Give me a clear and we'll go for it.

Bert: Clear.

First Asst: Ok. Let's do it. I'm clear what's it like up your end? Tom? Tom? Tom?

(Silence)

Fred: Tom did you hear that? He asked what's it like up your end? Cheeky sod isn't he?

Needless to say there was a bit of a delay whilst I pondered the question about what it was like up my end, with tears of mirth cascading down my face… as usual.

As I said, this acting game is really one of the best jobs around. I mean to say, where else can you get paid to kid on to be your hero. Maybe if I didn't look so like Steve Mcqueen, I would have been a big star of the big screen as well! Och well, I've done all right as it is. Thanks for tuning in, and long may you do so.

ABOUT THE AUTHOR

Tom Cotcher was born in Glasgow on 28 July 1950. At the age of seventeen he left school with four O Levels, enlisting as an Apprentice Ship's Draughtsman at Charles Connell and Co in their Scotstoun shipyard. But he had other ambitions, one of which was to be an actor. So, within a year he applied and was accepted into the three year action course at the Royal Scottish Academy of Music and Drama. His career in the business began with the familiar path of work in repertory theatres, notably three years with the Dundee Repertory Theatre Company, as well as season with the Royal Lyceum in Edinburgh and Perth Repertory Theatre.

Moving south he joined Farnham Rep, then went on to work at Basingstoke, Leatherhead etc., and toured England and India with the Cambridge Theatre Company. Then it was on to Denmark's London Toast Theatre where he also co-wrote a radio series, and then a tour of Holland with an American British theatre company.

From the Edinburgh Festival the play A British Subject, in which he played a newspaper reporter, was chosen for New York's East 59th Street Theatre as an off Broadway production for their Brits Abroad season.

Tom's many television roles include his portrayal of DC Woods in Thames Television's series The Bill, which he played for four years. From Lovejoy to Tales of the Unexpected, from EastEnders to Law and Order, from Making News to Case Histories, his appearances on the small screen have been numerous.

Film credits include Death Defying Acts, SNUB, Hope and Glory, The Magnificent Eleven etc.

Tom's voice is also well known for his work in documentary narration, most notably the History Channel series, Ice Road Truckers.

Tom is also the narrator for the following books:

Raw Spirit in Search of the Perfect Dream by Iaian Banks

Unabridged Rebus books by Ian Rankin

The Watchers by Ian Rankin

The Distant Echo by Val McDermid

The Testament of Gideon Mack by James Patterson

Tom is the author of two children's books: *Otto and the Sea Circus* and *Otto and the Kidnap*.

Tom and his wife, actress Cookie Weymouth have two sons and live in Brighton.

He is also an accomplished artist. Whilst his work encompasses landscapes and seascapes, his interiors are painted in what he calls his very own naïve Matisse style. He says, "Matisse because they are highly colourful, and naïve because I don't know what I'm doing."

You can view his work on *www.tomcotcherart.com*

Printed in Great Britain
by Amazon